Annoying Music in Everyday Life

Alternate Takes: Critical Responses to Popular Music is a series that aims to examine popular music from critical perspectives that challenge the accepted ways of thinking about popular music in areas such as popular music history, popular music analysis, the music industry, and the popular music canon. The series ultimately aims to have readers listen to—and think about—popular music in new ways.

Series Editors: Matt Brennan and Simon Frith

Editorial Board: Daphne Brooks, Oliver Wang, Susan Fast, Ann Powers, Tracey Thorn, Eric Weisbard, Sarah Hill, Marcus O'Dair

Other Volumes in the Series

When Genres Collide by Matt Brennan
Nothing Has Been Done Before: Seeking the New in 21st-Century American Popular Music by Robert Loss
DIY Music and the Politics of Social Media by Ellis Jones (forthcoming)
A Musical History of Digital Startup Culture by Cherie Hu (forthcoming)
Live from the Other Side of Nowhere: Contemplating Musical Performance in an Age of Virtual Reality by Sam Cleeve (forthcoming)
Ranting and Raving: Dance Music as Everyday Culture by Tami Gadir (forthcoming)
National Phonography: Field Recording, Sound Archiving, and Producing the Nation in Music by Tom Western (forthcoming)

Annoying Music in Everyday Life

Felipe Trotta

BLOOMSBURY ACADEMIC
NEW YORK • LONDON • OXFORD • NEW DELHI • SYDNEY

BLOOMSBURY ACADEMIC
Bloomsbury Publishing Inc
1385 Broadway, New York, NY 10018, USA
50 Bedford Square, London, WC1B 3DP, UK

BLOOMSBURY, BLOOMSBURY ACADEMIC and the Diana logo are trademarks
of Bloomsbury Publishing Plc

First published in the United States of America 2020

Cover design by Louise Dugdale
Cover image © Pictrider / Shutterstock

Bloomsbury Publishing Inc does not have any control over, or responsibility for, any third-party
websites referred to or in this book. All internet addresses given in this book were correct at the
time of going to press. The author and publisher regret any inconvenience caused if addresses have
changed or sites have ceased to exist, but can accept no responsibility for any such changes.

Library of Congress Cataloging-in-Publication Data
Names: Trotta, Felipe, author.
Title: Annoying music in everyday life / Felipe Trotta.
Description: New York: Bloomsbury Academic, 2020. | Includes bibliographical references
and index. | Summary: "Discusses the role of uninvited music in our day-to-day lives
and its personal and social impacts"– Provided by publisher.
Identifiers: LCCN 2019057845 | ISBN 9781501360633 (hardback) |
ISBN 9781501360657 (pdf) | ISBN 9781501360640 (epub)
Subjects: LCSH: Music–Social aspects. | Nuisances. | Noise–Social aspects. |
Sound–Social aspects.
Classification: LCC ML3916.T76 2020 | DDC 306.4/842–dc23
LC record available at https://lccn.loc.gov/2019057845

ISBN: HB: 978-1-5013-6063-3
PB: 978-1-5013-6062-6
ePDF: 978-1-5013-6065-7
eBook: 978-1-5013-6064-0

Typeset by Deanta Global Publishing Services, Chennai, India

Series: Alternate Takes: Critical Responses to Popular Music

To find out more about our authors and books visit www.bloomsbury.com and
sign up for our newsletters.

Contents

Acknowledgements

This book began to be written in Scotland, during the spring of 2017. The final dot was typed in Rio de Janeiro in 2019, also during the spring. Between northern and southern springs, the ideas developed here are the result of multiple encounters that began far before the writing process and certainly overlap with its end. Writing is a solitary activity. However, this solitude is filled with ideas, stories, situations, affects, emotions and the support of dozens of people. In this sense, one never writes alone, and every word is part of a wider set of relationships that reminds us of our personal belonging, friends, family and colleagues. Some of them are quoted in the pages of the book, both as authors and interviewees. Others must be referred to here, as a register of the thankfulness of their support.

First, I would like to thank Simon Frith for his direct encouragement. Simon not only agreed to supervise my research during the time in Edinburgh but also pushed forward the beginning of the book, reading the first pages and suggesting the path to its publication. His excitement with the project nourished the writing. In Edinburgh, I also met friends and colleagues at the Popular Music Seminar, led by Simon at the Reid School of Music at the University of Edinburgh. My thanks to all of them, here represented by Mark Percival, Matt Brennan, Tom Western, Nikki Moran and Sergio Pisfil.

In a long-term history of interchange and collaborations, I need to mention also the exciting ambience of the Latin-America branch of the International Association for the Study of Popular Music (IASPM-AL), where I met friends from different countries that are increasingly part of my references and biannual beer meetings. Thanks to Mercedes Liska, Malvina Silba, Martha Ulhôa, Claudia Matos, Pablo Alabarces, Christian Spencer, Natalia Bieletto-Bueno, Julio Mendívil, Ruben Lopez-Cano, Sílvia Martinez and Marita Fornaro, representing the whole branch.

Some key topics of this book have been largely discussed in an interinstitutional Brazilian web of research in popular music, where it has gained insightful contributions from my friends Simone Pereira de Sá, Jeder Janotti Junior, Micael Herschmann, Cintia Fernandes and Thiago Soares, among many other researchers involved with music studies. My special thanks also to my students at undergraduate and post-graduate courses in the Department of Media and Cultural Studies at the Universidade Federal Fluminense, who always challenge my thoughts with sharp questions that constantly change my way of thinking.

The challenge of writing in a foreign language made the process slower and harder than usual. Fortunately, I have had the luck of counting on the careful support of Simone do Vale, who not only translated the Portuguese quotes of Brazilian interviewees but also revised some parts of the book, making me more confident about language issues.

The research for this book had the decisive contribution of three research assistants, who did some of the interviews that are its primary data: Nicolas Sassi, who was an undergraduate student at the time and who made the first inquiries about 'annoying music'; Alec Cooper, to whom I was introduced in Edinburgh and who did several interviews with his Scottish fellows; and Luciana Pinheiro, an old friend that joined the team to help me with the balance between gender and social markers. Needless to say, without the interviews done by the three of them, this book would have taken a totally different format, and possibly some of the issues developed in the following pages would not have been part of it. I must include here a special acknowledgement to all the people that agreed to talk with us and to share their stories, feelings and memories.

The academic and emotive support of friends, family and colleagues has to be complemented with the materiality of money. Thus, I have had the opportunity to develop this research funded by three Brazilian government agencies: Fundação Carlos Chagas Filho de Amparo à Pesquisa do Estado do Rio de Janeiro (FAPERJ), Conselho Nacional de Desenvolvimento Científico e Tecnológico (CNPq) and Coordenação de Aperfeiçoamento de Pessoal de Nível Superior (CAPES), the last of which rewarded me with a visiting scholar grant in Edinburgh. It's never unworthy to reinforce the importance of funding, especially in a time when research in arts and humanities seems to be under attack in several places in the world.

Finally, outside the realm of professional and academic acknowledgements, I would never be able to write this book without the constant support of my family. Part of my personal energy comes from Gabi, the woman who changed my life two decades ago with an 'intense and calm love' that since then is the fuel of my own existence. The other part shall be credited to my daughters Ana and Nina, who are my daily inspiration to live, work and have fun. Without them, there would be no book, nor visiting time in Scotland, and not even me as I am today. Thank you!

Introduction

Music annoys. This statement is, at the same time, obvious and challenging. It is obvious because everybody has had unpleasant experiences with music. It is not difficult to remember several situations in which music has bothered or irritated us. Living in crowded cities forces us to deal with sounds from different sources. Car and bus engines, domestic and commercial machines, shouting, talking, dogs barking and several other sounds make up the daily sonic environment of our lives. Among all these sounds, music drives attention and not rarely becomes a major source of inconvenience. The omnipresence of music in everyday life is inescapable. Even though the purpose of music playing in most places is to minimize the messy ambience of contemporary public life, the lack of control over what is being played is very likely to irritate. In this sense, *obviously*, music can be annoying.

But this statement is also challenging because it can't be made without at least partially confronting the idea of music as the 'art of the muses', a shortcut to personal feelings and collective identities. Speaking about annoying music seems to dismiss the positive role of music in society as a device for sharing ideas, identities and belonging; as an activity that joins people together to socialize, to dance, to sing and to enjoy social encounters, festivals, parties. Somehow, it seems to deny the importance of music in interpersonal relations, as it helps us to shape our mood, humour, and corporal behaviour and to interpret our lives both as individuals and as social groups, nations, regions. For all this, it is challenging.

This book seeks to face this challenge. Without denying the pleasurable role of music in our daily lives, what is addressed here is the music experience that bothers us, that irritates, that makes us bored and annoyed. There are a few general questions that guide this investigation. What is 'annoying' in music? What do people identify in music experiences that may be defined as unpleasant? Are there any kinds of music that are more frequently referred to as annoying? What does the idea of 'annoying music' help us to understand about everyday life sociability?

Beyond the intention to answer these questions, what the reader will find in this book is an effort to interpret the multiple dimensions of what people define as 'annoying music'. As will be seen, the feelings it raises activate a wide range of issues and thoughts about life in society, issues related to ethics, politics, individuality and citizenship. Music is a kind of human experience that helps us to think and act both individually and socially. When it is felt as something annoying, it is the result of a mismatch between expectancies and experience, between ideas about what is right or wrong, adequate or inadequate.

'Annoying music' brings to the surface the issue of *control*. Most often, the positive force of music experience is closely related to repertoires and moments that we choose to listen to. To control the sound heard in a given place is to have a relative power within it. Music has multiple effects on the body, ranging from the vibrational materiality of sound waves to the symbolic and psychological interpretations triggered by it. Therefore, controlling music means controlling bodies both in their inner functioning (blood pressure, heartbeats, tissue and muscle movement and so on) and in their outer associations (memories, identities, belongings, sociability). As Domínguez Ruiz (2019: 100) puts it, 'Sound domination is a concrete manifestation of power, that not only reveals itself as aggression but also as an imposition of wishes'. Being exposed to music we do not choose means being forced to vibrate according to it, even if the set of ideas that are shared and interpreted hurts our moral sense.

In this regard, the use of music in public places is particularly interesting as a strategy to select who shall or shall not be there. Johnson and Cloonan (2009: 183) mention the report done by Newcastle-Upon-Tyne Metro that registered a drop in vandalism following the playing of Delius. According to the authors, this and other similar cases are reported on a daily basis across the globe, confirming the force of music to drive (undesired) people away from certain places. In a deep study about music in crime prevention, Lilly Hirsch (2012) describes dozens of situations where 'uncool' music was played as a measure to control attendance, driving away potential criminals or groups of youngsters. To have no control over the repertoire, the loudness, the adequacy and the duration of music experience put us in a disturbing submissive role. The power imbalance that unchosen music raises may, hence, be extremely uncomfortable, resulting in a decision to leave the place. In most reports of the use of classical music in public places to prevent the presence of youngsters, the strategy was referred to as successful (Hirsch 2012).

However, leaving the place is not always possible. In a bus or train, for instance, you are forced to withstand the unpleasant sound environment during the trip. In these situations, the music is an additional element of discomfort that may compose a multi-layered experience of annoyance. Within a closed place such as a train or bus, the body is subjected to vibrational and interpretative forces which make it move in synchrony. Forced undesired music makes us interact with rhythms and ideas spread by the repertoire, even if we disagree with them. In this sense, most music that is defined as 'annoying' is also 'unchosen'.

Notwithstanding, there are other layers in this equation. When people are invited to talk about 'annoying music', the issue of control usually appears closely attached to the issue of *taste*. Pointing out songs, artists or genres that they dislike is the immediate association that most people make when subjected to unwanted sound experience. Frequently, people try to find the source of disgust *in the music*, which appears in sentences such as 'that pop song is unbearable' or 'he played funk music very loud all night long and I couldn't sleep'. The classification of the music universe in genres that frame taste and identification is a starting point from which people listen to music, either chosen or not. As several authors have intensely discussed, taste is not a visceral intimate reaction to things, but a lifelong construction that is informed by sets of ideas, memories, feelings, senses of belonging and practices. When one is forced to listen to music, all these sets of values and learned features are called in for the complex process of interpretation triggered by the experience. Depending on the course this interpretation takes, the judgement about the experience will be framed. And, as Simon Frith (1996) puts it, this usually works around the terms 'good' and 'bad'. These magic words function as packages in which several thoughts are conserved, including prejudices, moral belongings, gender and racial segregations and a myriad of contradictory and confusing ideas about life in society. In this sense, it is not true that all unchosen music is annoying. It depends on the situation and, in cases where it matches our tastes, it can be surprisingly enjoyable.

Recognition and classification are operations done by the one who listens to music. Despite it being possible to demonstrate some features of sound organization that may be considered annoying, it is the listening experience that produces the interpretation of the experience as such. Changing the focus to the *listening* process allows us to unveil how music takes part in our interpersonal and collective experiences. We follow, then, an increasing framework of studies that emphasize the active role of the listener in sound experience. Listening is not a passive act but involves a knowledge constructed both individually and socially. It is a process informed by 'cultural and socio-political structures' that 'frame forms of perception', reactions and classifications (Bieletto-Bueno 2019: 118). Hence, it is related to present-time life experience, conditioned by available technologies that enhance and amplify sounds and music. Listening requires what Sterne (2003: 23) calls an 'audile technique', a set of practices of listening that are entangled with science and technology. Then, the active act of listening is understood here as part of a wider 'aural regime' and as informed by 'audile techniques'. It is the means through which annoying music is defined and felt. When music experience is classified as 'good' or 'bad' all these complex sets of knowledge, expectations, recognitions, techniques and dispositions are activated, revealing not only the position of the one who has had the experience but his/her role in it. The classification also points to the way s/he judges the interhuman relation within the experience, situated in time and space.

The dynamic process of listening leads us to the idea that annoying music is not a static object but a *relation*. The feeling of being disturbed by unchosen music puts us in contact with the presence of others who are soundly materialized in music. This relation is staged in physical spaces where the position of the listener and the controller is important in determining the nuisance. Position here is taken in a wide sense, both as a physical positionality and as a power role within that space. Of course, the one who has control over the sound operates a relative power on the acoustic relations that will be experienced during the time the people share the same space. Annoying music is, hence, the annoying other that is forcing his/her sound upon our intimacy, our body, our personal space. Going further in this direction, it is possible to state that playing music in a social space may be in itself a process of otherization since the one who has the control over the sound equipment is careless towards the others. In this relation, the others lose their individuality and become an indistinct, unrecognized collective that should either enjoy the music or leave the place. Of course, it is not always like this. A DJ in a party is obviously playing music for others and s/he is constantly aware and concerned with his/her audience's reactions, and also whether they are dancing or not. Nevertheless, in several other situations – most of those reported throughout this book – music is imposed on other people without much concern for their likes and dislikes. The others are diminished in importance, and their own desires and motivations ignored.

Not rarely, complaints about 'annoying music' are directed to a perceived violation of appropriate social behaviour, or, worse, a violation of individual rights. In these reports, people apply a vocabulary of violence that evokes the feeling of being violated by the other. The issue of music and violence is complex and has as well several layers. It can be simplified into the use of two words, defining roles performed in this relation: victim and perpetrator. The controller of the music equipment or instrument is the one who has the power and, hence, the one who perpetrates violence.

On the other hand, the auditor suffers the sound invasion in his/her body and place, being violated, victimized by someone else's music. Interestingly, most people are very keen to talk about their own experiences as victims of someone else's sound and music, defined as inadequate, loud, irritating or invasive. Annoying music is mostly defined as a weapon that victimizes the self. Hardly will one talk about a situation where s/he had control over the sound/ music and someone had complained about it or called the police. And when it does happen, usually it is in the middle of a non-important description of situations of fun, individual joyful moments or social gatherings. The selective interpretations of annoying music are revealing of how difficult it is to listen to the other. Although people regret the lack of solidarity of the other when s/he is playing loud music, we are usually deaf to that (im)balance when the situation is inverted. With few exceptions, the definition of annoying music is always a complaint about the other's low capacity of putting him/herself in my place.

Listening to the other is always an issue of *tolerance*. Tolerance is, in turn, conditioned by several elements that make up part of the annoying sound experience. How long, how often, how closely and how loudly bothersome music is forced upon us changes our capacity to understand and acknowledge the other's right to play music that invades our intimate personal space. Furthermore, if this other is a close relative, a neighbour or an impersonal agent, it also shifts the way we face the unpleasant situation and our threshold of tolerance.

This book deals with several layers and degrees of music experiences defined by people as annoying. It makes up part of a recent movement within popular (and unpopular) music studies that are increasingly addressing what could be called the 'negative' side of music experience and music practices (Johnson and Cloonan 2009). Music is a shared artefact that produces conflicts, enacts inequalities and brings prejudices, social struggles and segregations to the surface. Studies indicate that music has been used for a long time as a device in torture chambers, wars, group fights, intimidation attempts and several other violent acts. Hence, talking about conflicts related to music experience is not something new. Here, I'd like to invite the reader to enter this universe of nuisance and disagreements provoked by musical experience in everyday life. My focus is on the annoyance music causes in our daily experience while walking down streets, sharing crowded buses or trains, talking to friends at a bar or even arguing over who gets to choose the music at home. These daily and usually unimportant conflicts are taken here as shortcuts to interpret how difficult it is to live together in the world, while protecting our privacy, sharing our sociability and listening to one another.

Methodological notes and limits

In many ways, this book is inspired by Tia DeNora's *Music in Everyday Life*, from which I borrowed the title and the methodological approach. In her work, DeNora conducted several interviews that allowed her to describe and interpret how people use music in different situations. Following this procedure, the ideas developed here are the result of seventy-three interviews done between 2017 and 2018, both in Brazil and Scotland. The interviewees were selected randomly, first through friendship links and then through recommendations. The main concern while selecting them was to achieve balance among age, gender and social background (education, profession, place of residence). It is not a representative *corpus*, but rather an exploratory qualitative survey through which I could access arguments and ideas about annoying music.

The interviewees were encouraged to talk about their relationship with music, preferred genres and artists as well as songs and singers they don't like. They were asked to report situations when music has annoyed them and to try to explain why. Extracts of these reports are quoted throughout the book so that we can follow most of the main arguments. Some interviews were done by myself and others were done by my research assistants Nicolas Sassi (Rio), Luciana Pinheiro (Rio) and Alec Cooper (Edinburgh), who were interviewed as well. As these conversations took place in radically different cities (Rio de Janeiro and Edinburgh), some particularities can be noticed in the responses. Edinburgh interviewees tended to ascribe annoying music to public spaces such as stores, supermarkets and pubs, while few have mentioned conflicts with neighbours. On the other side of the Atlantic, Rio residents reported a wider range of noisy situations involving their neighbourhoods but also the sounds from the streets, bars and public transportation. Despite these differences, the interviews allowed us to acknowledge some general processes of nuisance triggered by music in several situations and places as many interviewees reported cases, episodes and feelings from their previous life histories. Often, questions about music raised memories of past experiences from, mostly, their childhood houses and cities. Therefore, the content of the reports transcends Rio and Edinburgh, reaching small cities in the countryside of Brazil, as well as places as different as Taiwan, Beijing, Laos, Barcelona, Cuzco and Buenos Aires.

The age of the interviewees ranges from fifteen to seventy-three, and most of them belong to what can be called a middle-class, well-educated social stratum. This is due to the selection criteria of the interviewees and some approach facilities provided by the closeness between interviewer and interviewee. However, some interviewees escape this definition, providing different sets of life stories and narratives. Although they are certainly the minority of the *corpus*, their responses were highly quoted in the book. Since it is qualitative research, I believe these limitations do not invalidate the conclusions but rather reinforce the widespread feeling that music can be a very disturbing social artefact.

Theoretically, the study was developed under a mixed approach that merges musicology with cultural studies, ethnomusicology, sociology and sound studies. The result is an interdisciplinary conceptual framework that hopefully can provide a wide range of topics and discussions. As a popular music scholar, working in a department of media and cultural studies in Brazil, the rigid limits of disciplinary fields constantly overlap in my research and my listening practices. In this sense, this book is fed by contributions from several disciplines, trying to get profit from this unsettled position to better understand complex phenomena.

Moreover, my belonging to the Brazilian and Latin American culture provides a place from where the questions are raised, which, I think, can contribute to a more diversified approach to the studies on music and sound nuisance in contemporary cities. In this sense, my references are filled with works published in Portuguese and Spanish, in an attempt to diversify the Anglophone bibliography on the 'negative' uses of music, sound and noise. The result, I hope, is a slight displacement in the ways issues and debates are developed.

An illuminating talk with Lourenço

Almost everyone interviewed for this book lives in a big city. Despite having references to previous experiences, some of them in the countryside, almost every report provided and cited here refers to urban music experience. Therefore, still as part of an introductory section, it could be fruitful to present the thoughts developed by Lourenço in his interview. Lourenço is a forty-nine-year-old rural worker who lives in a village called Colina, which is inhabited by approximately 500 people and is located nine kilometres from the closest city, Itamonte, a small city in the southern hills of Minas Gerais state, Brazil. He was one of the first people with whom I recorded a conversation-interview about 'annoying music', and the only one who lives in the countryside. Lourenço is the only employee on my father's property, and I have known him for more than twenty years. Despite going to my father's country house only once or twice a year, I have always liked to talk to him since we are from the same generation and have radically different lifestyles. He has always lived in Colina, and I am easily identified as a big-city middle-class urban person. Chats with Lourenço are usually filled with wise interpretations about life in society, moral issues and the differences between the countryside and cities. In this sense, my curiosity about music and sound disagreements in Colina inspired me to ask to interview him. However, as usual, he directed the conversation towards his general elaborations about lifestyle.

During the interview, Lourenço highlighted that he is never irritated by music. Instead, music for him is a kind of resource that puts away bad thoughts and feelings, providing shelter and filling life with happiness. In his words: 'It's much better to listen to music that makes you happy than putting your head in something that is totally unworthy.' This thought resounds some of Tia DeNora's findings that point to the role of music as an ordering device, 'as a means to creating, enhancing, sustaining and changing subjective, cognitive, bodily and self-conceptual states' (DeNora 2000: 49). In a sense, Lourenço credits music with the capacity of framing his thoughts, driving them away from what he considers 'unworthy' and focusing on feelings taken as 'good', such as happiness. Nevertheless, he admits some people can be annoyed by music. Interestingly, the example he provides refers to a personal concern regarding the way his teenage son Fabrício listens to music:

> I don't mind, but other people do, right? Sometimes, Fabrício plays really loud music at home. And his sound system really booms. And I feel it is bothering the neighbourhood. I think it's OK during the day, 'but don't play it at night', I tell him. People complain now and then. 'The music is too loud!' the neighbour nags. Then, I ask him to turn it down a bit, but all of a sudden he turns it up again. He enjoys loud music!

The loud sound that bothers the neighbours as described by Lourenço is one of the most often cited sources of annoyance related to music. At home, people expect control over the sound ambience, and outside music invades one's intimacy. What is interesting in this description is that the annoyed one is not himself, but the neighbour. His concern is about being the one who disturbs the other. Therefore, he assumes his position as the father who must keep his son's behaviour in accordance with the good rules of coexistence between neighbours. However, the negotiation has its limits. Little by little, his son changes the volume of the equipment and tries to impose his own way of listening. As Lourenço is not himself bothered by his son's loud music, he interprets it as a generation issue and tries to understand him, though worries about tolerance. He goes on in his elaboration:

> The neighbour doesn't like it for sure. There's a lady who lives next to my house and her family complain. That's why they don't even talk to Fabrício. Because Fabrício plays it really loud indeed! I tell him this because I think it's wrong. Sometimes, he spends fifteen or twenty days in a row without doing it, and there are times when he does it all week long. And always during the day! I mean, in the afternoon, until 3, 4 or 6 p.m. is fine. But I talk to him because I don't like bothering others, and I want him to do it my way.

Lourenço is quite aware of the relation between sound negotiations and the overall topic of bothering others (or not). Part of the difficulties related to 'annoying music' has to do with difficulties in living together in society. Music disagreements are, hence, informed and shaped through shared ideas about adequate or inadequate behaviours in public and private spaces. These ideas, though generally accepted, are not very clear and elicit different interpretations. Possibly, living in a small rural community like Colina makes him more sensitive to the role of interpersonal relations in a healthy sociable life. According to Lourenço, annoying the other is a 'mistake', a kind of misconduct that should be avoided in order to maintain friendly relationships with everybody around. If tolerance is always required to achieve this good coexistence, he stresses that proper self-behaviour is a key issue that allows people to respect each other collectively. Fixing time limits for blasting loud sounds leaked outside the house is a measure to reduce the problem and, at the same time, allows his son to enjoy the music the way he likes. Indirectly, it seems evident that his son is not totally comfortable with these limitations and, possibly, that he may feel his individuality is being disrespected. As will be seen, individuality is constantly challenged by music negotiations, both by the one who wants to listen to a given kind of music at a specific loudness and by those who feel invaded by the presence of the other's sound and music.

Lourenço uses music disagreements to reflect on how life in the countryside is constructed upon a respectful set of behaviours and conditions that differ from those in bigger cities. The shortcut to his elaboration is the issue of complaining. If one is bothered by someone else's attitude, actions or music, it is somehow expected that people have an urge to complain, so that the nuisance can be solved. In Colina, however, according to him, this happens very occasionally, and it is never a major issue between neighbours:

> On Sundays, no one complains. But people complain on Christmas Eve and New Year's Eve. And, when it happens, it's more than one person. 'Damn, they didn't let me sleep last night. This can't go on'. But nobody complains at the very moment. Everyone is very peaceful around here – they don't annoy each other pointlessly. But Rio is different, it is noisy and busy. Here, you don't get to spend day and night all stressed out, and that's why you don't mind the loud music, you're not in such a hurry. That's how one feels in the city. There, in the town of Itamonte, people complain more than they do here. They complain about loud music, cars, shouting. It's different here in Colina. One never gets stressed due to loud music [or at most] once in a while. Daily life makes people stressed.

Lourenço understands the stress as the fundamental element that makes people in the city less tolerant of sound and music. The constant rush and the number of sounds that are part of city environments are sources of stress 'day and night', leaving people more inclined to get irritated and to complain about others. In his interpretation, the messy and noisy environment of big cities is the scenario of less respectful interhuman relations, as well as a fruitful ambience to disagreements. In a sense, many people interviewed here echoed this perception. Lifestyle in the cities is characterized by huge concerns about the self, and this may be an important source of interpersonal mistreatment and complains. What annoying music reveals is a dual difficulty of listening to others, both from the one who controls the playing device in a given space and from the listener who has a short threshold of tolerance towards other people's sounds. Throughout the next pages and chapters, the multi-layered features of these complex issues will be discussed in detail, conducted by the contents of the reports provided by the interviewees. As will be seen, music and sound negotiations are spread in many moments of our daily sociability, being a fundamental element of everyday life, especially in big cities.

Book overview

Chapter 1 discusses the conceptual limits of the concepts of 'music', 'noise' and 'sound'. The terms applied by interviewees to talk about their unpleasant music experiences reveal a value judgement about this experience itself, an important point of departure for the questions that follow. Merging the idea of 'aesthetic disposition' (Bourdieu 1984) with the concept of 'auditor' (Daughtry 2015), it is suggested that the concept of 'auditor's disposition' might refer to the listening practice from which these terms are processed and evaluated. After that, the often-mentioned 'bus case' will be discussed, where a group of teenagers plays loud music, bothering other passengers. It is at the same time a presentation of a typical situation, the development of a conceptual frame and an invitation for a dive into a deeper debate about annoying music.

Space is a key element related to music – either pleasant or annoying. Music, as sound, is a physical phenomenon of air displacement through a place. It occupies a space during some time and interpersonal disagreements are entangled with expectancies about the (in)appropriateness of the sound within the space where it is heard. The issue of being invaded by sounds that come from elsewhere is the topic of the second chapter. It deals with situations where the auditor does not share the same physical space with the sound source, although the sound leaks into the space s/he occupies and produces disturbance. It happens mainly when the auditor is at home, where an expected control of the sound environment is the background of most irritation triggered by invasive sounds. The annoyance is the result of a mismatch between the space occupied by the sound and the physical space delimited by material objects such as walls, doors and windows. Sound surpasses these physical limitations and gains presence over other places. By doing so, it forcibly interacts as an element in a space that is not framed accordingly, raising the perception of intrusion and inadequacy. The physical position of the auditor is an important reference for his/her irritation towards music. If one is in a place assaulted by an outside sound, s/he is likely to be irritated by the situation.

The third chapter discusses the nuisance caused by music played in a shared physical space. Different from the situations examined in the previous chapter, in these cases, the auditor shares a physical space but is bothered by its sound, having no control to stop it. Music in restaurants, stores, public and private transport, and even domestic conflicts at home are the most cited situations where people are annoyed by the music being played in the same physical space occupied by them. Here, the idea of intrusion doesn't fit very well since, usually, the bothered auditor can leave the place. As will be discussed later, in some cases it actually happens. However, in other cases, one is not free to leave and is thus forced to stay in a place surrounded by unpleasant music, which can be highly annoying.

Most respondents associate unchosen music with the idea of violence. Chapter 4 will interpret the multiple ways violence can be understood as a conceptual tool that helps understanding conflicts involving sound and music. Violence appears in the accounts through the use of a particular vocabulary, filled with metaphors like 'I want to kill him' or 'it is like a bomb inside my house'. The figurative language works as a speech strategy to enhance the power of music and its disturbing features. Beyond that verbal resource, the debate addresses music itself as a device of violence, imposed on others in different situations. Violence also appears as a shortcut to solving conflicts, when, for instance, the threat of 'calling the police' is stated during disagreements. Fear, threat and invasions are elements of music and sound nuisance that are entangled with violence.

Chapter 5 is a debate about taste, mostly constructed through music genres. Some music practices annoy more than others or, at least, are mentioned more often than others. People in Brazil talk a lot about being bothered by 'funk', whereas interviewees in Scotland mostly mention 'pop'. Genres are classification marks that construct social barriers and differentiations, always intertwined with moral debates, prejudices and different degrees of confrontation. Music conflicts are also taste conflicts, experienced in an environment crossed by identity and belonging, where other issues such as class, race, gender, and income resonate.

With a titled inspired by Susan Sontag's book on photography, the final chapter reaches the complicated issue of the 'other'. It is the main argument of the book: music annoys mainly because it makes us face the other, against our will. Living together means touching people's bodies, ideas, smells and sounds. For its particular physical characteristics, sound leaks and invades other spaces and bodies, raising emotions that can disturb others. Negotiations about music and sound environment are power negotiations, closely linked to social conflicts and daily coexistence with the other. Annoying music is, hence, an experience in which our place in the world is challenged, raising claims for rights, individuality and citizenship. It makes us face the difficult task of listening to the other, of living together.

This book is highly informed by my personal experience with annoying music in some situations. Although discussed in more detail in Chapter 1 and the Epilogue, my own ideas about music conflicts cross every page. As a trained musician, I soon learned to acknowledge music as a fantastic device in daily life, one that provides pleasurable and joyful moments of collective and individual fun. Then, writing and thinking about annoying music has also been a personal challenge that somehow changed my practices of listening to music, the loudness at which I adjust my music devices and my tolerance towards unchosen music controlled by someone else. The questions and difficult issues dealt with in this book helped me to listen to multiple sides of music experience. It is not merely a matter of 'cleaning' the soundscape, as Murray Shaffer intended to do, but to understand sound and music experience as something that is at the same time pleasurable and disturbing, joyful and annoying.

The slippery classification of opposite poles of feelings towards music depends on how interpersonal relations are constructed within the time and space where the music is being played. Developing the research and writing the book have allowed me to dive into these complex issues and have shifted my auditor's disposition. Hopefully, reading it can do something similar.

1

Slippery concepts
Music, sound and noise

A few years ago, my daughter got, as a birthday gift, a scintillating red electronic spider-shaped toy. From the top of its 'body', two low-quality speakers played a loud sound while it moved on the floor, changing direction as it hit an obstacle such as furniture, walls, doors or someone's body. My daughter loved it. I cannot say the same about me and my wife, but that's not the point. I remembered this spider because, for me, it was a very good example of annoying music. The recorded file played by the speakers could be easily defined as 'music', once it was a recognizable *ostinato* with a rhythmic pattern, a melody and a sequence of three chords repeated exhaustively. Despite the poor distorted sound of the designed speakers, it was 'music'.

As I began to interview people for this research, I not only recalled the spider (which has somehow haunted my music memories since then) but also expected someone to mention children's toys as an example of irritating music-sound experience. Anyone who has had any contact with young children is aware of the number of noisy toys available on toy stores' shelves, and the disturbance they cause inside families' houses. Of course, one can say children are noisy, not only their toys, but also their play, which is filled with cries, chants and all sorts of human and non-human sounds. Children learn things through sounds, they make experiments with them, they cry and sing to call our attention. Shouts are the common audible presence of children and, usually, they have fun with sounded objects. My daughter was quite frustrated when the spider 'broke' one week after its arrival at home. In fact, we removed the battery and, as she was too young to understand, she only regretted that it had stopped 'singing'. Possibly, for a child, 'music', 'singing', 'sound' and even 'noise' are words that make up part of a set of designations used to define the sonic dimension of their playful universe. However, what called my attention was that in my interviews – done with adults and (a few) teenagers – nobody mentioned children's toys.

For me, this silence towards such a noisy universe may not be due to memory blanks or to a consideration that the nuisance caused by toys is of low importance, but to a conceptual fracture that splits the sound universe into separated definitions of sound, music and noise. Although the differentiation between these concepts is far from being clear, it is interesting how all the interviewees excluded children's toys from their memories of unpleasant *music* experiences. Perhaps they would not define my daughter's spider as playing 'music', but making 'sounds', or even making 'noise'. Therefore, before going further in the debate on annoying music, I think it can be worth it to discuss these definitions.

What do the words say?

At first, it is important to reinforce that this book is about *music*, not sound or noise. My initial thoughts during the beginning of the research were not to dedicate too much effort to the definitions of each term. For some time during the process of collecting data and talking to people about annoying music, I followed a common-sense understanding of the category 'music', a word that easily refers to most popular music (songs) heard on radio stations, on playlists, at parties, in stores and on streets and that also includes music pieces (not-songs) heard at concerts, on recordings, on TV shows, on soundtracks of films, in ads and in many other audio-visual formats. Music is music!

In fact, most interviewees did not manifest any doubt regarding the conceptual idea of 'music', talking about their music experiences in daily life without questioning its definition. However, some conversations pointed to the unclear conceptual differentiation between music, sound and noise. After some time, then, I realized the need for a deeper discussion about these terms. In everyday talks, sometimes the word referring to a sonic experience slides from one to another, revealing not only the kind of listening practice but also the movement of the definitions themselves and the relative value applied to each one.

When confronted with unwanted music, people often elaborate a value judgement on the kind of sound that is being played. This evaluation is made explicit through the language choices made while describing unpleasant sound events. Therefore, the words 'music', 'sound' and 'noise' are transformed into concepts related to hierarchical ideas about this experience. These concepts are applied to specific sonic events as resources for highlighting the subjective evaluation of such events. Far from being technical or limited concepts, the differences between music, sound and noise are blurred in daily talks, according to this personal judgement. Often, the evaluative force of the concepts points to the positive interpretation of the word 'music'. 'Music' defines not only a sonic phenomenon or a kind of artistic manipulation of sounds, but a complex process of evaluation and classification of sounds in everyday life.

In a widely known ethnomusicological definition coined by John Blacking in his often-quoted *How musical is man?*, what we usually call 'music' can be understood as 'humanly organized sounds' (Blacking 2000). In this definition, music is the result of an action done by humans, which implies ideas of organization and manipulation of 'sounds'. In his words, 'musical performance, as distinct from the production of noise, is inconceivable without the perception of order in sound' (Blacking 2000: 10). According to the author, 'sound' is the raw material that must be processed to become 'music'. Interestingly, Blacking admits that 'noise' may also be produced by humans, but he does not develop a more detailed debate about the distinctions between the two concepts. Following the same direction, Puerto Rican sociologist Angél Quintero Rivera states that this organization is an action that aims to control the materiality of life, playing an important political role in social struggles (2005: 34). 'Music', hence, is a human artefact that deals with power negotiations and inequalities, as the result of control over 'non-musical' sounds. Quintero Rivera develops a wide interpretation of the process of colonization in Latin America, in which missionaries tried to impose a musical heritage of church music on indigenous people. These musical procedures are defined by him as a modelling system of thought and values, manifested in sound organization as a device of power. In this sense, the resulting syncopated rhythm that he calls 'tropical music' is a negotiation of colonial power processed as a shift in sound organization. In this interpretation, the social human action of organization of sounds is conceived as a political tool that allows people to reshape power asymmetries through music-making. The force of this argument lies in the fact that the resulting concept of 'music' is defined as the consolidation of a power struggle in which 'sound' is the basic material. Organization is understood here as a form of control, adding an 'order' to the sonic universe and, consequently, controlling behaviours, thoughts and interactions. Once the 'order' is related to the definition of 'music', 'non-musical' sounds would be conceptually associated with 'disorder'. Often, these sounds are referred to as 'noise'.

The idea of order appears indirectly in the more neutral definition of acoustic sound, according to which a sound source that produces irregular waves is defined as 'noise' whereas regular sound waves are perceived as 'musical sounds', or 'tuned sounds'. Brazilian musician and scholar José Miguel Wisnik defines this difference in his often-quoted book *O Som e o Sentido* (*Sound and Senses*):

> Nature provides two major modes of experiencing the complex wave that sound is: regular, constant, stable frequencies, such as those which produce the tuned sound, with its well-defined pitch and irregular, inconstant, and unstable frequencies, such as those which produce noises, blurring, sound scribbles, and buzzing. (Wisnik 1999: 26)

Although this definition tries to avoid value judgements about the sound waves provided by nature, the positive value of the semantic field of 'regularity' encompasses the idea of order and organization, locating in the opposite pole the ideas of irregularity, disorder and disorganization, usually attached to a lower value. The association of noise as a disturbing element echoes certain approaches of the theory of communication, in which the 'clearness' of effective communication must be done without the interference of external sounds that may puzzle the sign or even block understanding (Shannon and Weaver 1964). These sounds are referred to as 'noise' that ought to be eliminated and purified so that perfect communication can be achieved. Although it can be argued that the idea of interference has been applied to communication systems inspired and funded by telegraph and telephone companies, the assumption that 'noise' is the word that defines sounds that blur the efficiency of communication is widely disseminated in daily speech. The force of the negative interpretation of the word 'noise' crosses different fields and authors, providing a strong common-sense agreement that is still applied by people in their vocabulary about sonic experiences and evaluations.

However, the distinctions between 'noise', 'sound' and 'music' are not always that clear. Sometimes, people slide from one word to another, depending on the feeling they want to highlight. Even in academic works, the distinction is often obscure. In his influential work about 'noise', Jacques Attali defines 'music' in the first pages as an 'organization of noise'. Throughout the book, Attali sometimes refers to 'noise' as a synonym of 'sound', defining it as the raw material of the organization or codification operated by 'music'. In his words:

> All music, any organization of sound is then a tool for the creation or consolidation of a community, a totality. It is what links a power center to its subjects, and thus, more generally, it is an attribute of power in all its forms. Therefore, any theory of power today must include a theory of the localization of noise and its endowment with form. (Attali 2009: 6)

The 'form' would be, according to the author, the music itself, conceived as a formation, domestication and ritualization of the 'noise' (2009: 24). Going further, he states that 'noise is murder and music is sacrifice' (2009: 28), trying to understand the sacrifice as a way to represent and dramatize actual violence. The conceptual intersections between music and violence in Attali's work will be discussed later in this book, but what remains relevant for now is the way he frames the concept of 'noise' attached to the concept of 'sound', and both opposed somehow to the idea of 'music'. In Attali's terms, there is no substantial difference between sound and noise, as he underlines the role of music as a device of control and organization. The opposition between 'music' and 'noise' within the realm of sound events appears also at the beginning of Bruce Johnson and Martin Cloonan's book about music and violence, precisely when the authors argue that it is needed to unveil the 'negative pole' of music experience in daily life. According to them, music is 'sound', 'and when it inflicts violence it does so not only by virtue of what it means but what it then is: noise' (2009: 4). This statement resounds common-sense agreements that put a qualitative meaning in the word 'noise'. The ideas of disorder, disorganization and disturbance in communication and violence are attached to the word 'noise' as it highlights the unpleasant or uncontrolled nature of sounds. Although it can be perceived as a human action, noise is usually described as 'something unwanted, inappropriate, interfering, distracting, irritating' (Hendy 2013: x).

Marie Suzanne Thompson (2014) suggests that this binary separation of the universe of sounds should be put aside once it directs the interpretations towards a 'good' and 'bad' definition. According to her, these common definitions are insufficient to describe the complexities of noise in everyday life, highlighting that this approach requires a listener who hears it as such (2014: 20). Therefore, she criticizes the simple definition of noise as 'bad', stating that this is framed through a subject-oriented perspective that ignores other powerful possibilities and usages of the term noise and of the noise itself. In her thesis, she proposes a non-binary definition, in which noise is not defined through what is it not (*not* desired or *irregular* sound waves), but as a 'productive, transformative force and a necessary component of material relations' (Thompson 2014: 6). Her attempt to understand noise 'beyond unwanted sound' is due to her interpretations of noise-music, which displace the idea of noise as disorder. In fact, thinking about noise-music is an interesting way to take noise as a floating category, that can be taken both as an undesired malfunction in communication systems and as a powerful tool to develop artistic creative works. According to Thompson, noise-music explodes the binary opposition held by authors such as Attali, who understands noise as 'the antithesis of music – it is what lies outside the realm of ordered, musical sound' (Thompson 2014: 177). In noise-music, noise is not only the material to be organized, but the result itself of this organization. In this sense, noise and music would be defined and perceived as complementary categories, beyond the common-sense definitions.

However, in doing so, we inevitably fall again into the subject-oriented approach she explicitly tries to avoid. Noise-music can be understood as 'music' only for those who are trained and able to listen to it in that particular way, those who are able to understand noise-music as 'organized sounds'. Although Thompson's arguments are very fruitful in enlarging the conceptual definition of noise, her theoretical approach is somehow detached from the everyday language in which noise is often defined and redefined. Yet she clearly states that she doesn't deny 'noise's everyday connotations but looks to add to them' (Thompson 2014: 18); the idea of noise as an unsettled category rather than an always negative term can be productive in emphasizing precisely the role of the listening in the process. In other words, the way people hear sounds is a key element in the process of defining music, sound and noise.

My point is that subjective perception doesn't need to be set apart for us to understand sonic experiences in a non-binary way. Instead, the form through which people apply different terms to specific situations is relevant in revealing hierarchies between the words and the concepts that define their experience. Usually, 'music' is referred to with a positive approach, but not always. Same as 'sound' and even 'noise'. Empirical data suggests a slippery administration of these concepts, framing spoken language with a subjective judgement of the sonic experience. Let's take, for instance, the report by Janet, a sixty-four-year-old Scottish retired pharmacologist who describes a situation in public transport that is not precisely related to 'music', but to a sound leakage of music devices that cannot be listened to as 'music' by her:

> Even on a bus, I can't stand people who play these in stereos. Here in Edinburgh, you go on a bus – if you go upstairs and somebody comes behind you and haven't got decent earpieces, you can hear this tiny sound behind you. It's leaked and I find that really irritating. Because all you hear is the din: you don't hear the music, you just hear the din. That's what I call 'impersonal stereos', because they are meant to be only for the person who is listening to music but when the sound comes out, some of them are really loud. I don't like it and sometimes I simply move away and sit somewhere else.

Janet puts it very clearly that she would rather have her trip in silence, but this sound half-way between noise ('din') and music is perceived as extremely irritating. Her sound experience leads her to define it as 'noise', although the owner of the earpieces obviously was listening to 'music'. Moreover, she raises an important issue related to our debate: the volume. Her perception of the sound that leaks from the earphone is merged with a judgement about its loudness. Accordingly, she can only hear the 'noise' because the person is listening to the music 'too loud'.

Technically, volume is the amplitude of sound waves, heard in a range of dynamics that goes from the low *piano* to the high *forte*. 'The intensity is an information on the *energy* of the sound source' (Wisnik 1999: 25), which always raises corporal sensations associated with an amount of strength and force. Very loud sounds can interfere in the body in several ways, with a growing potential to harm or damage alongside the increase of the volume. Discussing the effects of loudness in sound perception, Michael Heller (2015) points to the importance of thinking about the physicality of the sound experience, since radically different bodily consequences happen depending on the volume. Beyond the so-called 'threshold of pain', 'sound waves are no longer experienced as intangible or detached objects of hearing but confront the body through an experience of direct physical touch, force, or torment' (Heller 2015: 42). He argues that, in extreme loudness, a listener collapse occurs, provoking the auditor to lose the perceptual distinction between the self and the sound (idem: 45). The fact that very loud sounds can inflict pain reveals the importance of volume in everyday music experiences. The loudness of a given sound is an element of its materiality that changes radically the way it affects the body, and perception of it is framed by this corporeal effect. And so it is the sound judgement.

Moreover, volume is related to space. As Martin Daughtry puts it, sounds have 'size', they occupy an 'area over which they are identifiable as sounds [...] that are accessible not just to you but also to those around you, and therefore as events (or temporary objects) whose ontology is expansive and dispersed' (2015: 161). Therefore, volume can be defined as the amount of space occupied by the sound that allows it to leak from the source to other physical spaces. The higher the volume, the more easily it will reach other places (Heller 2015: 49). But, of course, reaching other places does not mean that it will be harmful to anyone or that it will trigger a change in the definition of the sound. This perception is balanced with the environmental sound as well as with the expectations of desired and undesired sounds within this environment.

Clearly, despite the fact that the sound leakage from the earphone could not be loud enough to impose damage to other passengers' ears or bodies, Janet feels bothered by the sound. As such, she slides the definition of sound from music to noise, emphasizing her nuisance and the negative feeling towards the situation. 'The problem is not the volume as such (measured by decibels) but the feeling that someone else's music is invading our space, that we can't listen to it as music, a pleasurable organization of sound, but only as noise, an undifferentiated din' (Frith 2004: 32). Janet is not wounded physically by the loudness of the earphone leakage, which leads us to reframe the nuisance of 'loud' volumes in a given space not only according to the volume itself but to a very unstable and subjective evaluation about the expected sound environment in a physical space. What I would like to retain here is that the slippery definitions of noise and music are somehow merged with the interpretation of the adequacy of the loudness in that space and moment. Still keeping the opposition between noise and music, but in a different way, seventeen-year-old Brazilian student Luane declares she does not like heavy metal music. Asked if music can annoy her, she states:

> Music annoys me when it is too noisy. I am not so keen on heavy metal. But, sometimes, you play a song and find out that, once translated, the lyrics are beautiful! They make statements, [are] revolutionary. The lyrics are beautiful, but that constant, repeating *ahahah* sound is something that irritates me, it seems like someone is banging on kitchenware all the time! I don't like it.

The direct association between 'noisy' and heavy metal in her narrative is interesting. The 'noise' is referred to as an element of the genre, as part of the set of sound organizations that make heavy metal music recognizable to her. Even admitting the lyrics may be beautiful (which she can only grasp after checking its translation), the 'sound-noise' of the background makes it unbearable. The significant comparison with kitchenware being hit and the vocalization of the noise she made while describing it directs her irritation to the loudness. As she defines the loud 'noise', she unveils her preference for lower volume music genres. In different ways, both Luane and Janet define music and noise according to the loudness of the sound, pointing to an unspoken desire towards quietness and silence.

The idea of silence encompasses a set of expectations on a given sound environment. A bus trip, for instance, is filled with several kinds of sounds, both from inside the bus (the sounds of the engines, people chatting, moving and so on) and from the street outside (horns, cars, other buses, indistinct talks, cries, dogs barking and so on). In this sense, the result is always 'noisy', never 'silent'. However, the evaluation of the sound environment is informed by the expectancy of some 'adequate' loudness of these multiple sounds. Heller invites us to 'imagine, for example, trying to fall asleep to a lullaby sung at the level of a jet engine' (2015: 42). In other words, the perception of silence is also the result of a judgement of adequacy and the loudness of a sound event. Moreover, this judgement is selective. In a noisy environment such as a bus ride, people select which sounds are acceptable and which ones are not. Possibly, for Janet, the street noise and the bus engine are tuned as non-important, as background sounds that don't bother her. The music leakage of the passenger beside her, on the contrary, is heard as an unpleasant sound that she would like to silence or to get rid of. This personal gestalt as processed by her suggests that possibly music-related sounds may be perceived as more intrusive and annoying than environmental non-musical sounds. Yet the border between music and non-music is flexible, and the recognition of 'music' brings to the surface a set of expectancies towards the sonic experience that informs the way that experience will be valued. Music attracts attention. Janet's irritation with the 'impersonal stereos' may be due to her idea that the music ought to be kept controlled or else it calls her attention and disturbs her trip.

However, silence is not always something perceived as 'good' or desirable. The musician Alec, thirty-four years old, reports a situation where he felt uncomfortable with a silent environment:

> The other day, a few weeks ago, I was meeting a friend in a bar and it was so quiet; it was like being in a library. I felt like 'come on, put some spirit into this'. If I go out I want to have a good time and I think that having music helps for that too. To shake up my mood.

Adequacy is the key idea. Libraries and bars are two radically different environments that are expected to have different sonic engagements. If a very low loudness is required and demanded in a library, a bar must be a bit 'noisy' to have 'spirit'. The idea of 'silence', hence, can be conceived not as a pure (and impossible) absence of sound, but also as an evaluative concept that results from a judgement of the sound environment modulated by loudness and by expectations of adequacy. In Alec's report, being in a bar requires a sound environment that is different from the one required in a library, and the music provides this adequate background sound.

The instability of the definitions of music, sound and noise directs our concerns to the role of the subject in the debate about annoying music, a subject who listens, an 'auditor' who has music tastes and sound expectancies in a given place.

Auditor's dispositions

In his book *Listening to War*, Martin Daughtry (2015) uses the term 'auditor' to refer to those who are in an earshot of a sonic event. Throughout his study on the sound environment of the Iraqi war, Daughtry argues that the 'belliphonic sounds' – sounds of guns and explosions that would not happen if there were not a war – are learned and heard by military staff and Iraqi civilians as a source of information, angst, fear and tension. As such, they carry messages about the direction, the force and the position of the sound source, allowing the auditors to analyse the risks and the possible actions. In this process, the spatiality of the auditor is a key factor to permit or not the right interpretation of the sound, as well as its capability to harm and injure. Moreover, the auditor's position is also determined by the role s/he plays in the war scene. A civilian will likely be at home, fearing the bullets and bombs outside, while a service member will be more often in the core of the detonation of the shot, being a possible target or triggering it. This is not to mention other people that the author could not talk to such as journalists or Iraqi rebels, who surely had other positions in the conflict and possibly other ways to interpret the sounds. The idea of 'position' can be taken, hence, both as a physical reference of the auditor in relation to the sound source and as an almost metaphorical sense that refers to the role an individual performs in any sound and music experience.

More than an operational definition of the sound as 'noise', 'music' or 'sound', Daughtry argues that the auditor processes a complex judgement of the sound event as a source of information. Mostly, they are dealing with non-musical sounds, and listening is a way of getting vital information about the distance and direction, and the kind of guns involved, which determines the risk and the adequate behaviour for the people in the extreme circumstance of war. In these situations, interpretation of sounds is a shared knowledge about the sound's physical characteristics that can save lives. Far from the war front, we could argue that these interpretations are also the result of a knowledge that is merged with our position in relation to the sound source in every situation. In mundane, much less dramatic situations, we extract from the sounds we hear information that is evaluated according to our interpretation. A key aspect of this process is our position in relation to the sound source. Take, for instance, the report from Rachel, a thirty-eight-year-old biologist who remembers a scene from years before, when she and her husband went to live in a far northern state of Brazil called Roraima:

> When I moved to Roraima, we lived in a hotel room for two weeks. But these two weeks were really hard for me, really bad. As we knew we were only staying for two weeks, we looked for a very cheap hotel. Wow, and what a comfortable, nice hotel – wonderful food! When we found out why it was so cheap we understood. Because our window faced the bus station, where people sell candies and play *brega* music on speakers. At first, I closed the window, left the air conditioner on all the time. It is very hot there. But I did so twenty-four hours a day! The sound was turned slightly down after hours, a little; but on weekends it was louder. People arrived there, waited for the bus and danced.

Rachel's narrative addresses two issues related to her position in that sound environment. First, the sound of the bus terminal invaded her private home filling it with undesired music. In this sense, she and her husband were not engaged with the music experience and, in their position at home, they expected a quiet sound environment. Although she did not define the intrusive music as 'noise', the loudness of the sound bothered her peace and 'silence' expectancy. Her role in the sound experience was as a hotel guest trying to rest peacefully (which means silently) and the music disturbed this expectation. Of course, passengers in the bus terminal waiting for their buses probably felt quite differently, using the music to help the passing of time and transforming the boring waiting time into a joyful entertainment. That's another position towards the music. In this passage, she did not mention the word 'music', referring to it first through the name of the music genre played at the terminal and then as 'sound'. 'Sound' is the term associated with her failed attempt to block the music outside her room while the music genre '*brega*' is the term she uses to refer to the music played.

This is quite interesting because it leads us to the second issue raised by her narrative. Her (negative) perception and interpretation of the music also resulted from her aesthetic and ethic expectations. As she refers explicitly to *brega* music, she reinforces her value judgement on that music, built, in turn, through her displaced situation as a migrant. Born and raised in Rio de Janeiro, one of the biggest and most important, cosmopolitan and famous Brazilian cities, she heard *brega* music as a strange and exotic genre she could not 'understand'. *Brega* is a genre of popular music in the north and northeast of Brazil that sounds like a mix of romantic ballad, bolero rhythm and pop song (Soares 2017). It is very successful among poorer strata of society, being labelled sometimes as 'maiden's music' (Araújo 2002). Her hearing of *brega* is, then, informed by her 'position' in the place, which in turn is a complex result of judgements and expectations of a young, middle-class, intellectual woman from a big and cosmopolitan southern city, then displaced to the far end of the country and having to face loud and unwanted sound-music in her private hotel room.

Conceived as a role performed by an auditor, the idea of 'position' can be enlarged to encompass another layer of meaning if we cross it with the Bourdieusian idea of 'disposition'. According to Bourdieu (1984), an 'aesthetic disposition' is the result of the amount of 'cultural capital' one possesses that allows him/her to admire a piece of artwork. Cultural capital is acquired throughout one's life depending on family background and the institutional years of formal learning at school. In the author's well-known (and criticized) theory, taste is the result of several layers that make up part of this lifelong training and learning, being the condition through which one is more (or less) likely to prefer legitimized artwork. Aesthetically speaking, high cultural capital provides the appropriate 'disposition' needed to admire and like highly evaluated artwork.

Without going further in the implications and contradictions of Bourdieu's theory regarding the value judgement of cultural goods, I'd like to focus here on the idea of 'disposition' as a set of shared conditions, values and knowledge that work in the specific relations people have with music in everyday life. It has to do with social position in a wider sense, encompassing class, gender and racial belonging, as well as territorial and professional marks. The powerful insight of Bourdieu is the general idea that our background as an individual in a social context conforms to tendencies to like or dislike artistic works. Although his work focus on the capacity to admire what he calls legitimate culture, it is possible to suppose that a wider aesthetic disposition is also informed by this kind of 'capital'. As Simon Frith argues, popular culture may have similar processes of accumulation of knowledge and discriminatory skill that also have hierarchical effect (1996: 9). For Rachel, her background, musical taste and cultural capital could not be set aside during her time in the hotel. For her, *brega* music was annoying both because of its inadequacy and because it was judged by her as 'bad music'. Her initial time in Roraima was defined as 'difficult'. However, later in the interview, she added that after living there for one year (not in the hotel), she could then 'understand' *brega* music, recognizing its value as an identity trace of the northern people and respecting it, if not liking it. This change is rather relevant to our discussion, as it reveals precisely the idea of accumulation and knowledge related to any music experience, which naturally changes one's interpretations of unchosen music. It changes the aesthetic disposition of the auditor towards a sound-music experience. Hence, it changes one's judgement.

When we choose to play some music, we are somehow dealing with tastes constructed throughout our lives, but also with a mood-making that corresponds to our desire in that particular moment. Music helps us to match our emotions in the way we define as adequate and this process happens at the same time as a momentary decision and as a lifelong memory triggered through that choice. In her influential work, Tia DeNora argues that music is a 'technology of the self', helping people to modulate feelings and sensations according to their will and moment. DeNora supported her findings with fifty-two Anglophonic women interviewed in the United States and the United Kingdom, highlighting that these women were clearly aware of music's role 'as a means for creating, enhancing, sustaining and changing subjective, cognitive, bodily and self-conceptual states' (2000: 49). Through music, people achieve desired moods in their personal experience, controlling affects and sensations. What I'd like to argue here is that for this process to happen, we must have a 'disposition' to be affected positively by the music, allowing the adequate response. Disposition which is not only related to a judgement of adequacy and momentary desire but accumulated during our lives as an archive of music pieces and positively evaluated associated feelings.

In the opposite way, it is possible to infer that a very similar process occurs when we do not choose the music to be heard. Depending on our background history and 'cultural capital', certain codes, preferences and tastes will be called on to interpret that music and to judge its value as well as to settle possible emotional responses. Our cultural aesthetic disposition will inform us so that we can like or dislike the music we did not choose to listen to at that moment. The case reported by Rachel, again, is a good example of this process.

At the same time, even if a piece of music that we do like is playing, our mood can simply not fit with the mood required by the music and the sound will be perceived as disturbing. We cannot affirm whether Rachel would have been less bothered by the noisy neighbour if the soundtrack had fit her taste. Sometimes, the inadequacy of music performed is so high that the fact we know and like the music does not overpass the nuisance (I'll discuss these cases in Chapter 5). In this sense, it is important to understand annoyance in levels, from slight discomfort to very high suffering. The music we like imposed in an inappropriate time and space is likely to be less irritating than the music we don't like. In her work about noise, Ana Lidia Domínguez highlights the different ways an unwanted sound is perceived, provoking rather different responses of irritation or nuisance:

Based on this idea, we can understand, for instance, that a neighbour's party may upset us more on a Tuesday than on a Saturday, or else that it may not upset us on weekdays as long as we are invited to join it. Or one may meekly accept the city chaos on a Monday morning but not on Sunday. The variance in noise perception is explainable by the fact that sound is an intruder only when it disturbs our habits or prevent us from accomplishing self-defined tasks. (Domínguez Ruiz 2015: 120)

Two things can be brought to the surface in this quote. First, the sliding of conceptual ideas revealed in those sentences. Domínguez Ruiz is concerned with city 'noise', and all her debate gravitates around the implications of noise in everyday cities. However, it is interesting that the example of the neighbours' party suggests the leakage of 'music', reinforcing the idea developed here that the definitions are unclear and highly subjected to personal considerations in each moment. The 'music' from the 'party' becomes 'noise' just like the hypothetical street sounds on a Sunday morning. This is a very common process. Josep Martí, in an insightful article suggestively called 'When music becomes noise', describes how in Barcelona the vibrant musical experience of the touristic Ramblas is perceived by residents as an 'undeniable nuisance' (Martí 1997:13). Indispositions towards a music event redefine the judgement of the sonic experience as undesired and 'noisy'. What is important to be highlighted here is the role of the auditor who judges the adequacy of these music-sound-noise events.

The second aspect in Domínguez Ruiz's quote is related to the idea of 'disposition' she uses to refer to the expectations towards the sound environment. With this word – yet not in a Bourdieusian sense – she reaffirms that not only is the physical position of the auditor to be considered in the evaluation of the sound but also her/his personal desire to listen (or not) to any music and sound at that moment. The key issue here is not only the quality of the sound or the cultural background of the listener but also a complex process that involves both aspects together with a judgement about the adequacy of the sound event.

Merging the Bourdieusian notion of disposition with the idea of positionality employed by Daughtry can help to highlight the complex process triggered by unchosen music experience, which is the result of one's *position* as well as his/her aesthetic and cultural *disposition* to that particular music. I propose to call this set of conditions 'auditor's dispositions', a set that involves the positionality, role, cultural background, sensibility, taste and judgement of adequacy of a given sound-music event made by a person who listens to it. This idea, of course, is not new. Jonathan Sterne highlights that listening is an active performance that involves a set of technological devices and a learning process that allows the listener to separate sounds that are important to be heard from others that should be ignored (Sterne 2003: 25). The concept of 'auditor's disposition' tries simply to emphasize the role of the cultural embodiment that informs these techniques and selective process of listening. Moreover, it highlights the role of sound judgements in the process, interpreted mainly through the word applied to classify the sound experience. David Hendy states that the idea of 'noise' 'is not always a sound "out of place", nor always strictly speaking unwanted, [but] can perhaps be thought of as a sound that someone somewhere doesn't want to be heard' (2013: 169). Again, the concept of auditor's disposition adds one's background knowledge and taste to the evaluative process of (un)wanted sound or music, mixed with an adjacent judgement about its pertinence and adequacy. It allows us as well to better understand music and sound conflicts as related to different positionalities that involve not only the moment of the experience and a physical position towards the sound source but also a constructed history of belonging and repulsion, and a momentary desire or expectation regarding what to listen to or not.

The bus case

Music negotiations are space-situated. Personal unpleasant experiences with music and sound are often mentioned by auditors merged with a description of the site where it happened. One of the most cited places where music is considered disturbing is on public transport. In contemporary cities, people spend a large amount of time going and coming from work, waiting for buses and trains, and being bored inside them. Public transport is a place to perform activities to 'kill the time' such as reading, thinking, chatting and… listening to music. Music began to make up part of these everyday journeys due to mobile technology, which allowed sound devices to be portable enough to be attached to our bodies. 'Personal stereos' are used to create an individual sound environment, 'replacing' the urban noisy background. According to Michael Bull, this replacement 'changes the users' relation to the urban environment, themselves and others together with their sense of presence and time' (2000: 18). Similarly, Tia DeNora argues that 'personal music listening offers a room in which to recharge one's batteries, avoid noxious stimuli in the immediate environment and dream, play and otherwise engage with an alternate world' (2013: 72).

Individual music listening is an action that has a powerful capacity to split one's personal space from the outside world. In his book about the use of iPods in urban spaces, Bull states that 'the urban sound confronts the subject as unordered, chaotic, and polyrhythmic' (2007: 24), and the use of headphones provides a desired 'isolation' from this unpleasant sound environment. One of his informants, Joey, describes precisely a situation in the New York City subway, where the device is used to 'block the noises', making him feel 'less irritable and impatient' (quoted in Bull 2007: 30). Throughout the book, several reports of enthusiastic iPod users reaffirm that its use allows a personal administration of the external noise, building a kind of comfortable and pleasant 'acoustic bubble'. Moreover, earphones mediate interpersonal relations in urban spaces, allowing a sense of undisturbed privacy as the environment sounds are blocked. Individual listening is, ultimately, a practice of individualistic behaviour, segregating the person from the outside world.

However, we cannot take this isolation strictly. Several degrees of permeability happen in personal stereos, making this 'bubble' much less isolated than some narratives may suggest. As we have seen in Janet's report, we cannot take for granted that the sound of personal stereos is always kept inside the earphones. Usually, it is possible to hear a leakage from the phones if you are a nearby passenger. And the opposite is true. Unless you have a high-quality (and expensive) pair of earphones and the music is being played in an unhealthily high volume, the external sounds are unlikely to be totally blocked.

In a critique of Michael Bull's idea of an 'acoustic bubble', Simone Pereira de Sá argues that, in many big Latin American cities such as Rio de Janeiro, one can never walk down streets without being aware of the environment. As Rio de Janeiro is known worldwide for its street violence, being visually and acoustically connected with the surrounding world is an attitude that may prevent assaults and robbery (Pereira de Sá 2011: 13). Hence, public transport behaviour regarding sound and music is related to specific conditions depending on the place, city and country where it happens. The interviews for this research, as I've mentioned, were done in Rio de Janeiro and Edinburgh, cities that have radically different systems of transport.

In Edinburgh, the public transport is administrated by Transport for Edinburgh, through two main companies that are, respectively, responsible for bus operation (Lothian Buses) and trams (Edinburgh Trams Ltda.), both under the regulation of the city's council. Although not exactly cheap, the system has reasonable fare options, which include family and day tickets and monthly payment. Taking a bus in Edinburgh is a comfortable experience, with a trustable timetable and good quality cars. The buses are quiet, as are most parts of the urban environment. Being not a very big city (513,000 inhabitants in 2017), the public transport system reaches most parts of the city and surrounding localities, with easy access. On the other hand, Rio is a metropolis with 6.7 million citizens within the city and more than 11 million in the wider city region. The bus system is the target of constant complaints of the population, being perceived as expensive, irregular and dangerous. Most of the buses are old and their maintenance is precarious. Several private companies provide the lines that cover the city transport, in a system administrated by a federation of companies called Fetransport. Corruption and suspicious relations between members of the government of the State of Rio de Janeiro and Fetransport have kept the precariousness of the system unchanged through the decades, providing high profit for the companies. As a consequence, taking a bus in Rio, especially in the poorer areas of the city, is a rough experience, with crowded and hot buses driven by irritated drivers who usually do not respect passengers. The situation is a bit different, of course, in wealthy districts, where newer buses equipped with air conditioners provide a much more comfortable experience. Nevertheless, as these are restricted to only some parts of the city, the overall experience is mostly defined as unpleasant and noisy.

Not surprisingly, despite the fact that some people interviewed in Edinburgh did mention public transport as a site of sound annoyance, the number of Brazilian interviewees who developed detailed descriptions of disturbing and irritating sound in buses and trains was far bigger. In this sense, to think about music and sound experience in public transport requires going beyond the idea of acoustic isolation and towards considering different cultural backgrounds and contexts where this experience happens. In the noisy ambience of bus transport in Rio, the use of earphones is but one of the possible experiences during the trip. Individual listening and shared sounds are overlapped in many different ways. Following these complex possible uses of music and sound in buses, Pereira de Sá describes a situation she had that points to other entangled issues. She mentioned her experience of taking a bus together with a group of youngsters that she heard lived in a *favela* in the south zone of the city. Living in a *favela* frames the youngsters as belonging to a low stratum of the population, which is always merged with racial prejudice (she noticed they were 'non-white') and social stereotypes:

> They picked a seat in the back and started playing *funk carioca* at top volume on a mobile phone. Talking about their musical preferences and making some kind of percussive accompaniment with their hands and feet, they spent the whole ride ostensibly showing that they were really enjoying the impromptu performance which invaded the acoustic space of the bus. They could have decided to listen to the track with earplugs. However, by choosing to 'open the sound' to the whole bus, they have forced the other passengers to share their musical taste and intervened in the ambient soundscape, since it was impossible to ignore them not only due to the volume of the sound but of the whole performance. (Pereira de Sá 2011: 12)

Music is a resource for building the self and reinforcing belonging and identity, but it is also an element of conflict that brings onto the sonic surface social inequalities, taste differences, moral disagreements. Life in a contemporary city is experienced in multiple ways and layers, in which 'dialogue, conflict and negotiations are part of a battle for the signification performed by its inhabitants' (Pereira de Sá 2011: 14). Music is part of these encounters. Hence, the bus situation described by Pereira de Sá highlights the dual process triggered by the youngsters who were enjoying the music. From one side, they were happy to listen to music and to share it among themselves and with others. This joyful performance is a way to deal with self-identification and collective grouping, merging their subjectivities in a playful gathering. In this sense, music provides 'a way of inhabiting the shared musical space and thus a means of projecting self into music and music into self' (DeNora 2013: 88). Located at the very back of the bus, the youngsters were reinforcing their common tastes, sharing ideas, sounds, behaviours, corporal movements and thoughts through music-making, performing their belonging and identification. However, from the other side, all this process is being imposed on the other passengers and, as such, the youngsters manifest a certain disdain towards the others' will and desires. And they do so while spreading their music into the bus environment, forcibly making everyone hear them. Politically, they are making themselves heard, possibly assigning musically a whole life process of silencing they suffer. And this leads us to another layer of this scene, which is the kind of music that is being imposed. As the music is played in the bus, a semiotic process leads the auditors to 'decode' the sounds and organize this perception, unveiling ideas and stereotypes about the repertoire being played and who is playing it. In Brazil, *funk carioca* is largely connected with young black poor people, acknowledged as music from the 'lower' strata. Played inside the bus, the music spread concepts of poverty, class, ethnicity and violence in the silence of the trip, shared by all the other passengers. Despite being marginalized in thousands of situations in everyday life, while controlling the sound equipment, the youngsters have the power to organize the mood of the trip and the sound environment of the bus (Murolo 2015). Not surprisingly, most passengers would judge their music as extremely annoying.

In her study about *funk carioca* music, Adriana Carvalho Lopes proposes inverting Gayatri Spivak's famous statement and questioning 'if subalterns can be heard' (Lopes 2011:94). She is thinking about the whole circulation of *funk carioca* in Brazil, especially in low-income slums where the vast majority of funk parties take place. According to her, despite the widespread presence of *funk carioca* in Brazilian music culture, the genre is not always successful in making their protagonists audible in the oppressive inequality of the country. In other words, it is at the same time criticized and celebrated as a 'music from the poor', which occupies the charts through the fringes. A more detailed debate about the role of music in confronting and negotiating social inequalities will be discussed in Chapter 5. For now, what is at stake here is that these youngsters in the bus are dealing with all these layers of silencing and prejudice towards them and their music. In that situation, they actually have the power to be heard. Without celebrating uncritically a supposed 'empowerment' of this marginalized youngster, the unauthorized manipulation of the music-sound environment brings to the surface of coexistence a social conflict that otherwise could be masked or hidden. Perhaps the subaltern can't actually speak, but s/he certainly can *play*. On the opposite side, the other people trapped inside the bus, after a possibly exhausting or stressful workday are challenged with an additional discomfort regarding not only the long uncomfortable trip itself but also the noisy youngsters playing music they didn't choose to hear at that moment. In this sense, the 'music' becomes 'noise' and the disposition of the auditors tends to deny or to be irritated with the music.

In her interview, after merging the term 'music' with 'sound' while describing her dislike of heavy metal music, Luane reported her personal 'bus case':

> I always take the bus to go everywhere. Most of the times when I get on the bus, as I pass through the roulette I can already hear someone's music. Then I go to my seat and sometimes even though the guy is way in the back of the bus I can hear it. Often they carry portable speakers, or at times they use a headset, and still I can hear it. Other times they use their mobiles as if everyone inside the bus had to hear it or liked the same kind of music. I don't think this is cool because I like MPB (Brazilian popular music), my friend might like funk, another one might like classical music. It varies a lot. There's a sign on the bus that says that you are not allowed to listen to music without headsets and people insist on going against that rule. It's very annoying.

In her perception, the music is an element that annoys her during her trip, making the sound environment of the bus unpleasant. Facing her discomfort due to the imposition of music she doesn't want, Luane claims for her *right* to control the sound ambience recalling the 'sign' that you can only play music with earphones. In fact, the 'sign' refers to a council law in Rio de Janeiro and several other cities in Brazil that states the driver can stop the bus and call the police to remove the passenger from the bus if s/he insists on playing music loudly (without earphones). Fixed in every bus, train and public transport of the city, the advice is intended to prevent disagreements during the trip and to support anyone who feels disrespected by someone else's music. Despite this legal restriction, actual action against noisy passengers is very rare. Most commonly, people manifest their discomfort through mumbles, corporal movements, gazes and other quiet and distant ways. The despair felt by Luane in these situations is shared by lots of people who use public transport every day in Rio. Andrea is forty-one-year-old house maiden who lives with her daughter Brenda, eighteen years old, in a *favela* in Rio called Rio das Pedras. In a joint interview, they agreed that people playing loud music in buses are very annoying:

> *Brenda*: It makes me feel like keeping a pack of free earplugs and saying, 'Dear, here are your earplugs', or hanging a sign saying, 'Mobile phones come with earplugs, OK?' Because it is unbearable. I often glare, but I don't speak directly to the person. Try saying slowly, 'Gee, mobile phones come with earplugs', and see if the person gets it. But it is as though you said nothing at all. If someone gets it, they pretend they don't, as usual.

> *Andrea*: I think it is horrible. When [someone] enters the bus, when we get it, and the guy carries one of those speakers that even have handles playing funk really loud in the bus. Another annoying thing is [the sound of] people talking on mobile phones, it seems they are screaming by our side. That is annoying. Once I got up and changed seats because I couldn't stand a woman shouting on her mobile phone. And for her it is normal, but it is annoying.

It is interesting that, in the way they describe the nuisance, Andrea slides her complaints from music to other people's speech as part of the same situation inside the bus. As pointed out above, a bus trip is a sonic event filled with several layers of sounds. In a study about the subway, Brazilian anthropologist Janice Caiafa (2006) argues that any public transport has etiquette rules that must be followed. Keeping a relative silence or at least speaking in a low voice and listening to music individually are a few of these learned rules, not necessarily put on any 'sign' or in any law. In this sense, speaking loudly on one's phone or playing loud music may be considered equivalent disrespectful actions inside the bus, triggering discomfort and irritation. Moreover, Brenda imagines a solution for the unpleasant experience, offering in her thoughts an earphone to the annoying passenger. Their auditor's disposition combines an evaluation of adequacy with a regret for being submitted daily to that annoyance.

However, it is not true that all passengers will react in the same way or will share the same discomfort with the music in the bus. A very good example of these different dispositions is given by seventeen-year-old Nathalia, who studies in the same school as Luane quoted above. Although it was not a joint interview, Nathalia listened to Luane's interview before talking with us and in turn developed some comments about related topics. By the end of the talk, after reaffirming several times that music *never* annoys her, she made a brief reference to the bus case reported by Luane:

> I even take the same bus as she does. Not with her, but we use the same bus line. Sometimes a bunch of guys from the public school, the same school I attended, get on the bus and they come in listening to funk music at the top volume, so I lay off cool and quiet just enjoying their sound, get it? And it doesn't bother me! Music never bothers me.

Both girls experience similar situations every day and feel the music in very distinct ways. Nathalia, having had some knowledge not only about the music played but also recognizing the boys who play it, is more likely to enjoy the imposed music than Luane. For her, the music played by the boys activates memories and ideas that fill the trip, providing a bodily engagement that she understands as pleasurable. This is due to her history with the music, its meanings and sounds, which are heard as familiar and joyful. In other words, Nathalia's disposition as an auditor allows her to get into the mood provided by the forced listening and not to be bothered by it. Interestingly, in addition, the way she refers to the music mixes the word 'music' with the word 'sound'. In very common slang, 'sound' is eventually used by youngsters and by musicians to refer to music, an entanglement that emphasizes its positive quality. To 'make a sound' or to 'like this sound' is to make or to like a piece of music. Here again, the concepts of 'music' and 'sound' cannot be taken as monolithic, as they assume different ideas depending on the situation. If previously we stated that 'sound' is a word used often as a neutral evaluation of the sonic experience, in Nathalia's report the concept assumes an overtly positive meaning, referring to a situation she enjoys.

Beyond the conceptual framing applied, the case of Nathalia and Luane reveals that the auditor's disposition is a complex interaction of several layers and conditions that cannot be reduced to social class, education or age. Despite sharing general identity markers, the girls perform radically different dispositions towards the sound on the bus, which means that the annoyance triggered by someone else's music and sound cannot be taken as a general procedure, but as a contradictory and multiple result of interactions between people, memories, background, situations, moods and forced listening.

The terms people use to classify and judge sound-music-noise experiences provide at the same time a framework of this judgement and a subjective perspective through which the auditor is feeling and processing the experience. It is, at last, an interpretation of ways of being in the world, of living out personal belonging and collectively shared ideas. In this sense, naming a sonic experience is a shortcut to dealing with the complex issue of privacy and publicness. The pedagogue Fredson, thirty-eight years old, while describing his annoyance in bus trips, points precisely to the idea of privacy:

> I live in Taquara and I take the bus. Sometimes, at eight o'clock in the morning, we find the bus is crowded, then someone decides to play funk, *sertanejo* or *samba*. Which I like, but I think that is not the time to share. Because I think of the other people. I think that in these moments you hurt others' privacy. It is a time when no one wants to listen to music. If you want to, use your earplugs!

Music helps people to perform their individuality, conceived as the result of complex interactions between self and others. Fredson seems to be aware of this process when he refuses the imposed music in the bus, defining it as an experience that can harm one's privacy. As he declared being concerned with the others, he unveils the force of music to build personality and collectivity. For him, it doesn't matter what music genre is being played, but the act itself of imposing music is understood as something potentially invasive. Music changes the environment and, in doing so, it negotiates ways of being in the world and occupying space, which is always a question of finding your personal space in a wider physical and social area. In crowded public transport, space is limited, and our bodies are adapted in a careful attempt to preserve some privacy (some space) to our intimate parts such as genitals, hands and face. Similarly, the eyes and ears of people around us are avoided, in a behaviour that aims at preserving our privacy and the others'. Music can break these boundaries and penetrate other people's intimacy, challenging the personal space carefully constructed. Fredson's complaint is directed precisely to this situation, where uncontrolled music is imposed on an environment where people are struggling to keep their privacy in a limited physical space.

Broadly speaking, privacy may be challenged by music in close relation with the physical space and condition of the experience. Although somehow simplistic, it is possible to think of two main relations between space and music that cause different types of nuisance to people. One is when we are in a place and the music comes from elsewhere. In this special situation, music is leakage and we do not have personal contact with the one who controls the sound source. The other is when we share the physical space with the sound source, yet it annoys us. The next two chapters will deal with these two situations in detail, describing cases and issues raised by each one of them.

2

Private individuals and the music from elsewhere

In the introduction of the edited volume *Music, Sound, and Space*, Georgina Born states that music has the capacity to 'forge connections across the permeable membrane between self and collectivity' (Born 2013: 44). Music has equally strong appeals to the body, the intimate and the private, as well as to the collective, the social, and the group belonging. Operating in this unfixed border, music experience blurs the limits between the self and the social, in a dynamic process where intimacy is something that needs to be achieved. In other words, music experience highlights that individuality and privacy are not static conditions, but rather moving ideas that need to be reinforced and reconstructed in every given situation and every physical and social space.

Privacy is challenged in many ways in our daily life, and we are constantly making body adjustments to keep our sense of privacy. Music, in its invasive materiality, is an element that frequently forces us to feel unsheltered in our individuality, imposing other people's presence on our ears, bodies and feelings. Of course, this uncomfortable intrusion doesn't eliminate the self or the sense of individuality. Instead, it exposes the fragile membrane between embodied ideas of self and others, the private and the public. As Norbert Elias states, the division between these two domains is artificial, since each individual person 'is tied by living in permanent functional dependence on other people [...] and it is this network of the functions people have for each other, it and nothing else, that we call "society"' (Elias 2001: 16). Music is, then, part of this complex network that at the same time reinforces our belongings and rejections towards other people's bodies, identities and sounds. In other words, music helps us to construct, in every moment, our personal ways of being part of society, providing us with 'an intensely subjective sense of being sociable' (Frith 1996: 273).

Going further into this direction, what I would like to bring to the surface here is the instability of privacy. As Judith Butler (1990) argues in her *Gender Trouble*, identity is not a closed idea but rather one that needs to be constantly re-presented, repeated and re-acted. In her debate about gender identities, Butler states that gender needs to be performed in order to be recognizable as such, providing elements that can fill (or not) some expectancies. Although she doesn't mention music experience, the idea of performative acts can be fruitful in thinking about privacy. In a very similar way, our sense of self needs to be constructed and reconstructed in many places and situations we face in our lives. Our privacy is always under threat while walking on the streets, taking public transport or entering an elevator. In these situations (and in many others), we shape our body and eyes to keep our private space, performing ways to construct our privacy and to save our personal space in the world. Music passes through fringes, forcing us to interact with unwanted sounds, defying our individuality.

Space is a key element in these moments, once our physical (and acoustic) relation with space provides a set of possible reactions and strategies that may be used to build a sound and body intimacy shelter. Public music in public places challenges private individuals. The consequence is that music is perceived as something unpleasant and irritating. These feelings reveal a tensive relation between public and private, where the individual is conceived as the most important part in society, demanding 'rights' and intimacy. Yet it can be a quite pessimistic approach, an idea that resounds the work of Richard Sennett, who argues that the emphasis on individual and private rights unbalances the intersections between public and private. According to the author, 'Behaviour and issues which are impersonal do not arouse much passion; the behaviour and issues begin to arouse passion when people treat them, falsely, as though they were matters of personality' (2002, position 383/9346). As such, individuals became 'narcissistic' and the intimacy becomes a 'tyranny', a 'political catastrophe' (2002, position 7024/9346). The negativity of Sennett's analysis can be smoothened by the notion of movement between the private and the public. Unpleasant music experiences in public reveal not exactly the high importance of the individual, but the provisional construction of individuality and privacy. In this sense, there are moments where the collective activity becomes very important in our lives, as we search for gatherings, crowded rock concerts, sports fans and dance halls. Music making is a key act in all these social phenomena. However, in other moments, we demand our privacy, struggling to keep our sense of intimacy, which, somehow, can be intrusively corrupted by undesired music.

When listening to people's complaints about others' music, most arguments are expressions of personal discomfort as the concern for sound privacy guides interpretations and feelings about musical public life. Even in public spaces like streets or parks, music creates personal spaces that are not always permeable to others, spaces occupied physically and psychologically by those who control the sound and mark the space through it.

A good example of this is mentioned by forty-three-year-old Bel. She lives in a middle-class apartment in the Copacabana district of Rio de Janeiro, a few meters from the beach. Once asked if there is any situation in which she feels bothered by the music, she recalled the beach:

> At the beach, for instance, there are people that bring their own speakers and turn them on loud. Normally I do nothing, and stay still at the same place. Unless I'm going to stay there for a long time, or they are playing some music that I can't stand. Then sometimes I just go somewhere else. Kiosks on the beaches of the northeast region, for example, they all have speakers. 'Oh no, let's walk a little more and move to another place'. It also happened here in Rio. Around these days we were near a little group of people, and they had a speaker on, drinking and talking so loudly. And I picked my things up, walked around and went away from there – I walked away. Besides the fact that they had speakers, they were too agitated and it wasn't pleasant to be around.

As a very popular and cheap place for leisure activity, the beach is usually acknowledged as a democratic space, where people from different backgrounds, income levels and formal education can gather together, enjoying the sun and the sea. Going to the beach is often a social event in which people meet friends and spend the day. Therefore, music is a constant presence in several parts of the beach, defining provisional territories in the open space of the sand. Usually, this sound and physical occupation is peaceful, but it is not uncommon for people to feel upset about some exaggeration that inevitably takes place. Music in public spaces such as beaches has the capacity 'to reconfigure public and private experience' (Born 2013: 24). In Bel's case, the space occupied by other people's music is perceived as an unpleasant intrusion into the private space she builds when arriving at the beach by setting up her 'things'. Music acts here as something she wanted to avoid, that is, the manifestation of the physical presence of other people imposed on her in her private ephemeral beach space. The solution for this intervention was simple: move on. And so she did. Nevertheless, it is significant that she recalled the scene, somehow registered as an unpleasant situation where she felt intimately invaded by someone's music in a public space. Thirty-four-year-old music teacher Belen, who lives in Barcelona, reports a similar feeling while walking down streets:

> I have lived that situation several times, when you are walking, and someone passes *auuu* [with music]. Your space or your walk is interrupted, it's like listening to an ambulance sound – you feel something wrong is happening. When someone arrives with music very strong, with a radio. I respect it, but I do not find the need. I look to see what happens. Normally I think it is a person who is calling attention. Above all, I feel, 'What are you doing?', what is the need of the music to be so loud? I thought they could put on earphones! I think it's important for them to say 'I'm here' and that they want to play it loud and they do not care.

The street is not a fixed place. Our perception of space, sound and environment is built in movement, while we walk thinking randomly about anything. However, this walk is informed all the time by sounds, lights, smells and the presence of other people, with whom, at least for very brief times, we have to interact. While walking, we create our personal space, settled according to our movement, body, sounds. When invaded by the loud music played by someone in the street, Belen is affected in her personal space, and her reaction is to judge the personality of the other person. According to her thoughts and feelings, the person must be somebody highly narcissistic, who needs to call attention and who doesn't care about invading the others' space. Her discomfort is due to an expectation of privacy during her walk through the street, stopped by someone's private pleasure imposed on everyone around. What is pointed in her narrative is a lack of balance between the rights of two individuals, where the public environment and the wider sense of being part of a bigger community are not important at all.

These two examples point to the fact that the public place is felt like a kind of threat against the private. The idea of the public as a realm of interchange and decision-making, as developed by Habermas, seems to be far from the notion of publicness mentioned by annoyed auditors in everyday life. Yet Habermas (1991) understood the public sphere as constituted by private individuals belonging to privileged strata of society (men and private owners), the notion of 'public' being overtly strong in terms of its political function, a social realm that confronts official government and law-makers. Instead, annoyed auditors mention the 'public' as a diffuse and unimportant concept.

However, it is still possible to grasp some ambiguity. From one side, the public is referred to as an intimidating space. From the other, it remains as the sphere of legitimized social organization and, as such, as a realm that needs to provide an adequate intimacy for private individuals. The degree of annoyance caused by someone else's music depends on how space is configured and how public it is. As the reports of Belen and Bel suggest, open public spaces conform to a music experience that can be irritating but is acknowledged as unavoidable. Even though both reported being annoyed in their sound privacy, they understand the beach and the street as a no-owner territory, where those who are bothered should move. A different relation to undesired music happens when the auditor does not share the same physical space as the sound source.

Invasive music from the street

Most complaints about 'noise' are related to an undesired invasion of external sounds in someone's intimate space. In these situations, people's rhetoric has a tendency of reinforcing the public–private split, usually from an auditor's disposition where one feels vulnerable to the public sound invading his/her private space. This process resounds the controversial opposition sustained by anthropologist Roberto DaMatta between the 'house' and the 'street'. According to him, in everyday life conflicts, 'house' and 'street' are the regular categories used to define private and public. The 'house' is associated with ideas of 'calm, rest, recover, hospitality', while the 'street' is defined as a 'land that belongs to the "government" or to the "people", always full of fluidity and movement. The street is a dangerous place' (DaMatta 1997: 52). This schematic split between two ideal places has been criticized for not including the complexities of society. As sociologist Jessé de Souza argues, how could DaMatta adjust his structured model for the case of a poor black woman, who, after an exhausting day working in a factory and facing an uncomfortable trip in a crowded bus, arrives to her house and is spanked by her husband? (Souza 2001: 53).

This critique highlights that we cannot think of a dualistic separation without being challenged by several contradictions and ambivalences that the ideas of 'house' and 'street' evoke. However, they do work as categories people use to refer to ideal places where we can find shelter (house) or face danger (street). Moreover, the idea of sound safety at home is often expected, and part of the nuisance caused by music and sound has to do with frustration in this expectancy. This split between house and street appears quite clearly in the narrative of twenty-eight-year-old Marina, who lives in a district of the north zone of Rio de Janeiro called Madureira, known for its celebrated multicultural atmosphere and birthplace of two of the most traditional Samba Schools of Rio's Carnival: Portela and Império Serrano. The environment of Madureira is filled with sounds and music from several genres, played live in bars and markets and through sound devices in every corner of the district. Being a busy and noisy district is both cause for pride in the cultural energy widely referred to in the city and regret for the exaggerated loudness the residents have to bear. After emphasizing that she rarely becomes bothered by her neighbourhood's constant music, she describes a situation that 'crossed the limit':

> Ten years ago I lived in an apartment next to the Market of Madureira, a place that after 6 p.m. dies, empty – it's dangerous even. The street in front of our window became a transvestite prostitution spot and a karaoke bar

opened there. That bar was a real problem. It has pitchy people screaming on the mic all night long and they had no limits. People singing badly is the same as noise. Karaoke is unbearable. There was so much trouble. Because it was a transvestite prostitution spot, there were disturbances. The police always made an appearance. The residents of the building went there to talk to the staff of the bar, they even called the police, but the officers told them that the person who made the complaint had to be there [to formally register the complaint]. Nobody called. And the things went down like this until the bar went out of business. That might have lasted one or two years. And it was during a workday, on Tuesdays. Maybe the owner of the bar thought it was OK to turn the music up so loud because it was a commercial area and the neighbourhood was empty at that time of the night.

The environment described by Marina feeds the characterization of the street as a noisy, dangerous and mixed place diametrically opposed to the familiar, quiet and private home. In her description, she merges the transgender prostitutes' activity with the music the customers used to listen to and with the bad quality of their karaoke singing. The result was a mix of 'confusion', fights, police interventions and actual disrespect for the neighbours. Of course, she felt offended and invaded by the irruption of the music every Tuesday night, disturbing her sleep, rest and comfort at home. It is also interesting the way she shifts the concepts of sound, music and noise, explicitly stating that bad music performance *is* noise.

Marina's narrative is the most common way to describe music as a nuisance. While almost every interviewee recognized music's importance in constructing particular moods and body regulations, they reported being affected by the others' music (noise) as they lost control of their personal sound environment. The general feeling is that they are deprived from a significant element of their personal privacy and, more radically, their own right to enjoy intimacy.

Fifty-one-year-old lighting designer Alberto, who lives in the Maracanã district in Rio de Janeiro, has a similar story. Asked if music can annoy, he argues that the discomfort is closely related to the loudness of the sound/music:

If the sound is loud, depending on the time of day, it can be a bother. There's a certain decibel level that is prohibited by legislation, which may affect your eardrum. I used to live behind a public school and at this school, there was a funk party that happened every Saturday. The guys put the amplifiers just by my house. It was impossible to rest on weekends. I had to go all the way there to talk to them. And it solved the issue, they moved [the amplifiers] to the top of the school.

Once again, in this description, part of the alleged nuisance Alberto reports has to do with his expectations of a quiet and safe sound space at home. Moreover, he feels that something must be done to restore his individual right to a sound-safe intimate space at home. This assumption is so widely accepted in our society that he successfully made the party organizers change the place of the sound equipment, allowing him to be somehow safe from the inappropriate sounds. In his interview, he declared not remembering how this talk with the managers of the party went, but he was sure the intervention resulted in a significant change in the 'sound' that invaded his house. Note he did not use the word 'noise', but referred to the music as 'sound'. This choice may reveal his respect towards the 'right' of people to make the party and can explain in part how he managed successfully to change the speakers' position, lowering the leakage into his house. 'Sound', as we discussed in the previous chapter, is a more neutral term than 'noise', which frequently suggests something wrong, inadequate or intrusive. Language choices bring to surface feelings and judgements related to our experiences, and they can be a shortcut to negotiate struggles between individuals.

In a sense, both the stories of Marina and Alberto point to the fact that this negotiation is not very easy once it deals with strongly settled ideas of individual rights and respect. Furthermore, they deal with expectancies towards quietness at home, challenged by the sounds and music that leak from the street.

This disagreement about sound is not new. In 1864, Charles Babbage dedicated a whole chapter of his *Passages of the Life of a Philosopher* to the problem of street music. Stating that the amount of street music had increased in the last decade, he assumed it had become a nuisance 'to a very considerable portion of the inhabitants of London'. In his words, 'If the annoyance is not absolutely prohibited by law, the number of the police must be at least double to give quiet working people any repose' (1864: 362). His claims were embraced by the businessman and member of Parliament Michael T. Bass, who proposed a bill that aimed for a 'better regulation on street music in the metropolitan district'. Most arguments in favour of the bill were published by Bass himself in the book *Street Music in the Metropolis*, also in 1864. The book is a fantastic example of the intense debates that cross the public and private realms through sound and music experience. In one of its five chapters, Bass reproduced several letters he had received from citizens who 'suffered' from street music in several locations of the city. One of the writers, Victor Baune, for instance, addressed the MP backing him in his claim for the 'mitigation of this daily torture' (1864: 7). The term 'torture' appears again in the letter of J. M. Rodwell, who manifested 'trust' in the success of the measure that 'may rescue the public from this most horrible nuisance' (1864: 13). As he puts it:

> I have had abundant opportunities of ascertaining the feelings of the low orders upon the music, especially the grind-organs which infest the courts and other places, especially when children can be congregated. I am certain that they are regarded as the greatest annoyance and interruption of the work, and that in case of sickness, confinement, &c., of which there are always some in every court and narrow street of London, that they are a source of the greatest discomfort and, I might almost say, actual torture. (quoted in Bass 1864:13)

The nuisance is associated with physical pain as well as a dangerous disease, provoked by musicians who are referred to as 'plagues'. Edw. W. Dundas reported to Bass that his neighbourhood is 'perhaps as much as any in the metropolis *infested* with organ-grinders, brass bands, &c., to our great annoyance' (quoted in Bass 1864: 23).

In a detailed analysis of the music and sound conflicts in nineteenth-century Britain, John Picker observes that complaints were directed mostly towards immigrants, raising strong xenophobia against them. At the same time, the depiction of street musicians by middle-class intellectuals allowed them to 'crystallize their own group identity and establish themselves as a formidable presence during mid-Victorian period' (Picker 2003: 80). According to the author, the complaints were stronger in the mid-nineteenth century, and Babbage himself, as well as other well-known artists such as Charles Dickens and John Leech, was a lead supporter of the movement against street music, aimed at ensuring safety and quietness inside their homes. Moreover, they were claiming to be recognized as 'brain workers', in an effort to legitimize their occupations. Here it is interesting that Picker makes a link between the idea of private property and profession upon the word 'occupation', while intellectual workers, artists and writers had the house not only as a space for rest but also as their office. Hence, their required 'peace' was a key issue that could allow them a proper condition for the practice of their profession. The defence of the home occupation was, at the same time, a struggle to keep the intimacy safe from external undesired sounds and to value their 'brain' occupations (Picker 2003: 53).

The letters addressed to Michael T. Bass raise in a very crude way one of the main topics of this book, the conflicts between social groups in society, overlapped by prejudice, intolerance and segregation impulses. The music all the writers would like to get rid is the music of working-class musicians, coming from poor regions of the city or from other countries. It is the music of the Other that occupies, without authorization, the domestic soundscape of bourgeois neighbourhoods. But they reveal also the limits of private property regarding personal and intimate safety. The middle-class intellectuals and artists were being challenged by street sounds that brought to the surface the instability of home privacy. Hence, the non-structured campaign against street musicians could also be understood as a political act that aimed at guaranteeing the acoustic safety of private spaces against the threat of public noisy sounds, an act that gained new tones as the technological development increased the volume and the reach of sounds played in 'public'. As Karin Bijsterveld (2008) notes, the increasing number of sound technological artefacts that began to make up part of urban sounds after the turn of the twentieth century complicated the differentiation of private and public issues regarding the music and sound. 'Noise' became, then, a public issue, being addressed by designers, architects, urbanists, law-makers and the police, among others. The main focus of most of these concerns was the issue of privacy. Professionals from different fields were searching for a way to keep the urban citizen protected from undesired sounds that may disturb him/her, mostly in his/her private space. The idea of privacy was, then, amplified to encompass not only the physical realm of the body and the social space but also the domain of sensations. The intimate space could not be properly safe if unwanted sounds were heard. In other words, to the material and corporeal intimacy was gradually added the idea of 'acoustic intimacy', 'a sensation of security in a place free of sound intrusions' (Domínguez Ruiz 2015: 119). The notion of an intimacy vulnerable to sound intrusion highlights that the sense of intimacy or privacy is not permanent, but rather an achievement. Hence, the physical space we occupy on each occasion will stage the struggle for this acoustic privacy, achieved (or not) through several acts and behaviours (closing windows, playing other sounds, complaining, writing to newspapers, calling the police, etc.).

Of course, in each place we enter, we bring some expectancies towards the possibilities of saving a private sound symbolic space. In a night club or at a party, we expect loud sounds and our possible acoustic privacy must consider this volume and deal with that. In quieter environments such as churches or libraries, we are expected to avoid conversations and corporal sounds that could be heard as invasive to the other people, settling a sense of privacy according to behaviour expectancies. At home, the sense of privacy is related to the right of property, once home is acknowledged as a place where the environment is under our control. Even though this control is used in highly different ways depending on the power asymmetries among people who share the same roof (which will be discussed in the next chapter), the expectancy of quietness inside one's home is high. As such, irruptive sounds from the external world may break this expectation, resulting in a sense of despair or irritation.

If nineteenth-century bourgeois auditors complained about the noise from musicians playing in the street, the technological sound reproduction devices increased the problem. Despite many efforts, studies, laws and campaigns, loud music played outside homes is still today one of the most common everyday problems faced by many urban citizens in contemporary cities. Take, for instance, the narrative of thirty-nine-year-old Carolina, an event producer who lives in Rio de Janeiro:

There's a street behind my apartment building that has a bunch of Portuguese clubs, Clube do Açores, Casa Portuguesa; and they host parties. This is something that really bothers me, they are getting drunk while I'm going deaf. But people need to understand that we're not alone in this world. It is a process, an invasion of music I don't like inside my house. I already politely asked them to stop with the loud music, when my mother was still in this world I used to say: 'C'mon, there's a senior lady in my house'. I went there to ask them, but it did no good.

Carolina makes very clear that she feels disrespected by the loudness of music played at the club parties, but the way she describes them resounds the rhetoric used by nineteenth-century Londoners' complaints against Italian grind-organists or German bands. The sound controllers are said to get drunk and behave individualistically, ignoring her personal space and her mother's health. Low-middle-class Portuguese immigrants that arrived in Brazil in the middle of the twentieth century settled in the country and usually owned small commerce stores, bakeries, barber shops and public bars. In a long-term process, the male Portuguese owners of these places were stereotyped as rough, bad-humoured and uneducated, setting a profile of prejudice that appears slightly in her complaints about their 'clubs'. Of course, the prejudice of intellectuals living in nineteenth-century London is far more explicit than hers, but what seems relevant to retain is that the invasive music raises reactions against the sound controllers that often is entangled with an ethical evaluation of the people who press the play button. In this sense, her narrative highlights that acoustic administration of privacy is tied in with interpersonal relations and a diffuse idea of public and private rights.

Another issue raised by Carolina is related to health. The idea that invasive music is harmful to health is usually embraced by people who suffer in these situations. Concepts of health and illness establish ideal models of normality that change throughout time. Nowadays, a holistic idea of health is highly accepted, one that embraces not only physical aspects but also a general idea of 'mental health'. Low 'stress', sexual and affective harmony, a regular social life and financial balance are some of the features that can be associated with the idea of a 'healthy' life. The psychological and emotional aspects of life experiences are key elements of our current notion of 'health' (Hanser 2010: 850). In this sense, music makes part of this search for well-being, triggering symbolic and somatic processes that can enhance one's health.

There is a huge academic bibliography that reports clinical cases that present music as an artefact capable of reducing stress, diminishing pain perception, improving immunological system functioning and changing bodies physiologically and emotionally to achieve well-being and even healing (Hanser 2010). Susan Hallam reinforces the idea that music reduces anxiety and stress, changing pain thresholds and post-operatory periods, mainly in ageing persons (2012: 494).

Similarly, Tia DeNora, in her *Music Asylums* (2013), elaborates a wide debate about the therapeutic uses of music, especially in mental health institutions. According to her, the idea of 'asylums' encompasses not only a place where one can find shelter and protection but also a means to keep and rebuild the self. Having control over the music played is an important aspect for the music to function like that. Medical uses of music are based on the idea that music affects bodies and emotions, getting advantage of these affections to enhance its healing potential or, at least, to establish a diffuse sensation of well-being (Västfjäll, Juslin and Hartig 2012: 420). For this to happen, controlling the music is fundamental. The argument is, hence, very easy to be inverted. If music acts over the body positively if adequately handled, it can also provoke states of ill-being and even disease. As James Kennaway states in his intriguing book *Bad Vibrations*:

> The physiological and neurological effects of music on the body are hard to disentangle from its psychological impact. Its power to evoke emotions, including melancholy, rage and despair, can clearly affect psychological wellbeing, and can be connected in that sense to psychosomatic illness. (2012: 8)

Kennaway (2012) traces a long history of regulations and concerns to prevent the use of music as 'pathogenic'. In his work, the idea that music can harm health is not reduced to a biological level but includes also general ideas related to collective well-being. The author describes both cases where music was associated with (individual) epileptic and nervous attacks and with situations in which it was understood as a realm of moral deprivation, perversion, brainwashing and mind control. Examining medical and political archives, as well as magazines and newspapers, the author criticizes the 'growing debate on music's dangers' (Kennaway 2012: 158) as a contemporary tendency to 'medicalize social and moral problems' (idem). Nevertheless, his study highlights that individual and collective issues regarding music in public places affect health in several ways. In Carolina's narrative, she uses her mother's illness as an argument to request the neighbour to lower the sound. As an old woman with a precarious health condition, she deserved proper rest at night, prevented by the music leakage. Sleep deprivation is one of the most frequent issues raised by interviewees. Andrea, the house maiden quoted in the first chapter, describes the way the sound of the *baile* in the *favela* she lives in reaches her house and disturbs not only her peace but her health:

> It is a row house and, as such, what annoys is a very loud sound. And *baile* funk, which echoes inside the house: the windows tremble, the aluminium doors rattle, the floor shakes and we can't watch television, even turning to maximum volume. Sometimes twice on weekdays and every Saturday and Sunday. Then it feels uncomfortable to sleep. In my case, for instance, I suffer from migraines and take prescribed drugs. It is terrible. I can't sleep, feel sick and the next day I can't work well. It is very complicated for me.

The physical impact of the loud sound in her house is associated with the precariousness of their neighbourhood, constructed with cheap aluminium doors and windows that hardly block outside sounds. At the same time, the loudness of the sound equipment of the *baile* is highlighted as the windows shake and the floor shivers. As she describes the architectural design and the physical consequences of the sound on it, she immediately reports her bodily fragility. The sound invades her house exposing the weakness of both the construction and her own body, subjected to the imposed sound and resigned with it. As someone who suffers from a limited health state (she regularly takes 'prescribed' medicine), the sleep deprivation makes her condition even worse. The tone of her voice while speaking made her despair with the situation transparent, revealing her illness. The most sensible consequence of sleep deprivation is the loss of mental capability, reducing concentration and hence work capability. Feeling sleepy during the entire day also diminishes the immune system, making the body fragile and less able to prevent diseases. In her case, the permanent unhealthy state is maintained by the uncontrolled sonic invasion that prevents her from resting at nights and during the weekends. And she is quite aware of the association of this sound nuisance with her (bad) health.

The interviewee Marcelo, thirty-nine years old, and who lives in another district of the north zone of Rio de Janeiro, also highlights the importance of the night-time hours. After emphasizing that he loves music and listens to music almost all the time (he actually had his earphones in and playing music during the interview), he said that, depending on the moment, music can annoy:

> Music bothers me at night when the volume is high and I'm trying to get some sleep. I listen to music, every weekend I listen to it. I have some neighbours that put the radio on top volume in the morning until the time they get sick of it. And it's not just one! I have a neighbour who listens to Pablo and Luan Santana all day long. It's terrible! Also, near my house, there's a community and the people over there put some speakers in the street and the sound spreads in a way that I feel like it's inside my house. At night, at bedtime, it bothers me a lot.

As a bothered auditor, Marcelo developed knowledge about the sounds that invade his intimacy, recognizing the musical taste of his neighbours as well as the kind of sound that comes from the street, leaked by the party in the 'community'.[1] It is interesting that the proximity with social markers of the neighbours leads him to define their music as 'music', whereas his perceived or desired distance from *favela* inhabitants shifts the music definition and he uses the term 'sound'. Here again, a set of value judgement of annoying music informed by class struggles and differences and appears subtly in the

---

[1]'Community' is a euphemistic term used in Brazil to refer to *favelas* in certain contexts. In some cases, the huge social prejudice against the poor people living in precarious houses within the *favelas* is smoothened by the word, but the stigma is not suspended at all. Nowadays, inhabitants of *favelas* have overtly used the word '*favela*', in a political act that aims at making explicit the amount of violence and poverty that its residents suffer daily.

word choice he makes. Nevertheless, in both cases, the nuisance is the result of external undesired music that enters his house and disturbs its expected calm and silence. The use of mechanical amplifiers is a key feature of these complaints, as, through them, sounds acquire a much bigger shape, targeting other physical spaces. However, it would be a simplification to blame only the sound technology devices for the annoyance caused by outside music.

Two different cases of live music in the streets

I believe it would not be too risky to assert that every city has at least one music public place that potentially produces some level of nuisance among residents nearby. As I pointed out in the Introduction, interviews done in Rio de Janeiro and Edinburgh raised sometimes different issues regarding the overall sensation of unchosen sounds. Nevertheless, it was possible to find some interesting similarities in complaints against music in the streets of both places. Despite quite evident particularities, two places in each city were mentioned frequently in these reports, addressing noise and music problems and negotiations.

The first case is the sound problem of Edinburgh's High Street, also known as the 'Royal Mile'. As one of the most important streets in the city, in the heart of the 'Old Town', the Royal Mile links Edinburgh Castle and the Palace of Holyrood House, two historical buildings in the town. The historic appeal made the street a central touristic location, hosting museums, guided tours and several 'Scottish shops' that sell typical objects such as whisky, kilts and other traditional souvenirs. Part of the touristic experience throughout the street is to stop and listen for a while to bagpipers who play on key corners fully dressed in their traditional kilts. Therefore, the music from the bagpipes has become a typical sound of the Royal Mile, an intrinsic sound shape of the touristic package. Argentinian musician Alec, who has been living in Edinburgh for five years, recognizes the pipes' music as a 'structural' element of the city centre. In his words:

> I find Edinburgh very quiet. Especially when it's not the season of tourism you can stand in the middle of High Street and you can hear the steps of

people and also the bagpipe in the background. For me the bagpipes are like a sonic structure of Edinburgh, like having the castle, and you know the points where you are having this, it is a fixed aspect of the sonic structure of Edinburgh.

Cultural connexions between music and spaces are reinforced by the music performed regularly in these places, providing a 'soundmark' to the landscape (Schafer 2001). As John Connell and Chris Gibson (2002) argue, music has a strong appeal to 'fix' identities and authenticities to places, through a process of reaffirming tunes, instruments and sounds as 'typical' of a country, city or street. According to them, buskers particularly 'rely on certain physical spaces that satisfy both aural needs (reverberating fragile acoustic sounds) and commercial intents (maximising passers-by)' (Connell and Gibson 2002: 193). Usually, places filled with live music are referred to as vibrant and desired by tourists and inhabitants (idem), as the music has a strong capacity to reshape the ambience and become 'an emotional and commercial tool' (Connell and Gibson 2002: 197). In the case of Edinburgh's Royal Mile, this shaping is informed by an emphasis on the idea of 'tradition', reinforced by clothes, artefacts and bagpipes. As a tourist, walking up on the street to get to the castle listening to the tunes played by the pipers is a charming experience of immersion in a performed traditionality that narrates Scottish identity in a deep sense, although highly stereotyped.

However, the positive feelings on the sound of pipes felt mostly by tourists are far from being a consensus among residents. Sounds played in public spaces are manipulations of the environment that deal with its acoustic properties, intensity and spatiality (Garcia and Marra 2016: 6). Bagpipes are traditional instruments with rudimentary mechanics that produce a penetrating sound, composed by a drone and a melody developed in a limited range. As a result, the typical repertoire does not vary too much and some few known tunes are played frequently in most bagpipe presentations. With these characteristics, a bagpipe performance in a public place can escalate irritation as the sound lasts for some time. In an article published in the Edinburgh News, shop owner Mr. Abe Wilson complains about them:

For the past three years up here, we have had a conveyor belt of pipers, starting in the morning and playing for two or three hours, then another one takes their place, and that goes on all day every day. It's terrible. You think you're hearing bagpipes in your sleep. (Edinburgh News, 29/01/2015)

Of course, it is not possible to measure how much time would be necessary for a sound to annoy or irritate people because time perception is highly subjective. However, a basic condition for music to annoy is to be sustained for some duration. The problem the complainers have with the bagpipe on the Royal Mile is not simply the penetrating sound of the bagpipe itself, but the continuously repeated tunes of the instrument in the sound space.[2] Repetition that can haunt one's sleep even hours after it finishes. Eva, a twenty-year-old music student, reinforces the role of repetition in this process. In her interview, after she asked, among laughs, *if* she could 'mention bagpipes', she unburdened herself:

I lived really close to the Royal Mile for a year and there was always a piper. Every time, every day. And like you wake up to the sound of pipes and you fall asleep to the sound of pipes. And after a while … and they play the same tunes over and over, because it is all traditional Scottish tunes. And by the end, you know all of the tunes, it is really annoying!

Although one cannot guarantee that if the pipers had a more diversified repertoire she (or anyone else) would feel less bothered by the music, the fact that there are a limited number of tunes the pipers do play on the street increases the nuisance. Moreover, her narrative confirms the usual complaints about the duration of bagpipers' performances at this touristic venue. The amount of time one is exposed to forced listening is determinant to the irritation it can cause. Eva counted the time in hours, but in other situations, the measure of time can be extended to months or even years.

The complaints made the City of Edinburgh Council interfere in the case of the Royal Mile, not only in relation to bagpipes but to all buskers. The first measure was to forbid the use of amplifiers during certain times and days. It has also launched a campaign to promote 'responsible busking'. Entitled 'Hit the Right Note', the campaign distributes cards to musicians on the street that advise them that the police can stop their performing 'when the performance is disturbing

---

[2] While revising this book, the copyeditor said he had lived on the Royal Mile for a summer, years ago, and the bagpipes continue to haunt him.

others'. The card also contains recommendations for 'adequate busking', which includes avoiding playing in front of doorways or cashpoints and keeping at least fifty meters away from other buskers. The intention to have the music on the street disciplined came from the many complaints against musicians who disturbed people living and working nearby. But the limitation of the use of amplifiers does not solve the issue of the bagpipes, for which electronic devices to increase the sound are never used. It is, indeed, a quite sensitive issue because bagpipes are a symbol of Scotland's national music, associated with a cultural heritage that makes up part of the touristic consumption of the capital streets. Nevertheless, the penetrating sound of bagpipes crosses walls and occupies not only the public space but also private homes and offices.

*   *   *

The second case is one of the surroundings of São Salvador Square, in Rio de Janeiro. Street music is the reason for years of struggle between residents and visitors of the square, occupied by several artistic and musical activities since 2009. At first, the square occupation was acknowledged as an example of the positive transformation of public space through cultural activism. The intense cultural movement was then welcome for having instigated a considerable change in the square from an empty and dangerous place to a festive and joyful territory. But, as the music and sound of the place became performed without interruption every weekday until late in the night, residents began to get irritated with the movement. Raquel is a thirty-eight-year-old biology teacher, quoted previously describing her problems with the bus station near her hotel when she lived in Roraima. In her interview, she followed a sort of autobiographic memory of music nuisance that reached up to her current experience of living on the thirteenth floor of a building just in front of São Salvador Square. She used to live in the square before the 'revitalization', and, after a few years out of the city (in Roraima), she went back to the place in 2014. She reports that she witnessed its transformation from a dangerous place at night to a celebrated cultural venue but claims that the occupation is out of balance:

> On Mondays there is the circus school, which is surreal! They are certain that the music they put there pleases everyone. They are the ones who

play the loudest music in the square; and they mix electronic music, with Brazilian music, with classical music. When it's classical music they play it even louder. What disturbs me is that they really think that is the best sound in the world. And we have to listen to it and put up with it. It bothers me a lot. [My son] Bernardo sits here in the living room to see a movie, a cartoon, and then suddenly he can't hear the characters speaking, and has to close the window. It's hot in here, so if he closes the window he has to turn on a fan that won't be enough to cool him. So he turns up the volume on the TV. It's disturbing. You get home and see your son in a house that is completely shut, with a fan on top speed and the TV louder than ever. You end up causing other problems because of the noise. [...] I spent a nice weekend and then on Monday they are busy, as it is expected on a business day. What then? What about my break? In this case, I feel disturbed and invaded. Still, I believe that these people have a democratic space that they can use. They could use it better.

Several issues are raised in her narrative. First, the way she uses the terms 'music', 'sound' and 'noise', in an increasing amount of nuisance. As related to the repertoire played by the sound controllers from the circus school, she refers to 'music', possibly assuming the pleasure felt by the school attendants. The genres are heard in themselves as artistic artefacts, hence defined as 'music'. In the following sentence, she manifests irritation with the attitude of the players, who impose their preferred music on 'everyone'. At this moment, 'music' becomes 'sound', a term that highlights the material element of music, separating it from the artistic domain. In the last part, her intimacy is being truly threatened as she finds her son stuck at home in a hot and unhealthy environment full of loud sounds (the outside 'music', the TV, the fan) that can damage his well-being. The result, then, is referred to as 'noise'. For Rachel, the potentially good act of occupying the public space with music turns into an aggressive experience where her privacy is invaded, forcing her and her son to change behaviours at their own home.

On the other side, the musician Alexandre Garnizé, who plays regularly in the square, argues that the music should not be used as an 'excuse' for the residents to complain about the occupation (quoted in Fernandes,

Trotta and Herschmann 2015: 6). For him, making music in public space is something good in itself. Garnizé echoes some arguments that deny the potentially harmful effect of music listening. Understood as a political act of artistic occupation, music in public space is taken as proof of the vitality and creativity of musicians who change the environment positively. The musician is part of a huge movement that encompasses the idea that citizenship must be experimented with through collective action in public space, as music performance is not only an artistic expression in everyday life but also a form of political activism, aimed at reshaping places and power relations (Herschmann and Fernandes 2014). In this sense, musicians engaged in these performances are highly reactive to some difficulties imposed on their acts, usually done by coercive forces (the state and especially the police), commerce owners and nearby residents. For them, the public surpasses privacy.

This opinion, of course, is not shared by residents. Luis Eduardo, for instance, is the owner of an apartment in São Salvador Square and struggles with the constant music activity. Interviewed for a newspaper article, he complains about people who occupy the square playing 'brass instruments, harmonica, trombone, saxophone'. And he adds: 'I've heard things such as "you'd rather move somewhere else" and they argue this is a public space' (quoted in O Globo, 23/03/2014). The conflict led some residents to make a Facebook page where they try to denounce the occupation and organize some reaction. On the presentation text of the page 'Praça São Salvador – Moradores' (São Salvador Square – Residents) can be read:

> We are a group of residents that, since 2009, have been watching the decay of the site (with the tacit consent of the City Hall, i.e. omission), unlike the frivolously disclosed propaganda of 'revitalization'. Daily events, including live concerts, be it samba or rock, using amplifiers, that ended up bringing an audience, due to its dissemination via social media, that the space does not support. An audience that think they're in the right to play their tambourine, saxophone, bass drum, triangle, to sing in the late nights, until 7 a.m. of the next day. Yes, we barely sleep, we don't have the basic right to watch TV or read a book, let alone listen to some music that we choose. We just want the law to be enforced.

Not being allowed to watch TV, read a book or control the music one is keen to listen to is recognized as a violent interdiction of one's basic rights. As such, they demand respect of 'the law'. As will be discussed later in this book, the claim for the 'law' is a claim for a regulative power that could balance different positions in conflict with each other. Moreover, it is the manifestation of faith in what could be the last sphere able to guarantee a friendly coexistence between opposite sides of a struggle.

Going back to Bass' book *Street Music in the Metropolis*, a letter signed by Alfred Wigan manifested concern with the writing of the bill proposed, arguing that there was 'nothing in it to prevent music in a man's garden, or fore-court, or balcony' (1864: 16). The author reported a case of a 'German band' that, being ordered off the street by the police, was taken up into his neighbour's balcony, where they played 'for about two hours' (1864: 17). Again, the duration of the music is a very important element in characterizing it as a nuisance. Prejudice against the 'German' and the problem of the loud volume they supposedly play are other ingredients of the irritating package. As Natalia Bieletto-Bueno (2019) puts it, street musicians are often victim of prejudice, and their work misunderstood as a mix of money-begging and unwaged artistic activity. But the concern Mr Wigan manifested on the possible uselessness of the bill is related to the fact that, in this case, the conflict was not between a desirable quiet home and an annoying noisy street anymore, but between two homes. This adds to the debate an even more complicated issue that he thought could be solved by the writing of another law that could protect him against 'the brutality of our neighbours' (1864: 16).

Neighbours

If street music bothering residents in their private space may be considered a classic opposition of public sounds challenging private silence, this is not the same for disagreements between neighbours. Initially, it is important to highlight that, in many cases, neighbours share similar class, cultural and economic conditions. For that reason, hierarchies related to class or social asymmetries would not play any role in the conflicts. This is worth keeping in mind because, in many cases, the arguments about someone else's music are filled with prejudices and power inequalities. At first, this should not be an issue between neighbours. However, crowded big cities put people closely together with others with very different backgrounds, heritages and musical tastes, creating a fertile ground for sonic conflict. In the most common case, somebody plays loud music in his/her house and the sound leaks into the neighbour's house. Let's analyse one fruitful narrative that describes how these conflicts take place:

> I have a neighbour who unfortunately makes me very stressed. And a thin wall separates us. She keeps her stereo on (loud). For example, Wednesday is my day off and I try to sleep until a little later and I can't, you know? Because at 8 a.m. the stereo is on and awfully high. A bang so high that I already get up scared and can't relax. Where I live, in the area, there's a commercial area on the corner, my building neighbours, people from the building in front of mine, with *music* all the time, always loud. I'm even used to sleeping with loud music. It's crazy! When there's no music, I even think something is wrong. I don't complain because I don't have the time. I said to Carol, the next-door neighbour, 'Gee, you won't even let me rest for a while', she didn't get a clue and giggled a little. People think that the *sound* is not bothering the other people because it is beneficial to them. They feel good with it. So they feel that this isn't bothering anyone. I can't relax, I can't rest. I'm already hyperactive, I carry a load of stress, and this continuous *noise* makes me more agitated. Unbearable. [...] Disrespect is the word that sums it up. I feel disturbed. I'm not angry because it's something that's assaulting me indirectly. Because you work all day long and wish to come home and relax, the place where you can find peace and balance, where you can recharge your energies, but unfortunately you can't.

The report from thirty-four-year-old informatics teacher Bruno is rich in several issues I've been discussing so far. First, he changes the classification from 'music' to 'sound' and to 'noise' when he began to get more emotionally engaged with his narrative. 'Music' is used in his description of a scene occupied by sonic interventions that people like to listen to. In a second moment, he regrets the carelessness people have while listening to their music, producing a 'sound' that can potentially bother other people. Here, he is not personally involved, but is only mentioning a hypothetical situation and a general behaviour. Then, the neutral term 'sound' was more accurate to frame the narrative. This sound becomes 'noise' as he associates it with his personal discomfort, sleep deprivation and despair. Moreover, other people's 'noise' is an element that damages his health, increasing his stress and annoyance. In his judgement, his neighbour's sound is a symptom of her individualistic behaviour. However, despite his intense discomfort manifested in sleep deprivation and a high amount of stress, he doesn't feel comfortable complaining directly to the noisy neighbour. Somehow, he understands the complexity of the situation where both he and his neighbour are arguably in their right to do whatever they want inside their private home, be it resting or listening to music. In Karin Bijsterveld's study of mechanical sounds, she points out that the Dutch Board of Public Health, in the 1960s, defined acoustic privacy as a 'right to an undisturbed tranquillity inside one's home as well as the right within the confines of one's home to express oneself freely, uncontrolled by the others' (2008: 183). It is surely a challenging postulation that could only be totally fulfilled if our houses and buildings were soundproofed. As this is far from being the case, acoustic privacy is not more than an idea to be achieved through everyday struggles and complaints. As technologic devices amplify the amount of sound produced at home leaking to the nearby houses, they also add a possibility of controlling it, to put the volume down. Neighbours annoyed by the sound that comes from someone else's house know that the music can be played at a lower volume and this knowledge has the potential to increase the level of irritation. Take, for instance, the report from Claudia, forty-six years old, who lives in a suburb of Rio de Janeiro:

> He plays it [the music] so loud that inside my house I have to close the door or go over there and ask him to turn it down, so I can watch some TV. Because it is too loud, and it bothers me. If he played it just for him to listen, it wouldn't be a problem, but he plays it for him and for the neighbours to listen. It upsets me. My husband is closer to him than I am, so he went there and asked him to turn the volume down, in a nice chat. So, he did it and now it's OK.

Claudia points to the significant role of individuality in everyday sound and music negotiations. She acknowledges her neighbour's right to listen to any music as long the music is played 'to himself'. 'To himself' means 'at an appropriate volume' that could avoid or at least reduce the leakage into her home. An important thing in this negotiation is that she knows he can control the volume and that he does not put it down simply because he doesn't care. Once he spreads the sound beyond the physical limits of his house, reaching her intimate space, he loses his very intimate right to listen to his music at home.

What we can observe here is not an opposition between public and private but between two private individuals who supposedly have the same right to a safe sound space at home. That's precisely what Claudia is demanding. However, her report also highlights a possibly successful mediation for solving the conflict. Talking to the neighbour was an effective measure to have the sound lowered, but, according to her, this chat was only possible because her husband had some degree of intimacy with the neighbour. Following Richard Sennett, this rhetoric exposes the higher value of individuality in the public domain. According to the author, individual personality became a social principle, organizing not only private behaviour but also public roles and political measures (Sennett 2002: Kindle 2380/9346). In this sense, the talk between neighbours can be successful if they can activate a process of personalization that can make the noisy party recognize the individual suffering of the neighbour.

But another interesting thing is the idea of playing 'to oneself'. Even in private individual listening, music is always informed by social contexts. There is always a collectivity associated with music experience, even though it may not be present in the situation. As we listen to some music, we get in touch with ideas, feelings and descriptions of cases and situations that deal with life in society, our individuality in the world. And a very common practice to experience this feeling of belonging is to share the music we like. Mike is a fifty-two-year-old kitchen chef who lives in Edinburgh. He provides a very interesting report on listening to loud music, recalling his younger days:

> I've probably annoyed people in the past, when I played too loud, especially when I was younger, and you don't respect neighbours. But I do know

when I listen to reggae I like to listen to it loud. You feel the music, it is just so good, and that's probably annoyed someone. [...] I remember playing music too loud. I loved it so much. I have deliberately played it loud through the windows to say, 'Hey guys, you've never heard this. This is amazing', and let the whole world know that I like this music. And I guess I probably annoyed my neighbours. There is so much music, and sometimes you become obsessed with a particular song and just play it and you can hear it for hours.

His narrative highlights the complicated relation between private and public (shared) music experience. He liked the loud music himself, but at the same time, he wanted to spread the music to the world in a juvenile (narcissistic?) explosion of joy and fun. Listening to music is also sharing the music you like, which nowadays can be done in several ways through technological devices, the internet and so on. Although he probably did all this, he also wanted to convince his neighbours about the quality of the music he likes, the happiness of his mood and the celebration of the ideas and values associated with reggae music (dance, marijuana, peace, worries about racial struggles and inequalities, and so on). At this moment, he really did not care about other people as private individuals doing their own things, possibly in different moods, sharing different values and with different expectations for the day. On the other side, his neighbours may effectively have gotten irritated with the inappropriateness of his individualistic sound and wondered whether or not to complain. If his neighbour had been thirty-nine-year-old history teacher Isabel, however, he would have been unlikely to hear any protest:

This neighbour thing is something that everyone complains about. Any noise nowadays is something extremely inconvenient. And there are parties! People in parties make noise. And my husband is one of the people that keeps complaining about it because there is music and there is funk, and when it starts playing he says, 'Here comes the bad music'. Then he gets stressed out. It affects him negatively. But hey, tomorrow can be our turn to throw a little party and we'll want to play the songs we like. Why can't we let this one slide? Got it? This is how it goes: today is theirs, and tomorrow is ours! The whole point is, is it really that uncomfortable? The discomfort is a reverberation of something inside of you. If you're OK, the music won't bother you. Hey, noise is out there, it's just noise, leave it be! If you're OK, you even do a little dance. But when I'm down, any fuss will bother me.

Even if we agree with the personal dimension of irritation music can cause, Isabel seems to ignore that it is impossible to check all your neighbours' moods to find out if your music will bother them. The balance between the right to do what you want in your privacy and the right of the others to have a quiet private space is a daily challenge. Of course, she points to a solution that is often effective depending on the regularity, the volume and the duration of the music, along with the time when it is being played.

There is an overall agreement, registered also in several legislations all over the world, that during the night the neighbourhood must be quiet to allow people to rest. Even though this assumption does not encompass the idea that during the day any loud sound is permissible, noise during daytime is more tolerated and accepted as 'normal' (Domínguez Ruiz 2016). Although this consensus obliterates several individualities such as night workers, babies and people suffering from specific illnesses, it is usually acknowledged as more acceptable to play loud music during the day than after sunset. Weekends and holidays are also considered days of silence and rest when noise should be kept to a minimal level. In this sense, the right to complain varies according to the time of the day and, furthermore, the day of the week. Marina narrates a situation where she, as a bothered auditor, felt she didn't have the right to complain to her neighbour, because it was a national holiday:

Wednesday, I was studying for a test for the university. I was trying really hard to focus and the neighbour decided to host a barbecue party and play her loud heavy metal. I was the one who was wrong! It was a holiday and it was her time to listen to her music. It happens. I was bothered by that, but I didn't feel entitled to go over there and ask her to turn off the stereo. I never went there. I was considering that she was right, on a holiday, putting music on at her little barbecue event.

Tolerance with your neighbours' barbecue during a holiday may be highlighted as a crucial element in being considered a 'good neighbour'. We could imagine that had she acted differently and knocked on her neighbour's door to complain, she would probably have been mistreated or ignored. But the important thing is that she didn't want to do so, recognizing her neighbour's right to have fun and play loud music in that situation.

If we put together the possible uselessness and the risk of the complaint, we can understand why several nuisances caused by the music are not even reported. Retired soldier José, seventy-four, describes his relation to music as 'very pleasant'. He says he likes every kind of music and that music can hardly bother him. Asked about situations that could be unpleasant, he remembered another barbecue case:

> *José*: Back in my apartment complex, there is a grill that the condo rents for residents. Many times in the afternoon, on Sunday afternoon, about 3 or 4 p.m., people there in the barbecue put on loud music, that really loud funk. It really bothers me. This has already happened several times.
>
> Q: Have you ever taken action about it?
>
> *José*: Actually no, because they were having fun and I kept it to myself. But it did bother me. But there was never any serious issue in that matter.

In this case, his personal desire to rest at home can be put aside in order not to provoke a 'more serious problem'. We cannot be sure about what he meant by 'serious problem', but it is possible that it refers to an imminent violent conflict that could be started by his complaining. Moreover, he seems to fully believe in the individual right of the neighbour who rented the space to use and enjoy his Sunday with friends. In his intimate judgement, to stop the fun afternoon of his neighbours would be worse than standing the unpleasant music in his living room. His decision to not complain is, therefore, both a calculated strategy to avoid a possible violent response and an acknowledgement that his neighbours had the right to have fun with their friends.

The case of José touches on the limits of the very definition of private space, closely linked to the idea of private property. The barbecue grill is a property of the building, shared by all the residents. It works as a private space owned by a group, and residents and owners can use it for meetings and parties normally upon reservation and/or some additional payment. The sense of privateness is interconnected with the sense of publicness, yet it would be more accurate to think in terms of a collectiveness, even though its use is only allowed for residents. Here, private and the public realms are blurred, and the sound conflicts appear as the arena where José (and, if he had a complaint, the participants of the barbecue) faces the difficult task of coexistence and cohabitation.

-

3

Sharing spaces and sounds in public and private

In the previous chapter, the complaints about music and noise were directed at sounds that invade someone's intimate space. In most cases, the home is occupied by unwanted sounds leaked from other physical spaces, and the irruption of this sound disturbs one's privacy. As such, the auditor's expectation of being at home safe from the outside auditory world is challenged as his/her place is invaded by the music (or another sound) produced somewhere by someone else. It is possible to think here of a kind of physical mismatch between the perceived physical space and the area occupied by the sound. The personal sensation of occupying a space is not fixed but determined by the materiality of the physical limits of the place. These limits are marked by walls, windows and doors that are expected to isolate the space from other adjacent places or divisions. Similarly, sound also has materiality and occupies spaces, limited by the physical capacity of sound waves to spread through the air. As we have seen in the first chapter, the amount of physical vibration of a sound determines how far this sound will be heard and, as such, occupy different places. Interestingly, the word 'volume' is applied in many languages (English as well as Portuguese, French, Spanish and possibly other languages) to refer both to the amount of space a body occupies and to the loudness at which a sound is played and heard. Sound and space are entangled not only in the sense of the vibrational energy of sound wave propagation but also in a subjective sense of being affected, pleased or annoyed by any sound, including music and 'non-musical' sonic events.

This chapter will focus on cases where the auditor shares the same physical space as the sound source. In these situations, the idea of 'invasion' is not accurate, since often the auditor is free to leave the place. Even if that is not true – and in some places, you are really not free to go away – the auditor is forced to listen to a sound or music but s/he is not in his/her private space or, if so, this space is also shared by other people with different relations to sound and music. Therefore, the expectation of quietness cannot be taken for granted as it may vary according to the situation. In most cases, it is possible to negotiate an agreement about the music that hopefully can be achieved. In other situations, however, you are deprived from any kind of control or interference in the sound environment, exposed to music you have not chosen and trapped in a physical space shared with other people. The musician Alec, quoted in the previous chapter, provides a very emotive and detailed description of an episode in which he felt very uncomfortable due to the music:

> It happened a week ago. I went to Newcastle to perform with a guy who plays table and who I don't know very well. I've only met him a few times. We were driving back; it was night time. I can even remember the feeling. I think the reason I find it hard to talk about this is that, in this particular episode (even though we are not close or anything), it is the way the whole thing evolved. We have gone to play music together but we were playing kind of as background music in a museum in an event, so there was lots of noise going on. This is kind of depressing for a musician, to be performing and no one is listening to you. You think, 'What the hell am I doing here, I'm doing something that I put so much effort on it and no one is listening'. This guy is a good player but he has not classical training, he played more like Bollywood style. He has no experience in accompanying a sitarist, and this is a totally different way of playing. I was trying to say, do it this or that way and we would sound better and I felt like he wasn't listening. So I felt, 'What's the point; even my musical partner is not caring'. I was not having a good day. And when we were driving back from Newcastle, he was the one driving, so he was entitled to pick the music because he needed to stay awake and make sure he was alert while driving. But I felt, 'OK, let's try to connect with some music'. We came all the way there listening to his music, so I said, 'Can I play some of my music and see if you like it?' And I kept

on going through all the music that I had and he didn't like anything and after while I said, 'OK, you pick the music'. And he put on this awful pop music really loud, and I felt like it emphasized the disconnection that we felt during the whole day. But also the fact that being trapped in the car, dark, at night, with loud unpleasant music. Honestly for a moment I felt kind of nauseated. I really felt something in my stomach like, 'This is such an unpleasant experience'. He is a nice person, I have nothing against him, but it was just this lack of connection that had been going on throughout the whole day and not just with him, but with all the situation.

His description exposes in a radical way the difficulties of being forced to listen to music you do not like or don't want to listen to in a shared place. In this case, he recognizes the right of his colleague-driver to choose the music, modulating the body, the vigilance, the attention and the general mood of his driving activity. Music, then, works as a device of self-regulation, chosen to build adequate body responses (DeNora 2000). But, after a difficult workday where music did not fit between them, Alec tried to restore some complicity by searching for a common repertoire for the two-hour trip back home. As the attempts were all frustrated, the end of the unpleasant day was translated into a music-intense experience of disengagement between them. Alec's story points to the indissociable connection between the feelings and the body as he related his painful experience of hearing unwanted music inside a place he could not escape. His case points also to the potential damage music can cause to the body. It is not only a question of taste disagreement that forced him to bear the 'awful pop music'. As a bothered auditor, Alec felt in his body an unpleasant symptom of nausea provoked by the forced music. As was argued before, if music can be a device to induce well-being and reduce stress, it also has a similar potential to produce unhealthy states and to escalate anxiety and stress. Alec may be a very sensitive musician who is particularly affected by music, a person that Judith Becker defines as 'deep listener'. In her study about trancing, Becker suggests that some people are more likely to have intense reactions to music listening, which can 'result in chills or tears, changes in heart rates, in their skin temperature, in their respiration, and in their brain chemistry' (Becker 2004: 54). What I am trying to argue here is that all these intense bodily reactions to music may also happen in not-deep listeners, yet at a lower level. Alec's intense feelings towards unwanted music in the car are illuminating when thinking about the damage an undesired music experience can cause. But beyond that, it also reveals that the amount of nuisance and even physical damage music can provoke is related to the kind of negotiation one is able to have when sharing a place with a music source that is heard as harmful or annoying. The car is, perhaps, an extreme example of a daily situation we face in our lives, having to bear unpleasant music in public places, parties, shops and restaurants.

Background music in public spaces

Public spaces are, by definition, spaces that can be occupied by everyone. Ideally, they do not have entrance restrictions and are designed to be used for a specific aim. Some of them fit precisely in this definition like squares, streets, beaches and parks, usually open-air spaces welcome to every citizen. In these places, music and sound conflicts are related to personal use of space for leisure as we have seen previously. If the nuisance is too high, the auditor usually reports simply changing place to be far from the sound source, and the enjoyment of the day is hardly interrupted or poisoned by these unwanted sounds.

However, there are some places that are conceived to be 'public' in their use, but are 'private' in their ownership. In these cases, the idea of 'public' has to do with its widespread use, but it is intermingled with the idea of privacy in the sense of property. Supermarkets, shopping centres, stores and restaurants are typical places designed for public use, yet they are owned by someone who defines the rules accepted within the walls. Inside their domains, the power to choose the music and to control the sound atmosphere is totally in the hands of the owner or manager. In these venues, someone is in charge of the music which fills the ambience according to this person's tastes and intentions. And that can be quite irritating for some attendants. Anthony is a seventy-one-year-old retired businessman, who presents a quite elaborate interpretation of the situation:

> I like obviously to choose my music because, like most people, I have my own tastes where music is concerned. I don't particularly like having music

thrust upon me, music that I haven't chosen, which occurs in most parts of modern-day life with Muzak. Or, [what] I call background noise [and] some people call elevator music: wherever you go in shops nowadays, in buses and trains, airports, it's almost impossible to get away from some sort of 'music' [the inverted commas were signed with his hands] – music you haven't chosen, and many times it is music that I don't particularly want. And it's not that I just want the music: I don't necessarily want any noise or background noise, whether it is music or not, in many situations. I'd rather have some peace and quiet. When I am going about my business, sitting in a lounge somewhere or on a bus sometimes is nice to have some peace and quiet. But in the modern world that seems more and more difficult to achieve.

The issue of choice is quite important here, not only the choice of the music that is to be played, but also the choice of the adequate moment to play it or not. Moreover, it is very interesting how he shifts the definition of the unwanted sound between the concepts of 'music' and 'noise'. As he refuses the classification of 'music' related to the background, the term 'noise' is used to highlight his audible discomfort with the situation. Here again, the vocabulary applied to refer to an unpleasant music experience brings to the surface a set of feelings towards unwanted sounds that are usually kept silent. His desire for quietness is referred to as a sound ambience of 'peace', a word that also has powerful possibilities to unveil the damage a sound can cause. The opposite of 'peace' is 'war', or, less intense, 'conflict', which opens a path to an intriguing debate about music and violence (the subject of the next chapter). Noise is a sound that invades his personal space and disturbs his 'peace'.

Anthony's report is directed at 'background music' and he specifically mentioned the word 'Muzak'. Muzak is the name of an American company specialized in background music that has provided recordings to several stores and places since the 1930s. From a brand name, it became a common noun used to refer to the kind of music the company used to produce, based on the idea of 'easy listening'. Despite its success and the spread of the term 'Muzak' to refer to any background music, the idea that music reshapes places and moods goes beyond the company and its products.

The widely quoted book *Elevator Music* by Joseph Lanza is perhaps the most significant study on background music. Lanza recovers a long history of ambience music, beginning with examples from Homer's *Odyssey* and Greek mythology, passing through medieval and classical music and arriving in a nineteenth- and twentieth-century explosion of demand and importance in everyday life. Reinforcing the perception of Anthony about the ubiquity of music, Lanza states that 'as restaurants, elevators, malls, supermarkets, office complexes, airports, lobbies, hotels, and theme parks proliferate, the background, mood, or easy-listening music needed to fill these spaces becomes more and more a staple in our social diet' (Lanza 1994: 2). In a frankly positive view about the phenomenon, he argues that background music 'makes us feel more relaxed, contemplative, distracted from problems, and prone to whistle over chores we might find unbearable if forced to suffer in silence' (Lanza 1994: 3). Although he does mention some critics directed to background music, Lanza is enthusiastic about its powers to define and settle moods in social spaces, modelling the affective environment:

> In a modest-size McDonald's in Connecticut, I witnessed the splendidly homogenizing effects of this process. At each time, the establishment was packed with groups of customers, each carrying on its own conversation in one or another language. This intolerable mishmash was somehow alleviated by the carefully assembled speakers piping in the near-subliminal music. The reconstituted version of a song like 'Both Sides Now' neutralizes nature's multichannel distractions into a single, benevolent source. The mono effect provides a paradoxical service of standardizing noise, enhancing private conversation, and even making food taste better. (Lanza 1994: 161)

His almost romantic narrative provides a clue to the different auditory disposition that crosses these public spaces. Once music can be considered a 'cultural material through which "scenes" are constructed' (DeNora 2000: 123), it is chosen to set an adequate ambience to the shopping experience, to manipulate time perception in waiting rooms in train or bus stations as well as in company phone-calls, to intensify connections between spaces and identities, ideas and thoughts.

Nevertheless, in a less optimistic approach, we can argue that in all these situations, what happens is, in fact, forced listening. And the responses to this are not always positive. In the sequence of the interview, Anthony reported a recent scene of a fishing trip to the Amazon he had done a few days before our meeting on which he did successfully complain about the background music:

> As soon as we got to the boat there was a big large speaker receiver on the bar and it was blasting music. And I actually said to the people who were there with me, 'Do you like this background noise?' And they all said, 'No'. But they almost seemed to be unaware of it. And I said to the young barman, 'Look, could you do me a favour? Turn it down or even better turn it off'. And he said, 'Sure, you are the customer'. And he turned it off and nobody realized he turned off. If I asked what they heard they probably wouldn't know!

Although Anthony is quite sure nobody realized the music had stopped, that is obviously a controversial statement. Instead, people on the boat were more likely doing what Anahid Kassabian calls 'ubiquitous listening', a mode of listening which is done together with other activities, usually as a secondary activity (2013: 18). Even though this mode of listening 'modulates our attentional capacities, it tunes our affective relationships to categories of identity, it conditions our participation in fields of subjectivity' (idem). That's why it irritated Anthony and that's why other people there didn't mind having the environment changed by the music interruption. What could have happened in the boat scene, instead, is that the place was flexible enough to assume either a sounded environment or a quiet surrounding. It would be hard to affirm whether or not the other passengers noticed the music interruption, although obviously the overall ambience of the boat bar probably changed deeply after the music stopped.

Another aspect that Anthony's narrative raises is the presence of music as a disturbing element in a place where people are supposed to talk to each other. The two sound activities (music and talk) dispute our brain attention, making the sound gestalt a hard task. Taiwan student Yu-fen, twenty-eight years old, reports a similar feeling in pubs in the UK:

> When we go to chat with friends we just go for a cup of tea, and search for a quieter space where we can have conversation nicely in a normal volume,

where we don't need to shout to each other. A very nice space for people to relax and chat. Since I mention that I really don't like very loud music, a high volume makes me feel very nervous. I feel that I can't properly stay in a pub here. I really don't quite understand why people are always doing social stuff in the pub, because I don't feel that's a proper environment for people to have a conversation in a comfortable way. I usually feel quite tired up to two hours after I go into the pub – I need to leave earlier. I just can't stay in a very noisy environment for a long time, I just start to feel tired very easily.

Like the car episode described by Alec, Yu-fen also declares being bodily affected by the 'noisy' environment of the pubs that calls her attention while she tries to talk to her friends. Her irritation here is triggered by the effect of loud music as an element of disturbance in the desired acoustic ambience for the conversation. Music in places like this is, for her, 'noise' in its communicative definition, something that stops or interferes in the normal course of talk. Sixty-four-year-old Janet (quoted in Chapter 1) describes a situation in a bank branch where music was intentionally used to avoid the leakage of conversations to other auditors:

> One of the main banks I have an issue with because it seems very loud was the Bank of Scotland. And I couldn't hear what the girl was telling me. And I said, 'Why? I have to complain about this music, I know it is not your fault, it will be a marketing decision'. And she said, 'It is for privacy'. But I said, 'It's not private because you have to raise your voice to speak to me and I am raising my voice to speak to you. So it's not suppressing, it is not helping with privacy'. It is the bank policy. And I actually wrote to the bank, and I got a reply but it was just a flange. I actually made the point just because of the hearing issue for me, but it could be a health issue for people with more impaired hearing and also it could distress people with autism, mental health problems. The music was so insignificant, it was probably fairly modern music, a rap. It was just insignificant, modern music. But the response was, 'Well, we are not going to alter our behaviour. Because nobody else has complained about it'.

The bank's justification for playing loud music reveals an authoritative mode of decision-making in several different chains. The adopted policy is decided by someone in the higher posts of the corporate organization and the reasons for this choice are never clear for employees below. As a consequence, they have to deal with the music in their daily life and answer, according to protocol, customer inquiries. Notwithstanding, in smaller venues, the person responsible for the choice is closer, and eventually one can argue directly with him/her. Retired sixty-five-year-old Dorothy reported one of these cases:

> See, you go to a café to meet a friend for a coffee. And I don't mind music in the background but if it is too loud [I do]. Just recently we were in a café with a friend and [we didn't want it to be] too loud. So we just asked if he wouldn't mind turning it down. We wouldn't mind music [playing], but if it is blasting, you couldn't hear yourself talk. We had to shout. [...] It was OK, the music; I quite liked it, but it was so loud, I and my friend had to shout. It's not very enjoyable. Maybe that's to say that we are getting older, the younger [people are not] bothered. You know, young folk don't care about it. I mean, I like music, but it's just about the situation, 'cause we wanted to have a chat.

Like many interviewees, Dorothy is relatively certain that the kind of music played does not matter as much as the inappropriate moment and volume. Music as noise alters the environment in a way that anything played is misheard. Also, as a bothered auditor, the music made her feel her own individuality as an aged woman, marking a possible generation gap between her and the young customers of the café. In fact, the interviews done with people aged over fifty or sixty reveal that most of them are bothered by loud music in public spaces. This is partially due to physical alterations on hearing throughout the ageing process (Cruickshanks et al. 1998), but also to a particular disposition developed by people towards sound in everyday life. Nevertheless, younger people such as Yu-fen may also feel annoyed by music in public places. The teenager Catarina, for instance, reports a scene she often experienced in a wealthy club in her hometown of Salvador, in Brazil:

> I like to go to a club that has a swimming pool and spend the whole day enjoying the sun and such. And people bring their own speakers. This annoys me a lot and I ask the waiter to ask them to turn off the music.

It's a place that everyone is enjoying and to play your own music doesn't make any sense. This is a public place – I mean, it's not public, it's just for the members of the club, but it is a place that many people attend. And some people turn it off, they feel ashamed that someone else complained. Probably they turn it off because of the embarrassment by the fact that the waiter had to ask them to do it, not because they realized they were bothering. If no one had asked, they wouldn't turn it off. If it was music that I like, I wouldn't ask to turn it off. But I wouldn't complain if someone asked to turn it off.

Like gender, age works as an important element that affords some tendencies in music and sound annoyance, although it is very difficult to trace a direct causal link between years of life and level of irritation aroused by music. As we can see from the report of fifteen-year-old Catarina, very young teenagers can be highly bothered by someone else's music if the place and the moment are judged as inappropriate for sound spreading. Again, the constant background music works as a mechanism of control, modulating the body and the feelings of everyone around. More than an age issue, perhaps it is worth thinking about the auditor's disposition, which involves not only background expectations but also taste and, importantly, a very complicated evaluation of adequacy applied individually in every forced listening situation. And, of course, different attitudes towards the sound are taken depending on this disposition and taste. As she mentioned, someone playing music she likes, even if considered inadequate to the place and moment, would not make her ask for the intermediation of the server to request it to stop. Music annoyance is not independent of personal evaluation and taste, and the kind of music together with loudness and judgement of adequacy are entangled elements in the sonic experience. An auditor's disposition is not simply a set of constructed values, tastes and expectations, but also prejudices and social conflicts. It will be discussed deeply how the kind of music interferes in the process in Chapter 5. For now, it is important to retain the idea that music evaluation in owned public spaces is the result of several layers of interpretations and dispositions of the listener. The idea of control is a central aspect of this process.

Stores: Branding and seasonal soundmarks

The ethics and the economy of control in public places owned and managed by someone is particularly controversial in the retail sector. Shopping centres and stores in general use music as an element of identity that both helps to keep the brand in customers' heads and informs the mood inside the space.

In a study done in eleven shops in a small city in England, Tia DeNora and Sophie Belcher found that music was employed as a resource 'for creating and heightening scene specificity' associated to the shop brand, which aimed 'to structure the aesthetic environment and, through this, the emotional conduct of consumers' (DeNora2000: 138). Several studies in the psychology of music demonstrate successfully how music does influence behaviours in shopping situations. Areni and Kim, for instance, conducted a survey in a wine store where they found that people spend three times more money when listening to classical music in the background than to top-forty hits. According to them, a possible interpretation of this result is that 'the classical music may have communicated a sophisticated, upper-class atmosphere, suggesting that only expensive merchandise should be considered' (Areni and Kim 1993: 338).

Recently, North, Hargreaves and Krause (2016: 793) revised part of the studies on consumer behaviour and stated that it operates in a tension between 'approach' (staying in the place, exploring the environment, facilitating interpersonal communication) and 'avoidance' (leaving the place, avoiding moving or touching, preventing interpersonal communication). Although music is (almost) always played in stores with the intention to produce 'approach', in many cases, the reaction of consumers is to be repulsed, avoiding the place and running away from it. Asked if music can be annoying, for instance, sixty-one-year-old retired public servant Laurence began to speak about what he called the 'dreary shopping mall syndrome'. As a trained musician, he complained about the 'quality' of the music in shops:

> I mean it is the shopping mall as a whole, the shopping thing anyway. Their attitude to music is as bad as their attitude to the physical environment, the temperature of the room, how they treat people. It tends to be dreary; it is not communicative. It is driven to the mood rather than engaging with

people or anybody. If I ever went there, hearing people singing Christmas carols on the radio system... . Again, to me, it is partly the arrangement [which] is so bad. It is the lack of any purpose behind the music which is being played other than the purpose of covering up the fact that people are having conversations and of manipulating what is going into these temples. But I don't go to these places.

To Laurence, avoidance is the dominant feeling towards background music, understood always as something politically harmful and artistically bad. His argument resonates the usual critics directed at background music, opposing it to music practices that could be somehow associated with the idea of 'art'. As Joseph Lanza puts it, once you simply mention terms such as 'easy listening' and 'background music', 'many critics will lash out with judgements such as "boring", "dehumanized", "vapid", "cheesy", and (insult of insults) "elevator music"' (Lanza 1994: 2).

Displaced to a semi-public space, filling the sound environment, the music occupies a secondary role in social activities such as dinner, shopping or waiting. Therefore, in Laurence's view, the music loses its purpose and irritates him. As a musician, he is worried not only with the adequate mode of listening but also with the quality of the music itself. His discomfort has to do with his vulnerability to others' manipulative powers on sound and music in some venues. This idea is shared by Nigel, a sixty-nine-year-old musician from Scotland:

Probably one of the most irritating things is that our entire mode of life got a backing track. And the backing track is everywhere you go. So, if you are on a building site the joiner next to you is playing whatever on Radio One. If you are going to B&Q they are playing a kind of music. For about three months before Christmas, in every department store, they are playing 'Rudolph the Red-Nosed Reindeer' or something like that. Almost always stuff that isn't actually the original! It is a copy of it to cut down on the amount of money the company has to pay the people who made the original music. But it is just awful that our lives are surrounded by sound. I don't say this as somebody who considers himself to be a musician. And I don't actually listen to a lot of music. I think that if you are going to appreciate music, you've got to actually appreciate quietness. To have an ear to what is happening. If you just go as background and wash, it is essentially like white noise.

Nigel and Laurence share some thoughts on what would be the adequate way one should listen to music, demanding not only attention but also a specific acoustic environment to achieve the 'right' hearing. As musicians from the same generation, their dispositions as auditors are framed similarly, avoiding utilitarian and mood-maker music practices. As music has become as integral a part of the 'artificial environment of the retail sector as climate control, lighting and interior design' (DeNora 2000: 132), they regret the fact that it is used inside these venues *only* to control the mood of the experience and not to provide any 'deeper' relation to music. And this control is usually heard as something intrusive and unpleasant. Isabel describes a huge irritation she had which, she realized, was modulated by the shopping atmosphere:

> It happened at the mall. It was at a time – I think it was some kind of anniversary of the mall, and they hired a DJ that was at the entrance playing songs. And they weren't necessarily songs that I didn't like. But I had just arrived from a trip to Teresópolis: contact with nature, only the sounds of the animals, the birds, a place where you can hear the sound of crickets at night, it is like your hearing was transformed. Once I arrived, I had to do something at the mall and I walked in and there it was, that thing, disturbing my whole body. I started to feel like my heart was accelerated, that made myself reverberate. And I was extremely uncomfortable and couldn't shop anymore. I simply couldn't stay in the mall. I had to leave.

The distinct mood between the shopping anniversary and her bucolic mood after a nice trip to the mountains had physical consequences for her. Emotions triggered by sound and music are both psychological and physical responses to the aural stimulus and are processed according to expectations and moments. In this case, the forced listening, judged as inadequate by her disposition as an auditor, provoked unpleasant nuisance in her mind and body, expelling her from the place. Corporal reactions include quite often an amount of disorientation that can have even more drastic consequences. This is particularly the case reported by Alicia and Peter, a couple with whom I have done a joint interview. Alicia had formal training in music and used to work as a music teacher before retiring. Both of them are in their sixties and have dealt for more than two decades with the symptoms of chronic fatigue, a disease that causes permanent tiredness, but which manifests also as hypersensitivity to light, stress and sound:

> *Alicia*: Sometimes I go into a shop and if they play some beautiful music I just stand to listen to it and then I walk out, 'cause I don't want to do any shopping when I've heard that lovely music. [laughs] We went to a shop just now to buy snacks [...] there was a waiting march [that played] on the system, mentally awful, full volume, so we ran away and no snacks. But very very often I walk to a shop and when I walk inside and hear the music I walk out again.
>
> *Peter*: Me too!
>
> *Alicia*: I can't handle it at all, it's just dreadful.
>
> *Peter*: For me it's not dreadful, I just can't get into that. I want to do my shopping, I can't start listening to whatever they seem to want me to listen to. That is not what I'm trying to do.

Although we could assume that the disorientation reported by Peter may be partially caused by his illness, narratives like the one provided by Isabel leave us little doubt on the corporal consequences that loud music can provoke when forced on consumers in those places. Being affected by this intense sensibility to sounds and music increases the problem and result in what Alicia defines as 'social isolation':

> What irritates me is that the music is so dreadful. I can't switch off my head. All the time. We are socially isolated because everywhere is full of this horrible music. So, the places that are closed to us [include] all restaurants, almost all cafés, pubs, shops; and the effect on me is partially because I am a sensitive musician and partially because I'm ill. The music is intensive, intrusive and ugly. Stressful and depressing. It's harmful to my ears, it hurts my ears and it causes me physical and mental upset. It causes extraordinary anxiety and fatigue.

Again, music here is associated with individual health, being a device with the potential to provoke illness and several painful symptoms. As she explicitly mentions being 'hurt', her narrative mixes an aesthetic evaluation (the ugliness of the music) with the 'intensity' of the sound and its imposition ('intrusive'). Taste, volume and inadequacy are pointed out as means that worsen her health, producing stress, depression, anxiety and fatigue. Her affliction is huge and partially associated with unwanted music listened to 'everywhere'. Yet she assumes her hypersensitivity is due to her illness, and she feels harmed by the ubiquitous music that constrains her very right to go out, meet friends or even buy food or clothes. As such, she felt set apart from everyday sociability, forced to stay at home, where she can usually be free from unchosen music and sound. While talking during the interview, Alicia expressed anger for feeling trapped in this situation as well as despair for not finding a way out of aggressive music. The issue of violence is attached to the perception of the pathogenic effect of forced music in public places.

However, it is not true that this unpleasant perception is consensual among customers. Fifteen-year-old Catarina, who was quoted previously complaining about the music in a club in Salvador, when asked if she gets annoyed by music in shops, answered with surprise:

> *Catarina*: In stores? I think that music inside stores is so quiet, so natural,
> creates an ambience. And sometimes it is like this, calm music, just
> rhythm, just instrumental. I work in a store, volunteer work, at the
> Capability Scotland in Leith. And usually I pick the music. Then I play
> Deli very soft, so the place won't be in mortal silence. Because if it was
> all silence, people would complain about the silence. It would be like
> this, people would walk in the store and it would seem like everybody
> was dead.
>
> *Q*: Is it you who chooses the songs?
>
> *Catarina*: If someone else chooses the music, I'll let it play. Every once in
> a while I pick it.

Music here plays an important role in avoiding silence. As Simon Frith puts it, silence is so rare in our society that it became something valuable, though it is surprising that at the same time it became something to be feared and to be filled (2003: 94). The fear is not so difficult to understand. As we have seen, the dynamics between sound and silence can be interpreted as a flow of degrees of movement, where the sound is the vibration (hence, displacement, dynamics, life) and silence is its opposite (steadiness, stopping, death). None of them is absolute, but they embody tendencies towards distinct poles of energy and quietness. 'Deathly silence' in the words of a teenager is something undesired, once associated with ceremonies and rituals as well as with grief and absence of life. Music is, then, a handy solution to avoiding silence and simultaneously to inducing a desired mood in the shop, framing the adequate ambience (according, of course, to the one who has control of the equipment).

The environment of stores and shopping is also determined by the year calendar, which determines seasonal shifts and moments where sales are expected to grow. Particularly sensitive in terms of the sound environment is the Christmas season. In many parts of the Western world, Christmas represents a time to buy gifts in an atmosphere of charity and wishes of well-being. Music is a strong artefact of this seasonal feeling, usually occupied by a repertoire of Christmas songs that often address positive interpersonal wishes. However, the omnipresence of some tunes during the weeks before Christmas evening in every corner of streets and especially inside sale venues is repeatedly reported as something annoying. I interviewed Janet on a grey day at the beginning of December, in Edinburgh:

> Christmas music, of course, is the goal of the moment; that is getting really irritating. Just because it is loud, rooting Christmas music, the same old tracks have been reproduced over and over and over again. I mean I know lots of people who complain about Christmas music. If you are not feeling in a Christmassy mood, it is irritating.

One important thing Janet addresses is the idea of a mood mismatch. Of course, if you go shopping in December to buy gifts embodied with the Christmas spirit, the imposed soundtrack of Christmas tunes may bother you at some moment, but you should be prepared for that. An auditor's disposition is made up of encounters between accumulated cultural background and positionalities towards the music played, which has to do with expectancies. In cases where you expect Christmas songs, possibly they will not irritate you that much. However, you may simply not be in the mood. In this case, the forced music experience is imposed and has a strong probability to irritate, as stated by Janet. Mood control through sound and music can be highly invasive and annoying.

Furthermore, Janet pointed to two issues that were also mentioned by other respondents who have complained about Christmas music. The first has to do with repetition. The limited number of tunes repeated in stores is irritating by itself. Moreover, some stores play the music loud enough to catch bypassing consumers, with speakers directed to the street. The intention is to set the season ambience through a determined repertoire of songs ('Jingle Bells', 'Feliz Navidad', Lennon's 'Happy Xmas', among others) that can work together with streets and house decoration, Christmas trees everywhere and the overall supposed faith in a better world. This adds to the fact that the majority of Christmas music employs certain musical procedures and elements (diatonic melodies and harmonies, synthetized xylophone-like keyboard sound, beat-upbeat smooth rhythm and so on) that make all of them sound similar. And this other layer of repetition is also irritating.

The second annoyance some people feel regarding the music of the Christmas season is the consumeristic chain that is triggered by the sounds. According to this causal thinking, 'It's Christmas, so you must feel solidary with others, so you should make donations for the poor and spend money to give gifts for your beloved ones. You must give presents as expensive as you can to demonstrate your love and your good feelings. If you have children in the family, toys and happiness for them can be purchased in the capitalist market available in every corner decorated with Santa's red hood'. Music is in every store to remind you to buy your children gifts, to buy new decorations, to buy Christmas cards, to buy. Christmas music reminds us of capitalistic consumerism, covered by religious charity and a desire for humanistic wellness. The irritation of not fitting the mood may be in part due to the perception of these contradictions that emerge in Christmas season.

Despite the intention to provide an environmental ambience that could help customers to be aware of the season and therefore to spend money and time in fairs and stores during Christmas time, the frequently mentioned irritation with the ubiquitous music of the season points to the emotions triggered by public music control. In other words, to control the mood of a semi-public venue is far from being an easy task and often the desired results cannot be achieved. Or worse, they can be diametrically opposite. In responding to whether music can annoy, Taivan, a twenty-four-year-old student, describes his previous experience as store employee:

> I worked for three years in a store and the music sometimes helped and other times got in the way. If the music was slow the customer felt that energy. If it was more exciting, they used to buy more, and stay more time. Yes, there are some customers that ask to turn the music down or even turn it off. It was a multi-brand boutique in the mall, and it was one of a few with music. We had a playlist and a Coca-Cola radio. It ranged from the young to the elderly, plus size, LGBT – the store embraced everyone. It was complicated because my manager said that the store had to have a nice environment, relaxing, comfortable. But I realized that some customers didn't like it when we had a DJ – especially during events, which were even louder. So, it was music, party and it really bothered people. There were customers that went in the store focused to buy something specific, but it turns out that they didn't even buy, didn't get in.

As a salesperson, he was aware of the contradictory effects of background music, both providing a cool ambience for some customers and keeping others away. The customer shopping behaviour is influenced by the beat of the music, as well as its loudness. And being influenced does not necessarily correspond to buying more or feeling pleased inside the shop. Once again, the volume is key in setting the mood of the place, but not the only one.

The problem is, of course, to find out what music can match properly to what store, and for whom this combination will work. Furthermore, the background music selection can allow sellers and managers to target specific consumers for their stores, keeping others outside. Both Lanza (1994: 227) and DeNora (2000: 18) reported experiences in which playing classical music in certain public spaces was a way in which security forces actively prevented the presence of youth criminals on buses and in train stations. On the other hand, in-store decisions may scare off not only undesired persons but also potential desired customers.

Pipedown campaign and the issue of choice

If for one side, it is possible to affirm that a significant number of people are bothered by music in public spaces, for another, many of these people develop individual ways to solve this nuisance. Leaving the place is the most often reported act of getting rid of unpleasant music in stores, restaurants or shopping venues. Some people try to talk to the manager or owner, like we've discussed in the case of Anthony on his boat trip. Sometimes, the request to turn down the music is successfully accepted, and the sound stops. But this is not always true.

In fact, a single complaint in a pub, restaurant or store is unlikely to be successful. However, a series of enquiries can eventually have some consequence. One interesting case of a political organization fighting against music in public spaces is the Pipedown campaign in the United Kingdom. The campaign was launched in 1998 by Nigel Rodgers as a response to his personal dislike of background music. He tells how it began:

> I was in a restaurant and the music was very loud so I asked the waiter to put it down, and he was quite sympathetic, but he said he agreed but he couldn't turn off the music. Then I talked to friends and other people and I realized that nobody liked the piped music, but people did not complain. So, I thought something must be done and I started the campaign. Today we have 2,000 members across the UK.

The idea that feeds the campaign is to 'do something'. According to him, 'British people are very reserved and hardly complain about something.' In this sense, his aim is to provide a collective sense of people's private nuisance, pushing them to 'act'. Acting means, at first, joining the campaign through a modicum annual payment that allows you access to the campaign mailing list. On its website (www.pipedown.org.uk), the information 'about the campaign' is an invitation for people to join it. The presentation text is self-explanatory:

> Do you hate unwanted piped background music? (also called piped music, canned music, elevator music, muzac, etc.) Do you loathe its incessant jingle? Do you detest the way you can't escape it? (in pubs, restaurants and

hotels; in the plane, train or bus; ruining decent television programmes; adding to the overall levels of noise pollution in public places). If, like tens of millions of others around the world you do, JOIN PIPEDOWN, THE CAMPAIGN FOR FREEDOM FROM UNWANTED MUSIC in public places.

Joining people from all over the country that share the same irritation about background music, the campaign uses the complaints to target some store chains and pressure them to stop playing music inside their branches. According to the website, some chains have reduced or even stopped playing music after the pressure increased. The campaign was replicated in other places, with more or less the same structure and approach. In Edinburgh, Dorothy Lewis organized a local branch but avoided the word 'pipe', fearing this name could be misunderstood with a possibly controversial 'campaign against bagpipes'. When asked about the beginning of the local campaign, she described a very similar situation as the one that, years before, motivated Nigel to launch the national Pipedown:

> I thought once I retired I am going to have lots of more time, I am going to be able to go into the shops and I am going to meet friends for lunch and chat when we wanted. And then I discovered I couldn't do because it is so noisy, the music everywhere. Everywhere, banks, restaurants, shops, even medical practices they play music. It is just everywhere! I did think it was just me, and I was in a shop with a friend and she said, 'I got to get out of here I can't stand this music'. Me neither! And I started to research and then I came across about the Pipedown, the campaign started twenty-five years ago. I think I wrote to him and suggested to have a local group here.

At first, the local campaign was named 'Quiet Edinburgh', but in 2017 it was renamed 'Quiet Scotland', in order to reflect the spread of the idea to other Scottish cities. Closely linked with the whole British campaign, Quiet Scotland is more active in one of the important axes of action aimed at the campaign which is sharing data and information about background music. They have a strong belief that most people do not like music in public places and that managers are misinformed by the powerful music industry to keep on playing music (and paying royalties). Moreover, especially on the local Scotland site (www.quietscotland.org.uk), it is possible to find links to several studies that challenge the idea that consumers like music in stores. Most links published on the website lead to newspaper articles or independent studies, but some of them mention academic journals in socio-biological areas such neuropsychology or psychology of music. The idea is to keep information updated on the debate about the negative effects of background music.

The campaign rhetoric is centred on the issue of music and health. Both on the websites and in many conversations I had the opportunity to have with members of the campaign, the connection between unwanted music and unhealthy conditions is often mentioned. As DeNora puts it, the categories of health and illness do not oppose each other. Instead, they are constructed according to cultural specificities related to 'our experience of being well or ill and for the quality of social arrangements that surrounds this experience' (2013: 10). Music, she argues, is one of the elements that shape our definitions of health or illness. Moreover, it is a resource people use to produce well-being, acting as a 'medium for removal from and refurbishing of social environments so as to make existence habitable, hospitable, better' (DeNora 2013: 138).

If this is true – and I have no reason to doubt it – so may the opposite also be considered. Music can be a device to promote an unhealthy environment, with direct consequences on people's bodies, emotions and affects. In this sense, a dense music-sound space may cause bodily reactions that some people could classify as unhealthy, as the Pipedown members argue. In 2012, Nigel Rodgers and Val Weedon, president of the UK Noise Association, launched a small booklet in PDF format entitled 'Whose Choice Is It Anyway?', where some of these concerns are detailed. Divided into two brief chapters that address problems of music at workplaces and in hospitals, the booklet adds to the health problem the issue of 'freedom'. After mentioning that the contemporary world allows us to have freedom of choice in many subjects such as education and health, they add:

> One freedom has, however, become far less common over the same period: the freedom to shop, eat, travel and work without having to endure non-stop, inescapable music. Unwanted music easily becomes noise, and noise is

a growing if still under-recognised pollutant. To call music a pollutant might seem absurd but it is often true. When welcomed, of course, music is far from being a pollutant. For most people it is one of life's greatest pleasures. It also has undoubted therapeutic uses, when used correctly. What turns a pleasure into a pollutant – a real pain in the ear – is lack of choice. Music freely chosen or accepted is one thing. Enforced and inescapable music is quite another. (Rodgers and Weedon 2012: 2)

The idea that music becomes noise resounds our debate on the terms evoked to refer to sonic experiences. However, they go further in this negativity of noise, classifying it as a pollutant. In their narrative, 'noise' poisons the air and the ambience, becoming an unhealthy element of daily life. Once framed as a close connection between health, freedom of choice and 'music' (transformed into 'noise'), the arguments of the campaigners acquire strength and relevance. In fact, unchosen music in any shared physical space usually produces anxiety and some level of stress, mainly due to the lack of power to avoid the sounds or to press the stop button. The body is affected by the sounds and minor changes in behaviour are instantly required such as speaking louder to be heard, following the rhythmic pattern of the music with light bodily movements, or, in a semiotic-psychological sense, being forced to interpret the meanings and values spread by the music. All these inescapable adaptations of our bodies in these situations may not necessarily be unpleasant, yet they are highly likely to be so. And if so, the music may be a serious threat to someone's wider health condition.

Therefore, one of the campaign's main targets is to remove music from hospital and healthcare places. In the final pages of the beforementioned booklet written by Rodgers and Weedon, the associations they represent (Pipedown and the UK Noise Association) recommend the government to 'prohibit piped *music* or television *noise* in public areas of hospitals', and to 'carry out comprehensive study of the long-term ill effects of piped music on employees, to discover what psychological and physiological impact it has on those who hate it' (Rodgers and Weedon 2012: 8).

With all these actions, Pipedown plays an important role in the everyday struggle on background music in contemporary life in the UK, providing information, sharing studies and putting pressure on venue owners and public authorities to minimize the disturbance caused by music. The belief in the law to provide security on such issues comes side by side with a direct intervention in pubs, restaurants and stores, filling a wide range of fields where the debate can be raised, from the everyday face-to-face conflicts to the social media realm, passing through juridical and legislative spheres.

This unusual case of music activism against the music is somehow weird. In order to avoid any confusion on their motivations and opinions regarding music in society, both Nigel and Dorothy emphasize all the time that they love music and their campaign is not a campaign against music. On the contrary, they fight against unwanted *recorded* music in public spaces. With this, they leave apart two frequently reported situations of music annoyance: the music that comes from the neighbourhood and the conflicts about live music. That's, of course, a political strategy that aims at the same time to target a very specific problem and to highlight that they are sympathetic to musicians' work. Musicians playing in streets are 'doing their earnings', as Janet stated, and, as such, one can be more tolerant of their art. Live music deals with a direct interaction between musicians and their audience that smoothens the eventual disagreements or annoyance that may happen. Quiet Scotland campaign coordinator Dorothy Lewis admitted that live music may also be annoying and disturb the place, but she argued that streets are open places that people walk through, and, as such, you are not trapped in a place for some time. As we've seen in the case of bagpipers on the Royal Mile, this is not exactly true in every situation, but remains as a strategy to fix the target against recorded music and make their sympathy towards musicians' practise very clear.

The campaign arguments are built on an opposition between a very well-defined idea of 'public place' and the notion of 'individual right'. While entering the owned physical space of a restaurant, store or hospital, one must be assured of his/her intimate right not to listen to any music. Even though this right may conflict with other people's right to hear what they like, the assumption is that you are not in a place that you can control or where you can determine every element of the environment. In other words, you are not in your own home. And, not being at home, one cannot be allowed to impose sounds on everyone who may have or want to frequent these public places.

Following these thoughts, the public and private realms appear again to be linked with the ideal concepts of 'home' and 'street'. The expectation of a safe intimacy at 'home' is, however, far from being applicable to the concrete reality of the house.

Domestic conflicts

Although public and private are important notions through which most debates and conflicts on music and sound are fed, there are some situations where sound leakage is not exactly associated with outside (public) music. Some interviewees reported disagreements and struggles inside their own homes. These conflicts show how power relations are experienced in everyday intimate life, exposing at the same time the different arrangements of cohabitation in our contemporary society, some of them quite distant to the typical bourgeois family model. Far from being silent and peaceful, the home must be heard to also as a stage of repressed struggles that make it 'a site of teenage angst, domestic violence, and sleepless nights' (LaBelle 2010: 65).

In his insightful essay on 'bad music', Simon Frith (2004: 24) confesses to 'being most irritated at home by one child's habit of playing Bob Dylan's *Greatest Hits* in the kitchen – too loud! – whenever he gets the chance to do so'. Domestic disputes on music and volume are particularly frequent and intense. Let's take, for instance, the interview done with Alexandre, a forty-three-year old geologist, who lives in the worldwide famous Copacabana district in Rio de Janeiro together with his wife, daughter (nineteen years old) and son (fourteen years old). When I asked him about home sound conflicts he described taste disagreements:

> There's a conflict with children, generation conflicts. They don't like much my music preferences, except when it's MPB [Brazilian popular music] or samba, but when it is some heavier rock 'n' roll or something like that they get bothered. Often when he's listening to those heavy funks that are not of my liking, also there's a conflict of interests. We complain a bit but accept it, each in their own time. But when we are travelling in the car, there's the

moment of Henrique's songs and then I may be hating them, but we'll listen. And then there's my turn: I play my music, and it's their turn to keep quiet.

Generation conflicts are frequently experienced as music conflicts. As has been well documented in bibliographies about youth, music is a central artefact that produces a sense of belonging and shared ideas about the world between young people, playing a very important role in helping them define themselves in terms of age, sexuality and ethics. Different repertoires and attitudes towards music are connected to some listening practices (hearing loud certain dance genres) that are largely shared to be an element of what we could call a 'youth lifestyle'. 'Family members (teenagers most notoriously) mark off their own space with their music – volume as a barrier' (Frith 2003: 103). Nevertheless, the problems Alexandre reports point to repertoire negotiations that involve the whole family. As music is a powerful device for changing an individual mood, radically different mood expectations will lead to diverged music repertoires and genres, being a fruitful pathway to home conflicts. Thomas Turino, in his book *Music as Social Life*, describes a personal situation:

> As we drove to town my children began to squabble. 'It's my turn!' my twelve-year-old daughter cried. 'It's my turn; you got to decide last time', my son, fifteen, answered. 'I want to listen to *my music*', she insisted. 'We always listen to your music', he responded, forcefully blocking her move to control the radio dial. And so the battle continued, voices escalating as if lives were at stake. (Turino 2008:93, original italics)

According to the author, control over the sound was a way to reaffirm the self within the family, a way to 'project oneself throughout the house' (idem). While emphasizing the teenagers' movement to occupy the environment and to reinforce tastes and belonging, Turino reports the conflict as the main part of these processes and negotiations. Thirty-nine-year-old Carolina described how she and her elder cousin used heavy metal and grunge music as a tool to show their personalities and teen mood to their grandmother when they met in her house for weekly lunch. According to her, the family had a very close connection with Afro-Brazilian religions and music practices such as *samba* and *jongo*. Through these traditional music genres, they cultivated a very strong sense of blackness and Brazilianness, fulfilled by shared ideas, values and feelings and reinforced by the music and the music events. Listening to rock music in this environment against the family background was an act of transgression and defiance:

> Then Rafael would come (at lunch) and said, 'Let's listen to something'. We listened to Iron Maiden. And my grandmother said, 'Who is this person screaming?' At that time, at seven years of age, I became a headbanger. Because of my cousin. We used to sing 'six six six, the number of the beast' and he took a while to explain to me what that meant. Because of Iron Maiden I started getting very curious with this rock business, which wasn't the taste of my family. Listening to Iron Maiden at lunchtime bothered them. A lot. We tried to leave it on, but there wasn't much negotiation with my grandma. She just turned it off. Our music was disturbing to the rest of the older people of my family. Today I won't even go anymore. If you ask me to go to a heavy metal concert I pretend not to listen. That was really a rupture process with what we always listened to at home. And from heavy metal we went searching for other kinds of music and other styles that made us feel more cosy – let's put it in that way. I like rock. Today I no longer listen to heavy metal, but I still like a few songs of the grunge era.

In her memories, the music provided a way both for her to understand herself as a girl and to direct her interests to repertoires and values not shared by her family. Despite the undoubtedly imbalanced power relations between the two youngsters and the grandmother (who actually turned off the 'shouted' music), it is interesting to highlight the way she associates the music repertoire with family conflicts that probably would not have been raised without it. Moreover, she emphasizes that rock music was a moment in her life that worked as a tool for her to go beyond her family restrictions in terms of music and, why not, in a wider perception of life.

Beyond the generation gap that is dealt with alongside different hierarchical positions inside the house, music conflicts reveal disagreements between individuals that are not often brought to the surface of daily life. And sometimes, they point to emotional links between family members, as appears in the case narrated by Quinhan-Chen, a twenty-six-year-old musician, recalling her childhood in Beijing:

> My father singing. After we came out of the restaurant, then my father starts singing, upbeat song, and my mother said, 'How can you be so annoying?' I guess it is because it is not really bad, but it was the moment. I cannot stop him from singing. The music he sings, it's just like *talaltaltlat*. I guess I call it annoying because my mother called it annoying—she transferred it to me, maybe when I was at primary school. He did that to annoy my mom [...] My mom said, 'Can you just be quiet? We just had a good meal, make my belly feel comfortable, in the car' [...] It's annoying but it depends, really depends. If my mom is happy with my father singing, it is OK, but if she is annoyed, I found it annoying. But it is not the other way round. If my father got annoyed I don't mind. I must be more connected to my mom. It is so childish, him doing this. My father cannot help making sounds all the time, and it is annoying, and he keeps making noise every time.

In her memories, her dad's annoying chant showed not only a 'childish' disagreement between her parents but also her closer connection to her mother. According to her affective description, his annoying behaviour was intentional and aimed to irritate his wife, possibly functioning as a device to negotiate tensions between them. Furthermore, the way she recalls this conflict points again to the idea of adequacy. After a good meal in a restaurant, trapped inside the car, the music was an intrusive element spoiling the family harmony. But her interpretation goes beyond the car and her father's music-noise, being described as a constant element of a disturbance at home, as he 'keeps making noise every time'. What was at first narrated as an unpleasant situation changes into an interpretation of her father's character, revealing possibly deeper conflicts in their relations. The nuisance was, hence, made worse as it was felt by her mother as a lack of respect to the moment and to each other. Respect is a keyword in sound and music conflicts. That is what Victoria reported in her interview:

> We need to have respect. I live with my uncle and he enjoys listening to rock. I don't like to listen to heavy rock. I rather stick to my indie music,

Lana Del Rey, extremely calm, in a very 'I wish I was dead' mood. And he doesn't! He likes it heavy. And then we must respect one another. You have to listen to music in your space, without bothering others. That thing he does always bothered me.

Nineteen-year-old Victoria inverts some of the conventional expectations of music consumption between youngsters as she prefers calm repertoire that arguably differs from her uncle's musical taste. Moreover, she demands 'respect'. Respect for her individuality and her private right to be safe from the other's music, even though the 'other' is her own uncle and the place where this disagreement happens is her house. Soundly speaking, the idea of 'respect' would be playing music at a volume that would not leak to the next room inside the house. It means controlling the spread of the music throughout the house in order not to impose it on her ears. Once she is forced to listen to (loud) music that she doesn't like and/or that she doesn't have the power to stop, she felt her subjectivity forcedly changed, having to share the vibe of the 'heavy rock' she does not want. The mood split between her uncle's 'heavy rock' and her 'calm indie' appears to be felt by her as both a generation conflict and a personal offence.

Musicians frequently experience sound negotiations at home. Since instrument learning requires considerable time spent making sounds that are not exactly pleasant to anyone's ear, practising at home can be an element of disturbance. Belen gives an interesting narrative about her teenage years of clarinet training:

I remember my sister when I played clarinet at home, when I was practicing it. Because I had to study every day and it was a kind of a nightmare to her. 'Another time playing the clarinet: no, please!' It was long notes like *tuuuuu*, and it was a little bit annoying for her. My mother said, 'No, she has to play the clarinet'. I had a separate room to practice but our houses are not soundproofed, and you are playing and the other can listen perfectly. [...] Normally these exercises are technical exercises, very repetitive, like *too tan too tan* – I think it is really annoying.

Her story reveals how the management of sound in domestic relations is connected to power relations. The disagreement between sisters was solved through the intervention of her mother, who imposed Belen's right to play the clarinet despite her sister's protests. This case reinforces that the idealized idea of home as the space of shelter and security against the noisy and dangerous street is far from being true in every situation. Conflicts inside one's home are the everyday tissue of family relations and part of this primary intimate public sociability. Within our homes, hierarchies are tensioned and negotiated daily, in many cases with struggles over sound and music. Another case of sisterly disagreements was provided by project coordinator Olivia, also as a memory of her time growing up:

> My sister is a professional guitarist in a rock band and she used to listen to music all the time, like around the clock. I think it must have bothered me because we had a bit of an imbalance at school. I was doing OK at school, and she wasn't doing so good in school. And she was really into music, which is great – it's become her life. But she used to do all her school work listening to quite intense rock music. She just wasn't getting a balance, and you know, the music probably was distracting her. And it was annoying me. I know that you are slowing your brain down if you're trying to do the two things at once. That's what I thought the intention was.

While remembering this case, Olivia develops a link between the music played and a much wider sense of behaviour and expectations towards life. Their imbalance in school performance would be dealt with by her sister in a mix of envy and anger that materialized in 'intense rock music' 'all the time'. According to twenty-seven-year-old Olivia, her sister's intention was precisely to annoy her and reinforce a different path in life, a different choice to be made. Music works here as a device to expose and clarify behavioural conflicts, as a tool to mark distinctions and positions, helping to say, at the same time, 'I'm here and I like this' and 'I don't care about you or your choices'.

Every human relation involves negotiations on expected behaviours that are done according to power hierarchies and tensions. Within a typical family, the adults usually have more power to impose their sound on the others in the house, depending on how these negotiations are done. But this is not that simple. If we think about crossed relations in every family, several hierarchies appear and are defined in each situation, according to moments and moods, and to dispositions towards arguing and disputing. Isabel remembers a regular family disagreement on music in the yearly celebration of Christmas (again!):

> Every Christmas my family had a fight over the music. It was at my grandmother's house; she used to gather everyone. Four sisters and their husbands, alongside their children, every single one of them used to go there. I had an aunt who was very lively and always put Roberto Carlos on to play, which was always the album he had just launched for Christmas. She used to turn the stereo to the top volume, and sang along with it for us to dance, but there was a grumpy uncle who didn't want to. Another aunt had the TV on and didn't listen to it. And it always turned into a fight. The most vivid memory we have of Christmas at my Grandma's is these fights. Nowadays there are no fights anymore, because my fun aunt lives in Brasilia and hasn't come to spend Christmas in Rio. But it was fun, this thing of playing music and everybody dancing, it was really good.

In wider family meetings, some unmatched preferences, past feelings, uncured fights and hearts among family members may appear and be dealt with through music tastes. Again, the disagreement is over who will or can have the control to define the proper mood of the moment, be it at a Christmas party or on a regular Sunday morning. When the power hierarchies are not very clear, the dispute can be more intense and explosive.

This is precisely what happens in other cohabitation situations, where power asymmetries can be less clear and, as such, more likely to trigger conflicts. Sharing the same house implies sharing several intimate habits that can eventually be felt as invasive, inappropriate or undesired by others with whom one lives. These include cleaning habits, food menus, entertainment preferences, timetables and, of course, sound and music practices. Twenty-seven-year-old actor Diego describes a nuisance merging both the outside neighbour's sound and the inside one's music in the next room. Asked if music can annoy, he answered the following:

> It is disturbing if the music is loud, if a neighbour is listening to a song that I'm not in the mood to listen to, whatever it is. Or even right here at the hostel. I live in a hostel, it's a shared house, and sometimes someone puts on

loud rock, maybe to show their rock-liking personality, I don't know. But I don't wanna listen to that rock music and it bothers me a lot, even if it's a song that I like.

Negotiations on sound and music in a place like a hostel or a collective flat tend to be more difficult due to the inhabitants being in close proximity to each other. Twenty-year-old Aidan reports a very dramatic situation where he changed his entire daily planning in an attempt to avoid bothering his flatmate:

Right now I'm learning sitar and one of my flatmates has forbidden me to play for all the hours she is at home. I have to change my day around to play when no one else is at home, which is really annoying and made me very angry. I can easily go on about how angry I am with that kind of thing. For me, I'm not bothered by someone playing music in the same building or room that I'm in, because I think it is such a good thing to play music. Because I know how spiritual for me it is to do it. So I don't wanna stop someone from doing it. I understand my flatmate doesn't have this background, maybe doesn't relate to music the same way I do, obviously. I try to be at peace with that in my life because I am not going to be moving out soon. I respect this person. I don't want to be disrespectful. I want to be at home. It means that if I am at home I'd like to play music. I'd like to have a conversation with her about it. I was playing one night and she knocked on my door and said, 'You have to stop, it's too late'. I was like, 'OK'. She texted the group chat and said no music after 8 p.m. And I said, 'OK, that's reasonable'. And I was playing when she was home one day, and it was 5 p.m., and she came out to my door. I actually had left the window open, and so she used the window as a pretext and she came out and said, 'Don't leave the window open because it's freezing the house'. And she said, 'But also you can stop playing now because I'm home'. She was so rude. Like she told me to shut up, it's like, 'Shut the fuck up', very rude the way she delivered it.

In this case, the conflict irrupts from the music, but the damaged report is not from the bothered auditor, but from the one who was actually playing the sounds. This inversion reveals how conflicts in domestic situations are a fruitful terrain of interhuman negotiations. Probably Aidan's flatmate feels she is in her right to demand a quiet environment at home, and the sound of the sitar somehow disturbs her. In her auditor's disposition, she hears the sitar as an intrusion in her intimate place, and she seems to be angry that Aidan plays it at home, being assertive in her complaints. We can speculate she is not only irritated with the sound leakage itself, but also with the kind of music being forcedly heard throughout the house. Surely, she felt disrespected by Aidan's sitar, which made her be 'rude' in her request to stop. On the other hand, Aidan reports a mix of feelings that go from disappointment to anger. He is constrained by her and also feels disrespected not only by the repeated intolerance of his playing but also by the way she complains about it.

Aidan's feelings resound the car situation reported by Alec at the beginning of this chapter. In both cases, they feel trapped in a physical space where the music conflict is inescapable. In Alec's case, the music was played by his colleague, against his will and taste, making him literally sick. In Aidan's case, he is the one who is playing and bothering his flatmate, although he feels victimized by her aggressive way of imposing silence. Sharing spaces with other people means facing behaviours that could collide with yours, in a tensive administration of tolerance that is constantly being challenged. Moreover, as in Aidan's narrative, the conflicts that emerge from these situations raise the issue of violence. Cases of violence, some of which have already appeared in several descriptions provided by interviewees quoted so far, will be discussed and further developed in the next chapter.

4

Sound, music and violence

Music and violence are entangled in several ways. Music can offend, harm, irritate, cause anger, despair, fear. Music events may instigate physical violence in the form of fights, shouts and even killings. Music choices can also trigger violent negotiations of conflicts, usually linked to social issues beyond the sound experience itself, like territorial, class, racial and sexual prejudices. At the same time, music is sometimes a shortcut to promote solidarity and conflict resolution (O'Connel 2010: 12). Making music together is a powerful collective act that engages people in promoting empathy and friendship. The latter aspect is usually reinforced in popular music studies, emphasizing the force of performing music in enjoying the trivial and necessary experience of being together. Notwithstanding, it is possible to identify an increasing number of published works in recent years that face the uncomfortable entwinement between music and violence (Fast and Pegley 2010: 27).

In its common sense, 'violence' refers to an act engendered *against* something or someone with the explicit intention to inflict pain, damage or destruction. Described as an act, violence is conceived as something related to the physical. Moreover, this definition points to the idea that violence involves two protagonists (perpetrator and victim) and intentionality. Someone commits violence against someone else with an explicit intention to do so. Violence is, then, the resulting consequence of a power asymmetry that is measured by physical force. Such definitions somehow put the concept of violence far from music studies. When we follow the news talking about 'rates of violence', it is murder, robbery and other physical assaults that are framed, and not sound leakage from an apartment to its neighbours. However, if we define a broader approach to the term 'violence' it can encompass other forms of power and control struggles involving the sonic. If violence has to do with power and control, annoying music is music you hear without having the control to stop or change it. Controlling the sound of a social space is, hence, having the power to impose your sonic choices over the others.

Ethnomusicologist Samuel Araújo and the research group led by him – Musicultura – have been working with the interactions of music and violence for more than a decade. In a long-term project of active research with youngsters in Favela da Maré, one of the most violent and poor districts of Rio de Janeiro, they are developing a set of reflections on music practices in contexts of permanent violence. According to them, 'conflict' and 'violence' are usually associated in ethnomusicological studies, or as a 'social or personal disturbance of an implicit social order, or an eventual denial of a given order that produces effects on music makers and the music they produce' (Araújo and Musicultura 2006: 289). The idea of order resounds the perspective of Jacques Attali discussed in the first chapter, who defines music as an action of ordering in the world, against a pre-existing chaotic disordered nature (2009). In this framework, music is understood as a kind of antithesis of violence, a device that has the power to 'solve' or 'eliminate' it.

Instead, Musicultura's approach to violence and music suggests considering violence as a central condition of knowledge production, 'which includes the production of musical knowledge and cultural analyses of music and music-making' (Araújo and Musicultura 2006: 289). Therefore, violence cannot be considered something outside music and cultural experiences, but as an intrinsic part of them, framing the way interhuman relations will be developed in a given space and time. Moreover, this framework points to violence itself as a conditioning mode of knowledge, which has several implications for the study of music in social life. Following this path, violence is a category that pervades unpleasant music experiences in several ways, being part of a daily narrative of music performed by auditors.

When confronted with unwanted music, most interviewees reported a general feeling of being violated. Hence, violence, as music, is something felt and suffered, and something that challenges and disturbs intimacy, privacy and body. And it does so both for the physical encounter between sound and body and for the psychological interpretation of the meanings of the sound. Furthermore, it activates a process of judgements about the one who has control over the sound, resulting in inferences about his/her personality, lifestyle and preferences. Beyond all that, annoying music triggers a complex reflection about life in society, usually described using a vocabulary of violence.

Vocabulary and imagination

In the narratives people develop about negative music experience, it is possible to notice the use of a set of language resources that deal with a vocabulary of violence. It is applied as a means to enhance the emotional element of being violated by music and sounds. Using violence metaphors helps people not only express their disgust but also develop a therapeutic *voice* for their feelings. Let's take, for instance, the narrative of Ernani, a sixty-eight-year-old psychologist who lives in a middle-class district of Rio de Janeiro:

> Often, music is used as a form of violence, it is a sonic violence. You can see that when you're driving. You see some guys who get out of their cars, playing stupidly loud music in their cars, usually those blunt, challenging sounds, etc. And they ride what I consider a musical war tank – that is a sonic missile for me. Whenever I see that it annoys me.

While describing this generic case, which is a result of several similar situations witnessed by him in his mobility through the city, he changed his voice and tightened his muscles to emphasize the discomfort with the situation. In his body and ears, the loud music of cars was felt as a 'sonic missile', acting as a weapon pointed in his direction. He is, then, the 'victim'. This experience is related to a wider violent situation of driving in big cities like Rio. Traffic jams and individualistic driving patterns are elements that make up part of an environment that is far from being calm and peaceful. Nevertheless, people passing by in their cars with blasting music leaking outside them is a behaviour that irritates him. The metaphor of a musical war tank playing 'challenging' sounds reveals the force of his unpleasant music experience.

But this metaphorical violence voice is often a way to *interpret* the daily situation of being forced to listen to someone else's music. While remembering the blasting cars, Ernani manifested despair and tried to elaborate on the reason why people do things like that. It is a reflexive attitude similar to that expressed by Belen (quoted in Chapter 2) when she described her inability to understand why people walk down the street with loud sound devices, and imagined their need to show off. This interpretation is a way to elaborate ideas and feelings towards the other and his/her music, judging his/her choices, personality and public behaviour. In this sense, music and violence are entangled as categories that construct knowledge about public and private life.

Furthermore, as auditors feel violated by the other's challenging music, they sometimes develop a hyperbolic discourse that allows them to *imagine* violent solutions to the assault suffered. The desire to destroy inopportune sound devices or even to kill the one who is controlling the music is mentioned by some interviewees. These three strategies – talking, interpreting and imagining – are not clearly separated, and many times the verbal elaboration that includes violence signifiers is at the same time a way through which people develop thoughts about unpleasant sound experiences as well as imagine violent acts that could interrupt the nuisance. As Ruth Finnegan argues, 'Music provides a human resource through which people can enact their lives with inextricably entwined feeling, thought and imagination' (2003: 192). In the case of annoying music, feelings are sometimes expressed through violence metaphors (voice), elaborated in consonance with shared thoughts (interpretation) and, in many cases, 'solved' by imagined violent acts against the sound source (against a device and/or person).

Emotions are at the core of the music violence vocabulary. It is highly accepted both in common sense and in empirical data available in studies in psychology of music that music raises emotions (Juslin 2016: 199). However, the word 'music' is usually associated with 'positive' emotions such as happiness, calm and interest (Juslin 2016: 200). Emotions such as anger or anxiety are reported usually in social contexts (idem), which is a clue that the issue of choice is something that changes how people interact with a musical event. When music raises emotions associated with violence, metaphors borrowed from war and conflict vocabulary are applied by auditors as a way both to define their deep feelings and to imagine solutions. As people feel harmed by someone else's music, an intense process of administrating emotions is triggered, oscillating between tolerance, control and discharge. The reactions towards the feeling of being invaded by the other's sound vary, usually according to the ambience and the overall characteristics of the individuals involved. Carolina expresses contradictory thoughts in her complex administration of emotions and self-control:

> *Carolina*: Another nuisance are those [useless?] 'babblers' who listen to music without earplugs in the subway, in the bus. I don't know how I didn't freak out so far. I wish I could hit the mobile phone like this, throw it on the floor and step on it. Damn, that's lack of respect!
>
> Q: And what about you, have you ever said anything?
>
> *Carolina*: No, because I will lose it quite easily. I will lose it in a way that the person will jump on top of me and I will jump on top of him. I know I won't hold back. Sometimes, I stand still, staring. I wanted to develop a strategy and carry around some earplugs to give them way: 'Here, take these earplugs'. And there are people who use earplugs, but they play the music so loud that one still can hear it! Do you understand? It is a nuisance!

Feeling disrespected by the mobile sound in the subway, Carolina imagines the violent act as a possible solution to the situation. The extreme act of smashing someone's mobile phone may be considered a sort of childish reaction that reveals a lack of tolerance and that triggers other layers of violence. Knowing she should not behave in such a way, she *imagines* the violent act but avoids even complaining or asking for the person to turn off the mobile. She fears losing control and provoking a physical fight.

Life in contemporary societies is regulated according to several norms that are both imposed by external agreements (the law, the affective links with family, friends, etc.) and internal self-constrains. According to Norbert Elias, the 'process of civilization' enacted a long-term negotiation of manners and desired behaviours that resulted in a setting apart of those human activities defined as animalistic, and aimed to control instinct and feelings (Elias 2000: 365). As a consequence, alternative and symbolic forms of social regulation became more important than the explicit threat of physical violence. In his words, 'The individual is largely protected from sudden attack, the irruption of physical violence into his or her life. But at the same time he is himself forced to suppress in himself or herself any passionate impulse urging him or her to attack another physically' (Elias 2000: 370). That's why Carolina compared her possible violent physical reaction with a kind of madness. 'Acting like a crazy woman' and 'losing her mind' are, then, undesired reactions that must be avoided as they express strong emotions that ought to be hidden and controlled. They are emotions associated with animalistic and uncivilized behaviours.

It is worth mentioning that violence and the way people deal with unpleasant sonic experiences are framed in cultural and social contexts. While talking about being mad or uncivilized, Carolina reveals her personal belonging to Brazilian culture and its complex way of processing the idea of civilization. In countries with a history of colonization, the idea of 'civilized behaviour' is attached to the contradictory desire to be like the European invader, controlling acts and corporeal movements that could be understood as inadequate. It is a process that was led by the colonial elite especially during the nineteenth century and that included a sound administration of public space. As Natalia Bieletto (2018) has argued, the desired mode of listening by the upper class in colonial society, at the turn of the twentieth century, enacted a form of social control, excluding the body and, especially, the racialized bodies of indigenous and black people. Bieletto is talking about the initial decades of the twentieth century in Mexico City, but her argument can easily be applied to a wider geographical and temporal realm, encompassing twenty-first-century Rio de Janeiro and Carolina's complaints. The issue of 'civilization' is experienced in similar ways throughout Latin America, being a much-explored topic that is still used to classify people within society nowadays. Of course, I am not stating, with that, that European countries do not have problems with inadequate, loud sounds heard as violent or uncivilized. On the contrary, the idea of civilization is the result of the encounter with the other, especially after the sixteenth century. According to Anibal Quijano (2009), coloniality is a process of the imposition of a power pattern on the world that resulted from the colonization of the Americas and Africa, supported mainly through racial segregation and racism (Quijano 2000: 218). As such, the Western world power distribution is divided between exploited colonies and imperial centres located in Europe that defined not only the relationship between them, but also the knowledge through which this relation is interpreted. Civilization, alongside with catechization and slavery, defined human beings and social relations according to a perspective that aimed to avoid what could be felt as non-human. Slaves, Indians and other human beings were classified as non-human and all sorts of violence could be imposed on them. This moral frame of colonization defines not only the colonized 'other' but also the (white) European as the one who has not only military but also symbolic power: the knowledge, the science, the religion, the civilization (Quijano 2005).

The relevance of this discussion to our debate lies in the fact that the idea of civilization became a commodity in social struggles, which induced respect and power to those – mostly considered 'whites' – who could be seen and heard as 'civilized'. The frame of civilization makes distinctions not only in international asymmetries between countries and populations, but also inside each country between the elite and the 'people'.

Soundly speaking, civilization means, in many situations, silence. The opposite of it, spreading sounds and music in a place regardless of others, is acknowledged as uncivilized and the response can be an irruption of physical violence – also interpreted as an animalistic and unreasonable reaction. With all this turmoil in mind, Carolina can only imagine a violent disclosure for her annoyance, bearing the soundly invasive trip in a silent and 'civilized' manner. Her reaction is also shaped so as not to appear far from the civilized expectation, in a complex administration of feelings and belongings that merge music, culture, emotions and desired behaviours. The individual consequence of all these feelings is a struggle to suppress violent reactions, inflicting somehow a kind of a self-violence.

Janet makes an interesting reflection on how multiple and confused feelings affect her behaviour and produce angst. Asked how she felt when experiencing a situation where music is annoying her, she said she feels

irritation, along with a level of stress as well, that possibly becomes anger. I feel more frustrated because I think it is just the anxiety and stress that produces what you need [to find a way] to deal with. And the best thing is moving away. Fine, you adjust your behaviour to remove yourself from the stress and the irritation. But you can't always do that. It is more than irritation on occasions; it really ends up being, you know – you feel quite tense. You are quite irritable inside, it builds up because you feel harmed as an individual. Some people would argue actually you are gonna have to control this because it's causing you a lot of angst.

Her vocabulary of unpleasant feelings is filled with different words – irritation, angst, stress, tense – in an attempt to express the violation she felt. In her way of interpreting the nuisance, she evokes a supposedly expected emotional reaction that, somehow, she could not achieve. The issue of having control over your feelings is again set as a condition for a better life in society, where she could feel less harmed by the music. Tolerance with others' sounds and music would be, according to her, a desired sentiment that would allow her not to suffer so much in these situations. But the fact that she cannot do that always 'builds up' personal stress highly harmful to her health. The issue of controlling emotions comes together with the sensation of failure when one can't do that.

Janet and Caroline deal with their emotions in different ways. While Janet takes the unpleasant situation to think about herself and her tolerance threshold, Caroline imagines an explosion of anger that could be seen as a mad act, but that could solve her annoyance. They both manifested a considerable level of irritation but imposed self-constraint to avoid any external reaction, which is in itself a form of self-violence. Even though life in society is always filled with rules that block the free expression of emotions, the circuit of violence in their unwanted listening experiences involves a dual movement of being affected by the sound externally and internally. In the case of Caroline, the imagined violent solution adds another level of entangled violence.

The idea of imagining a way to get rid of another's music appears again in the description of Andrea and Brenda about their neighbours' habits:

Brenda: I feel so angry, I feel like grabbing a bomb, not to throw at them but at the speakers. I feel like getting a sign and saying 'no sound' – anything to explode the sound (laughter). I don't even look at them. I pretend they don't even exist. I actually despise them. I just don't want to interact. Pretending they don't exist is OK for me.

Andrea: I wish they vanished from the street. Yes, I wish they went somewhere very far away, vanished. They are unbearable.

Bombs, explosions, magical disappearances and contempt are some of violent ideas used by them to interpret and imagine solutions for the strong nuisance. In this brief passage, Brenda provides a full range of verbal resources to express and elaborate on her anger. Not only does she talk in a violent way, but she also thinks about the situation, expresses her deep emotions and imagines the end of her deprivation by sending her neighbours far away. Although she avoids even imagining a direct physical act against them, she talks about the desired destruction of the sound device. Music and sound are the elements of her contact with the neighbours, mediators of an unspoken conflict, filling her with feelings of anger and despair. Her actual reaction is to ignore them, but her wish is to get rid of them and their intrusive sounds.

This imaginative solution through perpetrating a violent act against the sound device or its owner is sometimes radical. Sometimes it takes an extreme form, when the respondent verbalizes being tempted to *kill* the other person. Obviously, it cannot be taken as a threat or a real possibility but it works as a rhetoric resource to emphasize the amount of irritation the situation produces and to 'solve' it. Intention and guilt are strongly related ideas in criminal processes involving violence perpetration. However, violence can only be considered an actual crime if effectively committed by someone, which excludes the imagination. In this sense, speaking about an intention to commit a murder is often a path to enhancing the emotional aspect of the situation and not to a proper crime:

Really, I still prefer loud music than loud television. Even though it is music from hell. The vocals annoy me more than the music itself. As it has the rhythm of the instruments, that lulls me. But the television sound, especially if it is a violent noise, gun shots, whatever. It can be something about memory. Music also has to do with unconscious memories it activates in you, which drives you mad, willing you to argue with the person, wishing you could kill the person. That generates an extraordinary hatred, an abjection. But I think it is because it might trigger some memory within us.

Several issues can be highlighted in the narrative provided by forty-six-year-old librarian Marise. First, it is quite interesting how she mixes different nuisances in a perceived violent environment. Different sound sources are heard and interpreted in different ways, using words and qualifiers that express her value judgement. She said she prefers loud *music* to the *noise* that comes from the TV, especially those noises defined as 'violent'. The noises she identifies as violent are the sounds associated with physical violence such as shots and explosions. By applying these terms, she highlights the artistic element of music experience (especially rhythm) comparing it positively to the annoying human presence of the voice. Somehow, in her speech, 'voice' and 'noise' are opposed to 'music'. However, she keeps the word 'music' to refer as well to her hate against the person who is controlling the sound, revealing that even the language choices used to refer to unwanted sound are sometimes confusing. 'Music' can at the same time embrace and annoy her in such a way that she even images killing the controller. In a sense, she begins saying that 'noise' from the TV irritates her more than music, but she classifies the cause of her desire to kill as 'music'. Although a bit contradictory, like most human experiences, these intense feelings she reports towards sonic experiences reveal mostly her anger and her sense of belonging.

As she is very aware of the influence of life experience on the way sound annoyance is interpreted and felt, she made very clear the importance of what I am calling auditor's disposition. The set of ideas about music and sound is the result of her previous experiences with music and sound, strongly connected, in turn, with expectations of an ideal sound environment in each situation. A part of this disposition is informed by background experience, national and regional belonging and other personal elements such as gender, race and class. The irritation music may cause is also connected to these memories and they can actually trigger violent sensations and reactions. Of course, killing the sound controller is hyperbole. These exaggerations are part of the imagined violent solutions described by auditors while remembering unpleasant moments of other people's music. As they deal with overreactions towards something they acknowledge to be not so important, and which should be dismissed, in many cases it turns into something laughable.

Most conversations about annoying music and its violent metaphors are accompanied by laughs. Humour works as a kind of shortcut in some complicated debates, allowing access to something that otherwise could be difficult to say or to talk about. Also, humour and irony are cultural resources that may open room for criticism, providing a shift in the seriousness of acts, behaviours and situations; transforming these into something funny can raise one's awareness of them (Billig 2005: 25). And the opposite is true. The laughable content in narratives about music nuisance reveals that this nuisance should not be taken as so important.

But there is another issue regarding humour in music unpleasant experiences. Laughing at a complex situation may be fruitful in interpreting a situation and adding complexities in apparently simple and unimportant things, but it can also stop the further development of ideas, the laugh being an end in itself, keeping uncomfortable things as they are or even feeding prejudice and intolerance. Racist and sexist jokes are frequently removed from public spaces as they seem to perpetuate racism and sexism, instead of criticizing or problematizing them (Billig 2005). As Pickering and Lockyer argue, comic discourse allows a 'contraband cargo' of offence:

> Comic discourse obviously operates in ways which are distinct from other forms of discourse, and it would be foolish to try to reduce it, or make it conform, to the conventions and values of those other forms. At the same time, it doesn't operate in a completely separate realm, a parallel world without connection to the one we routinely inhabit. It accompanies us all along the way within this everyday world, whether in conversations with friends or in responses to the media. (Pickering and Lockyer 2005: 13)

In this sense, music violence and humour are more complex than they seem to be at first glance. Exaggerating the reaction to someone else's music is a way to show your irritation as well as to share this unpleasant feeling with friends and colleagues. And it may be funny. But the critique stops at this point, closing the path that could lead to further debate on music and violence. While laughing at the situation, the seriousness of the personal feelings is transformed into a mere funny joke, accompanied by the subtext 'let it be, you will not be upset because of it, right?' Johnson and Cloonan (2009: 188–90) highlighted that media coverage on the use of music as torture in the Iraq War by US soldiers against Iraqi detainees was often filled with laughs and jokes that dismissed its importance, even though what was being reported was 'the studied destruction of a human being' (Johnson and Cloonan 2009: 190).

When we are dealing with violence, humour may be on a slippery ethical tightrope, balancing unevenly over a critical terrain. At any time, laughs can be transformed into shock or astonishment as we face situations in which the overreaction to sound and music conflicts did end in death.

Violent acts and sound violence

In December 2017, Brazilian On-Line News *G1* published the case of a murder at a party that followed a discussion of the volume of the music:

> According to the agents, officer Jorge Luiz Aguiar attended a party in the neighbourhood and demanded that they lower the sound, but the guests refused to do so. He fired fifteen shots at a woman identified as twenty-one-year-old Hayssa Alves, with whom he had had an argument minutes earlier. 'The argument between Jorge Luiz and the victim Hayssa which led to the murder of the victim Hayssa was due to the police officer's complaint about the kind of music [funk] which the victim and her friends were playing in the celebration. Indeed, an acquaintance of police officer Jorge Luiz, who was with him, was the one who invited Hayssa and her friends', said Fábio Cardoso, the chief police officer of the capital's homicides division. (Lívia Torres, G1, 8/12/2017)

Whereas the narrative may sound absurd, the extreme violence against the one who was playing the sound in a party (fifteen shots!) is not an isolated case, but a possible though not common response to this kind of disagreement. In this case, we move far away from the imagined violent solution to an actual violent act, consonant to common-sense definitions which point to its physical dimension.

An interesting report is provided by thirty-one-year-old Peruvian musician Sergio. As he recalls his younger years, he remembers that his music preferences differed radically from his friends', who used to listen to reggae every time they met. After highlighting that he 'hated' reggae, he remembers a situation where he tried to 'impose' his musical taste:

> I do remember a trip I took in Cuzco. I would put that music on, I brought my little sound system, anticipated the situation on music… and [played it] loudly in the dorm that we share with probably with my closest friends. And yeah, my friends tell me just, 'Man, turn it off'. I said, 'No, like you guys do it all the time, put your reggae music on and I try to be cool. Now I want to put my own music on as well'. Yeah, kind of a dick actually. I do remember, because I was probably so unpleasant about it. And in that situation, I was alone 'cause my friend who liked punk was in another room. My friends grabbed my iPod, the only iPod that had the same songs (it was more than fifteen years ago), and threw it against the wall and broke it. I've always been very small, no way I could fight, but I was like [yeah]. But that episode definitely stayed in my mind, kind of those violent actions of trying to impose your sound … my … he broke my iPod!

The extreme act of throwing the device against the wall is obviously an example of violence related to music in which the physical act happens beyond the music but is caused by it. Johnson and Cloonan (2009: 65) elaborate on a distinction between 'causality' and 'adjacency' in the connection between music and violent acts. After mentioning several music events – concerts, festival, parties, singing in pubs and so on – where acts of violence were perpetrated, they refuse the simplistic idea inculcated by security forces, governments and media that music could be the direct cause of the violence. 'The logistics of the music events bring together the participants [of the violent acts], but how far the violence of the event is actually caused or made more likely by the musical force-field is debatable' (Johnson and Cloonan 2009: 81). While it is possible to agree that the direct relation between music and violent acts is uncertain, the idea that music can be an element of mere adjacency is hard to sustain. If we agree that music and sound produce physical and psychological changes, it can be difficult to imagine social situations where some music is being played without influencing the behaviour of the participants. Unless we dismiss the power of music to induce moods and interhuman interaction, then music becomes, in any place where it is being performed, a conditioning factor in auditory perception. If any physically violent event happens, music is always connected to it. The problem with this way of putting things is the simplistic conclusion where music is blamed for the violence. Although it is obviously naïve thinking, it is not uncommon for authorities investigating crimes to trace a direct link between music and violence. What is darkened in this process is the difficult task of understanding that behaviours are complex and, despite the fact that music does shape them in a sense, it is impossible to make direct associations between the sonic ambience and the violent physical act.

In Sergio's case, music was an element of disagreement between him and his friends, working as a background of a possible irruption of violence. As he describes the scene, he makes clear that he premeditated the conflict and tried to 'anticipate' it by 'imposing' his sound. His imposition was a shortcut to a doubly violent event perpetrated both by him when imposing music his friends didn't like and by his friend who broke the iPod. While it is a situation that reveals some complexities in defining who is doing violence against whom, the music cannot be dismissed as an unimportant element of the scene. Nor as a mere adjacency. At the same time, there was nothing in the music that could induce violence in the way sound ambience could be said to be the cause of any violent act. While facing cases like this, Johnson and Cloonan refined their argument by proposing the idea of 'arousal', stating that the violent act can be triggered by the sound, lyrics or context where music is played. 'Relations of power (who chooses the music, and the conditions under which it is experienced), can enable any music to arouse aggressive forces' (2009: 146).

The idea that the context is significant to the arousal of violence opens the path to another issue that is present in many of these reports. Music, as sound, has a materiality that can be violent in itself. In the beginning of this chapter I quoted Ernani's description of his annoyance related to music leaking from cars in the street and highlighted the use of a vocabulary of violence he applied to talk about his feelings. The hyperbolic usage of violent words is important in his narrative, but, additionally, we cannot erase the way music sounds actually affect him and his body. When he compares the sounds to war tanks, he reports that he felt actually harmed by them, and this damage is not metaphorical. As

Martin Daughtry puts it, 'Sonic events engender an immediate experience of sound as bodily invasion or assault' (Daughtry 2015: 163). As such, they are intrinsically violent, especially if imposed.

A growing number of publications about the use of music in torture point to the fact that imposed music can have a strong effect on the body. Imposed music listening modulates the body movements and the conditions of the relation between the self and the external world. As Suzanne Cusick (2006) states in an influential article about music as torture, the music, as sound, penetrates the body and forces the listener to vibrate according to the sound waves. The idea of vibration as a dynamic force in music perception is reinforced by Steve Goodman (2010: xx), who claims for what he calls a 'politics of frequency', ranging from silence to noise. Sound vibrations are acoustic phenomena that cannot be stopped by our personal will. In this sense, imposing music is imposing a corporeal reaction on the listener, who is forced not only to deal with the psychological semiotic interpretation of what is being heard but with his/her own uncontrolled bodily resonance. Taking this path, the report of Ernani is not simply the narrative of a bothered auditor made uncomfortable by being forced to listen to unwanted music, but a description of a bodily violation felt by him in this situation. However, how this resonance will be felt and to what extent it can damage the auditor depends on several elements involved and judged by his/her disposition. The following quote from Alicia's interview deepens these ideas. While recalling her lifelong experience with pop music, she defines it as something violent:

> *Alicia*: But I felt that pop music was violent. And I was learning to play the piano and I loved hearing Bach and Mozart. I used to be very shocked that my parents allowed me to hear this pop music. It thought it was violent and dirty.
>
> Q: But violent in what sense?
>
> *Alicia*: Anything that has got a regular thump, a strong bass. I hate it. Unless it serves a very particular purpose. In Wagner, you're ready for it. If something has been building up, [like in] Stravinsky, *The Rite of Spring* – you don't just go and listen to *The Rite of Spring* just as a background. It's a very significant experience. It is not something that

you have on a plane, when you're going on a hop or something. And you have to be prepared for it, and ready for it. But this sort of regular beat (beat beat) that goes throughout 90% of pop music – you're supposed to just ignore it.

Clearly, she recognizes *in the music* some elements of energy described as violent. Rhythmic patterns, high volume, dissonances and 'strong bass' are music elements usually associated with violence. Energy is a key issue here. All these musical procedures described by Alicia are ways of increasing the loudness of sound waves, suggesting the idea of an energetic and powerful musical event. As the volume increases, the corporal impact of the dislocation of the air is more intense in our ears and tissues, intensifying the invasion of the sound into the body. Thus, she considers: for instance the 'strong bass' is nuanced by the ideas of intention and preparation. Presumably, this preparation is something that is done by the composer and executed by the performer, but we can add a set of expectations she directs towards the music experience, her auditor's disposition.

The example of Stravinsky's *Rite of Spring* is illuminating of this process, since its *première* in 1913 is usually referred to as an astonishing event of an explosion of violence as the audience refused the innovations (strong rhythm, intense dissonances, unusual choreography) and the force of the piece. The turmoil of this event was the result of a mismatch between the audience disposition and the music delivered. Even if the uproar of the riot may have happened much more due to Nijinsky's choreography than to the music (Chua 2007: 6), it is undeniable that the score has plenty of sonic elements that evoke and activate bodily energetic arousals. Moreover, the ballet in itself is a dramatic narrative of a sacrificial murder, which brings us back to the conceptual division between noise and music developed by Attali's work. According to him, music in festivals and ritual acts as a 'channeliser of violence', 'an attribute of power' capable of 'ordering the noises of the world' (Attali 2009: 23). As such, music is a 'minor form of sacrifice' (idem: 25), and its power lies in the fact that this sublimation of murder in its dramatization creates social order and political integration (idem: 26). While the irruption of physical violence in *Rite of Spring*'s debut contradicts this statement, what is important to retain is the connection between a specific sound organization within a music spectacle and the way it can be listened to by the audience, the way it can be understood as an unbearable corruption of a desired experience that is involved in several layers of violence.

In the case of Stravinsky's most famous work, what is interesting is that, as the years passed, the barrier somehow was broken, and spectators began to understand the ritualistic elements of the work and recognize how the music 'prepares' the violent irruption of bass patterns and dissonant harmonies. One hundred years later, accepted worldwide as a masterpiece, *Rite of Spring* can be used as an example of how to insert violence into music without bothering the auditor.

This leads us to the second issue of Alicia's narrative, relating to the use of music. She is particularly affected by background music, insisting on the idea of adequacy. In previous chapters, we discussed how music invades personal spaces at home and occupies public spaces as an inescapable mood conditioner. What Alicia's argument adds is a feeling of being harmed by the simple presence of these unwanted sounds. She does not imagine any violent solution for that, such as making the neighbour disappear or shouting at the shop owner to turn off the music; she simply feels wounded by the violent intrusion into her ears, powerless to get rid of the music. The shortcut of this kind of despair of the bothered auditors is to evoke a superior and violent force to intercede in their favour. In other words, to transfer the solution to a regulative power that hopefully can make the sound stop.

Complaining

The act of complaining about someone else's sound requires effort. You must either take your phone and call some mediator (the building administrator, the doorkeeper, the public authority, the police) or leave your own home to knock on the neighbour's door and ask him/her to turn down the volume. This second option represents a degree of risk, many times avoided by the auditors. As teenager Luane (quoted in Chapter 1) said, referring to her being annoyed by the music played in buses, 'I will not complain, because society is very violent, and we don't know how the person could react'. The fear is part of daily life in most contemporary cities, especially in certain districts in big cities.

In this regard, the following quote by Isabel is quite illuminating, as she lists several noisy situations that result in mistreatments:

> I went into a shop to buy a dress and suddenly it was playing music and really very loud. I was holding on, then I [thought], 'All right, then, I'll come back later'. Another case: I went to a restaurant, the music was loud and I asked them to turn it down – I couldn't eat or think. It is the tenuous line between stimulating and disturbing the cognitive. They turned it down, but I was the only customer. Another day, I was having a tomography and there was a television which was on although no one was watching it. And, in our society, you watch TV in the elevator! I feel as though we're in an American movie, a bunch of zombies. The other day, I was listening to the radio on my mobile phone and in the middle of a song that I love it stops and talks about the woman who got shot. One becomes worse than oneself and everybody gets a little crazy and hostile.

Astonished by the unceasing music-sound that invades every space of her day, she blames the noisy environment for making people crazy and unkind to each other. The sound is, for her, the agent of what Zizek would call 'systemic' or 'objective' violence, 'which is not attributed to individuals and their evil intentions, but [which] is purely "objective", systemic, anonymous' (2009: 23). The author suggests we stop looking for 'subjective violence', usually graphically irrupted in physical acts of daily life, and instead pay attention to the general and invisible violence caused by inequalities, poverty and capitalism itself (Zizek 2009: 13). This idea resounds the often-quoted article by Johan Galtung (1969) that provides a broader definition of violence, stating that the violence is present 'when human beings are being influenced so that their actual somatic and mental realizations are below their potential realizations' (1969: 168). Isabel seems to be precisely feeling this stifling sound violence when she enumerates several situations of increasing music everywhere, preventing her from fully achieving her potential in daily life. Forced music forbids her from having a peaceful meal, thinking freely or shopping without being bodily driven away by it. But her narrative also points to the direct violence of the sound, affecting and invading her ears and body without her permission in such way that she cannot help vibrating together with the constant sound environment that attacks her. As Ana Maria Ochoa Gautier states, 'One of the characteristics of violence is the redefinition of acoustic space' (2006), which takes the form of several acoustic restrictions and invasions with which we have to deal every day. Isabel reports feeling harmed by unpleasant acoustic spaces that trigger bad sensations and force her to negotiate sound and music as she negotiates her place in the world or her movements through the city. Facing someone else's music is never, then, a mere confrontation between two human beings in search of their respective and contrasting rights, but a social encounter located in a very complex environment, informed and influenced by hierarchies, violence, behavioural values and feelings.

Life in contemporary cities is threatened daily by different kinds and levels of violence, from the coercive force of the state and its armed arm – the police – to the fear of robbery and physical assaults that may irrupt on every corner, passing through power asymmetries between people and social groups in workplaces and several other sites. Social conflicts, fears and threats are often experienced through sound and music negotiations that embody ways to deal with power relationships in daily life. Taking violence as a condition of existence in contemporary cities (Araújo and Musicultura 2010), sound and music negotiations are staged in a violent environment that determines the way the conflicts are dealt with by people, always intermingled with feelings of anger, fear and indistinct threat. As Argentinian sociologist Beatriz Sarlo has pointed out, in contemporary big cities 'fear organizes public space' (Sarlo 2014: 85). And our circulation and conditions of existence in cities are contexts that determine how these fears and violence are experimented with. For Messias, forty-three, who works as a doorman in a middle-class building and lives with his family in a *favela* in Rio de Janeiro, complaining about his neighbour's music is not something allowed. As a resident of a poor area of the city controlled by drug dealers, he tries to avoid any closer relationship with his neighbours, to keep him and his family safe from the violent environment. As such, neighbours' music must be tolerated:

> We just have to put up with it. We hope that common sense speaks up so we
> don't get into an argument. We just shut the door and the noise is slightly

better. We get disturbed, but never say anything to avoid confrontation. You go out in the alley, with fifty houses: about twenty of them are keeping the stereo on, always loud. It's a clash of all kinds of music: if someone is listening to *forró*, the other listens to funk or *sertanejo universitário*. We go by ten metres and there's one kind of music, another ten metres it changes to other types of music [...] I feel disturbed, but I can't complain. There's the concern about someone doing something bad to you if you complain, because you don't know what kind of neighbours you have, even though you may know them for years. You don't know what kind of relationship they have with 'those guys over there'. I've been living there for fifteen years. But we basically just greet each other with 'good morning', 'good afternoon', 'good night'. My friends are my family. I just go from home to work, from there to my home again. I know everyone in the community, but only by name. People even call me 'uncle', 'daddy', respectfully, and say to each other 'stop messing around'. But I always keep a low profile.

In order not to be disturbed by the 'guys there' (the drug dealers), he must withstand the loud noise to keep his safety. His report reveals how different habitational situations provide different ways through which tensions regarding sound and music can be held. Andrea has a similar narrative. She also lives in a poor area of Rio de Janeiro, facing at the same time the constant threat of drug dealers that rule the borough and the architectural structure of the houses, which are built very close to each other. According to her, complaining about neighbours in her 'community' (a very frequent euphemism to refer to a slum or *favela*) is something totally useless because 'they' do not respect your right to silence:

In the community it is very difficult to ask a neighbour to lower the sound because not everyone is well educated. If we do, they can be aggressive, calling us 'snobs'. They don't care if we are going to wake up early – what matters to them is that they are having fun. They don't respect us.

Andrea adds, to this issue, that violence appears not only in the risk of someone doing something evil but also in the form of aggressive language or public shame. What hurts her more is the feeling of being disrespected in her right to rest inside her home, harmed by sleep deprivation and by rude comments on her attitude and behaviour.

Social inequalities appear here not only as a general difference in income or kinds of job or residence, but in the daily possibility of intermediation to solve conflicts. If, on one side, this mediation is blocked by fear in *favelas*, in other places complaining is possible and eventually effective. Forty-year-old teacher Monica reports a situation that took place in a quiet city in the mountains near Rio de Janeiro:

> I was already married when I was writing my dissertation. And I have a neighbour who is the housekeeper next door. Whenever the owner of the house wasn't there, he hosted pool parties, with extremely loud music, especially with Paula Fernandes's songs such as 'Amor por favor' and 'Não desliga o telefone'. Anyway, there was all kinds of music, from midday until 2 a.m., at a top high volume. I live in the countryside: there's no need for amplifiers. Then, I asked [my husband] Luiz to talk to him: 'Please, I need to finish this chapter, I need you to put down the music'. I knew it would sound bad, but then Luiz went there and explained, so they turned it down. It was a very awkward situation. Then they came to ask me if I finished my dissertation. He did it every Saturday but on that day specifically I had to ask him to turn down the music.

It is interesting that she pointed out being ashamed when asking them to turn the sound down. This shamefulness is the result of the feeling that she could be stopping someone else's pleasure by imposing her necessity of quietness. In a sense, it is an inversion of roles on who is bothering whom, but some people did report the same doubts. The difficult task of convivence in cities and even in the countryside is exposed by sound negotiations when the music leaks from one house to another. In most cases, people wait for the nuisance to finish and do not complain. But sometimes, the irritation overtakes the patience and people feel pushed to negotiate directly with their neighbour.

Another element that appears in Monica's case is gender. Gender issues are always merged in social relations and can hardly be erased or hidden. If she was alone at home or if it was she who knocked on the (male) neighbour's door to ask him to decrease the volume his reaction may have been different. We cannot speculate about what the consequences of her mediation would have been, which could indeed still have been successful anyway, but it is important to highlight that the decision to complain directly to the neighbour represents some risk that is usually higher when power asymmetries are evident. In our sexist society, masculinity is constructed mainly through violence, force and energy. As it is performative, like every gender role (Butler 1990), men's behaviour in daily life should correspond to what is widely accepted as 'hegemonic masculinity', refusing what could be considered unmasculine: 'being peaceable rather than violent, conciliatory rather than dominating, hardly able to kick a football, uninterested in sexual conquest and so forth' (Connell 2005: 67). The reference of football playing is worth mentioning due to the close association of male performativity within the realm of a team's fans. Argentinian sociologist Pablo Alabarces (2014: 159) interprets the native category of *aguante* as a point of convergence of several stereotypes of masculinity that ought to be achieved within a club supporter: 'courage, strength, violence'. Following the same concept of *aguante*, Eduardo Herrera (2018: 474) states that the collective chant is a fundamental way through which masculinity is performed, 'acting and sounding in synchrony'.

The performance of masculinity is usually shown socially through sounds. Music repertoires that explicitly evoke high volumes and energy are usually commonly associated with male fans. Not only do the narratives developed in lyrics often describe gender imbalance, but also, through dance and the body, certain music genres are more likely to produce a macho pleasure performance (Trotta 2014). Soundly speaking, occupying a sound space is to enact a power within it, and male gender behaviour is usually attached to the fulfilment of this stereotyped though expected role. In this sense, interrupting a male neighbour's pleasure of hearing loud music can have some violent consequences. Men's desires and pleasures are, hence, defended with energy and violence, making gender a key issue in sound and music negotiations.

Talking about the loud music played by her current neighbours, thirty-five-year-old nurse Candice reports 'becoming agitated' and 'anxious' as it begins, which makes her revisit the memories of conflicts over sound that filled her childhood:

> When I was younger, with my parents, we had really bad neighbours; like neighbours from hell. And one of the things they did was to play music

and my dad just physically couldn't cope with that level of stress. He likes a calm, quiet house – he was quite regimental. So I think it obviously brings back anxiety feelings from that, that something bad may happen. So I think I connect that kind of music, and someone listening to music like that, to those kind of memories. Well, he was quite a violent person. He had quite a temper on him. As soon as you knew the neighbours are going to be noisy with that kind of music you knew something bad is going to happen. So as a child you felt frightened, and nervous and scared 'cause you knew that the atmosphere in the house was going to change. And often it would end up that he would go downstairs and they would argue, and quite a few times physically fight. Actually, it wasn't really about the music, it was just about the irritation between them. But it then escalated. But the music was the pinpoint that started it.

Her narrative reveals that complaining about someone's music is an act that may be risky and result in unexpected reactions. In defence of their private space, (male) individuals may get aggressive as they feel threatened in their (masculine) rights. Physical fights between men are a permanent possibility for reaffirming masculinity and power relations. Possibly, Candice's father performed in a very direct way the imposition of force in the construction of his masculinity. Similarly, his neighbour may have used loud music to construct the same male power within the neighbourhood. Controlling the sound is an act of power that could be interpreted as a masculine right. As such, the sound invasion within her house was understood by her father as a violent intimidation of their home safety. As a traditional and violent man, he was supposed to keep his family and his house safe from other menaces, from other men, both physically and sonically.

Beyond the gender issue, in these cases the idea of 'public' loses relevance as the powerful sound of the one (male or female) who controls the volume is imposed on the others, without worrying about who those others are. If the potential violence of these negotiations cannot be underestimated, the individual harassed by another's sound is empowered by the idea of having his/her rights disrespected and might claim for the restoration of a friendly and respectful sound coexistence. In doing so, s/he enters an uncertain terrain that could explode in violence or simply fail. Thirty-two-year-old Nayha also reported being disrespected in a situation when the neighbours' party kept her awake all night long:

> All of a sudden the neighbours moved in and they were playing techno music, but the way they did the transitioning of the music the beat stayed the same, so it was just constant. Through the night, you couldn't hear the melody but you could hear only the beat and feel the beat. When I asked them to put the volume down they said the volume was not that loud. I think it was that type of music where the beat, the resonance, was really loud. I couldn't sleep. [...] I think [they could have lowered the sound], given the fact that we had asked so nicely, and we tried to explain we work. What really annoyed me was that they kept playing all through the night and all through the next day. And I find the word I would use is 'disrespectful'. I found it very very disrespectful, because I thought if I was disturbing someone's sleep I would turn the music off or I would listen in my headphones. I didn't understand the necessity of listening to the music with the speakers when you could use headphones. Luckily, I was moving on in a week.

In her interview, she said she did like the electronic music and she used to listen to it, but she highlights the specific regularity of the music beat, which became disturbing. It is the specific organization of music elements as well as its loudness that made her experience annoying. Although she liked to listen to (chosen) electronic music, in that situation it was invasive, making her feel violated. Moreover, an important part of her annoyance was the fact that she perceived she had been 'nice' in asking to turn down the sound, and she was ignored. Violence is always an ingredient in personal interactions, especially when one is complaining about the other. Therefore, being 'nice' and respectful, even in a situation where she felt disrespected, is an attitude that she thinks should have been considered in the course of the negotiation.

In a moment of personal reflection during his interview, Anthony expressed hopelessness in directly negotiating someone's else volume. In his words:

> If I go down and very politely ask him not to do so he can go and say, 'Go away'. People tend to be that way, whether or not you ask very nicely. [...] I have

occasions when I asked people to turn down the music and nine times out of ten you get some gratuitous offence as a response, sadly. I'm afraid the reality of modern life seems to be like this. In my experience, no matter how polite you are, most people take offence at being asked to change their ways. Even if what you do is 'please, a favour: turn the music down or turn it off at midnight'. Because they feel they've been told to do so, even though in fact they've been politely asked to do something. That tends to be the reaction. It's quite rare to have 'I'm sorry, you're quite right, sure I'll turn it down'. Pretty rare!

He reinforces the notion that, despite being polite, the neighbour seems to be irritated with his request and reacts with disdain. Being exposed to this carelessness makes him feel even more disrespected than the musical nuisance itself, once it becomes clear that the neighbour considers his own individual pleasure far more important than other people's possible irritation.

However, this lack of hope in successful negotiations is not a general rule. Alicia reported an almost pedagogical approach to her neighbours when complaining about their sound:

These flats we live in are on top of each other – you have to learn how to live in flats. It's partially our job to teach them, because there are many students, many people who come just for the first time away from home and it's our job to help them grow up a bit, isn't it? We go and knock on the door and say, 'I'm really sorry, but I have to go to bed now, would you mind turning your music off'. This happened with the girl we are on top of: she said, 'Oh, I'm so sorry, am I disturbing you?' 'Best if after ten o'clock you just don't play music'. Fine. They're not doing it on purpose, they are just young, living on their own for the first time, coming from somewhere else – used to live in a house, suburbs. They don't realize that families with babies would be disturbed by loud noise. The sound does go all the way upstairs. There was one time when music was played from the flat on the very bottom, the ground floor, and we thought it was the next door. We went to knock on the door. Usually people want to be good neighbours.

Contrary to Anthony's opinion, she manifested hope that most people want to live side by side with each other in peace. What is not clear is exactly what it means to be a 'good neighbour'. In many situations, to act as a good neighbour means to censor your personal pleasure of listening to music at home in the way you would like. And, again, this can be felt as a kind of self-violence. Indeed, some kinds of music and some kinds of auditor have a personal demand to hear music at loud volume, be it for the music to be felt in his/her body, or to better listen to the details hidden in the audio mixing. Nevertheless, being aware of the sound leakage is a desirable element to be considered. Respect the other in order to be respected. We can think here of a blurred limit between pleasure and nuisance, in the background of interhuman classification as 'good' or 'bad' neighbours. What Alicia highlights is that complaining may be a successful means of negotiating these limits, based on her experience that neighbours want to be respectful with each other. Of course, it is not always like this. And, when unsuccessful in this attempt, people eventually call the police.

The police

In our societies, the state is the strongest regulative force that can effectively respond to these claims. And the response usually happens through the coercive force of the police. Max Weber's highly quoted statement that 'the state is a human community that (successfully) claims the monopoly of the legitimate use of physical force within a given territory' (2008: 156) provides a fruitful way to understand the mechanism of mediation enacted by the police. According to Proença Junior and Muniz, public awareness that the police have the prerogative to compel a solution on its own in any police encounter 'shapes the behaviour of the public towards the police' (2006: 242). In other words, the presence of the police in a given place to mediate conflict makes people change attitudes once it is known that the police can 'act'. Intimidation is the most effective solution the police can provide to a bothered auditor. In other words, the police have the right to use physical force to solve problems, but the mere presence of the police officer is enough in many cases to mediate conflicts and prevent criminal acts.

  Furthermore, a police intervention demarks two distinct roles performed by the victim (who believes in the institutional protection provided by the police force) and the perpetrator (threatened by its presence). To call the police to act in a music and sound conflict is, therefore, at the same time a manifestation of a belief that the sound nuisance can be interrupted by the authoritative force and a threat. Erica, twenty-seven years old, explains this common logic:

> I had a neighbour in Recife and she was evangelical. On a Sunday, while everyone wanted to sleep, she was listening to gospel music at 6 a.m. loud enough so everybody heard it. I don't know if, on some day, I have bothered anyone else – it never occurred to me. Because I respect these hours, that's what I want others to do for me. I do it for the sake of others. In the right volume and at given hours. I am more concerned about the time. I don't judge her for the gospel style, but for the time. After 10 p.m., if I arrive and the sound is still loud, I call the police.

Although dismissing the gospel style as a source of annoyance – genre issues will be discussed deeply in the next chapter – Erica describes a sound invasion merging the inadequacy of the loud music on Sunday morning, the music genre itself and a general simplistic classification of her neighbour's lifestyle ('she was evangelical'). Together with all this, the evocation of the police works here as a threat and a trust, an extreme means to stop the music that violently invades her private acoustic space. Worden and McLean argue that the act of calling the police involves a customer-like relation with the state and its armed force:

> A citizen who calls the police to report a stolen bicycle or a loud party, say, resembles such a customer in some respects. He seeks a service – official recognition and recording of a crime of which he is the victim, or third-party intervention to resolve a situation that he defines as a disturbance. His contact with the police is at his initiative and is largely voluntary; he could instead choose to forego any assistance in recovering the bicycle or making an insurance claim, or to tolerate the disturbance that the party represents to him until it ends without intervention. (Worden and McLean 2017: 52)

Moreover, the citizen-customer believes in the availability of the police to re-establish a desired 'order' and eliminate his/her personal disturbance. Calling the police is less risky than knocking on the neighbour's door and implies a safe way to solve the nuisance immediately. In a study on the data provided by the Department of Public Security of the State of Rio de Janeiro, sociologists Marcus Ferreira and Livia Almeida reported that the most frequent claims of 190 calls received by State Police of Rio de Janeiro are related to 'disturbance of work and sleep'. From January to May 2015, according to the authors, 51,405 out of 345,964 calls registered by police data demanded the mediation of problems with sound. Most of them (34 per cent) were directly related to neighbour sounds (Ferreira and Almeida 2015: 47). Moreover, 59 per cent of these calls were registered during the weekend and 51 per cent of them were made during the night (idem: 50), confirming that the economy of work and rest is a determinant factor in everyday negotiations of unwanted noise. However, the police many times failed to solve the problem. In the conclusion of their article, Ferreira and Almeida (2015: 53) find that, although a considerable effort was made to respond to these calls, the efficacy of the police was inconsistent.

Although it is possible to point out several similarities among the procedures people follow to call the police to solve daily conflicts on music and sound, it is undeniable that the kinds of action the police take differs from place to place. In this regard, the differences between the two countries studied for this research are astonishing. This is due to radically distinct state structures and histories that shape the way people deal with state authorities. In Scotland and most European countries, the police are acknowledged as an arm of the state whose presence is welcome to protect and guarantee safety in the streets. It is a state force that can be trusted to solve everyday life conflicts, such as noise and sound nuisance. Historically, police in Scotland have always had a community focus, with strong links with local governments and a general idea of their role in the welfare of local communities (Scott 2011: 122). Although several changes have been processed within the last two decades, mostly due to the 'devolution' act, which reshaped the autonomy of Scotland in United Kingdom politics, the police force is still widely trustable for many Scottish people to whom I have talked. Alicia explains how she eventually called the police when she was bothered by 'dreadful neighbours', regretting some changes in the policing structure of Edinburgh:

I called the police. Not [anymore], but it used to be that if you rang the police three times in one night, then they would come and take away the music equipment. They would do that! [On the night in question, the police] came just once and it scared [the neighbours], so they stopped. But it used to be that if they had to come a third time, they would take the equipment away. That used to be the law. Anyway, maybe there was a party but not necessarily. They were just playing loud music. We couldn't sleep. We talked to them first, there was no effect and then we rang the police. We used to have something called 'community policing' in Edinburgh on the local police station – now it's all centralized and this is all gone. They didn't know who was complaining; the police didn't tell. There are several apartments and other people also have knocked the door to complain.

Her case is very typical of the evolution of a night of nuisance. Once she realizes that she is being bothered by her neighbour's music, she decides to knock on the door and ask for the music to be turned off. After a while, she notices her claim was useless and asks for external help. The police come, and the neighbour is intimidated into turning the music off or else s/he could have the equipment confiscated. The threat does not need to be made explicitly. The simple presence of the police is enough to settle the behaviour.

Despite its expected efficacy (not always achieved), calling the police is not a regular decision for many people. As I've previously stated, Edinburgh is a quiet city and public problems on sound and music between neighbours may occur but hardly are referred to as a constant issue. And very rarely do they become such a nuisance that one feels the need to ask for external force. Moreover, the idea of tolerance is reinforced by many interviewees, who report bearing the sound if it is not a frequent problem.

By contrast, in reports from Brazilian citizens the police authority is more frequently cited as a possible mediator, which is somehow surprising due to the fact that people there do not trust the police, who have historically been involved in thousands of cases of disproportionate violence, crime, abuse and misconduct. Teresa Caldera (2000) argues that police violence in Brazil is inscribed in a long-term history of abuse perpetrated by authorities, from its slaver colonial past up until the militarized institutionalization of today's corporations. As such, policemen are often pointed to as perpetrators of torture, illegal invasions, beatings, murder and corruption, most of the time against poor people in poor areas of the country's crowded big cities, the so-called *favelas*.

A very clear description of the sound and music negotiations in Rio de Janeiro's *favelas* is provided by Andrea and her daughter Brenda, in their joint interview. Like many others in the city, the *favela* where they live is controlled by drug dealers and police interventions inside its narrow streets and lanes are usually very violent, with shots and killings. Living in *favelas* means always being threatened by violent irruptions of shots both from drug dealers and the police. Talking about the extremely loud volume at which their neighbours listen to music, they do not hide their despair on the situation, even having called the police:

> *Brenda*: There are days when they spend twenty-four hours playing the same songs, in the same order. It is the same music all day. I don't study at home. I used to go to school earlier so I could study there – they gave me a room there – or I went over and left earlier in the afternoon and even at night to study at school. If I arrive home now, early in the morning, they will be sleeping. They don't start the noise when they wake up, it seems they don't work and swap night and day. Their party starts at midnight, and the noise goes on until the following day. No, I have never called the police.
>
> *Andrea*: It is complicated. I have called the police once. They went there and turned the sound down. When the police left, they turned the sound up and the policemen said they couldn't do anything because it was a *favela* community. Then, because I have called the police, they turned to me and said, 'She is crazy, she is sick, she takes medicine', and I became the old crank of the street. I was slandered, disrespected; today, I keep my mouth shut and am unable to call the police and do anything. I can't run away.

The overall situation described by Andrea and Brenda points to a larger complexity involving the connection between music, sound and violence. Living in a violent *favela*, they face on a daily basis the danger of being too near criminals targeted by the police. In other words, structural violence in *favelas* is experienced in a quite dramatic way, conditioning different aspects of everyday life. Violence negotiations are, then, done on very unstable terrain with a constant threat of physical violence. In these situations, calling the police is risky because it can make clear your disgust towards someone else's music and some kind of retaliation can be perpetrated. In their case, they had to face a gossip consequence that followed the police call, making the situation even worse. As the police reported not being able to do anything else about their case, they had to bear the loud sound and the aggressive talk of neighbours against them.

Favelas consist of territories where the official state hardly rules. As such, their famous *bailes* (parties), organized or authorized by drug dealers, are spaces that escape from police control. The loud sound of the equipment becomes, then, a real torment to nearby residents who struggle to sleep in these days. Messias describes the weekly *baile* that happens only 200 metres from his house:

> In Santo Amaro there is *baile* funk every Saturday. It begins around 11 p.m. and goes on until 7 a.m. They are annoying, but stay there and [we] have to accept it. There are people who say that it is a living hell for them, but we can't do anything. When I get there and see no *baile*, the hill feels like a wasteland. Because there is *baile* every weekend.

The assumption that there is nothing to be done in this regard has to do with the criminal environment of the *bailes* and the *favelas* in general. In these situations, calling the police seems to be useless and even dangerous. However, as the sound leaks to the neighbours outside the *favela* limits, eventually the police may be called by some resident disturbed by the *baile*'s sounds. Thirty-nine-year-old Paula reports a case where she did call:

> I lived in the corner next to the Ladeira do Tabajara's ascent. When it was the traffic dealer's birthday, the *baile* was more intense, the sound was louder. It was annoying. I called the police twice. They took notes but it was held at the Turano's court, so they said, 'Which court'? They don't go there. Are they going to mess with the *baile* funk? Of course they won't! Maybe I am selfish, but that's the kind of sound that takes away my right to sleep. I worry so much about that, about not being selfish or not taking away the

right of others to have fun, that sometimes I think I'm being selfish. Why on a Friday night, right? But the funny thing is that the *baile* doesn't begin at 9 p.m. It begins at midnight! Besides the *brr brr* sound, there is a guy who yells into a microphone. He must be the *baile*'s D.J. I can't understand what he says. You begin to fall asleep and he starts screaming *grgrgrg*. Son of a bitch!

Her doubts on calling or not are related directly to what I've been arguing to be an individualistic thinking that pervades sound and music nuisance. Although she is aware of a possible selfishness in her act of calling the police, she is at the same time invested within the idea that her private right to sleep and rest is stronger than the collective right of having fun in a Friday night. Even trying to balance these two rights, she decided to call hoping the intervention could restore her required quietness at home. As the police withdrew the possibility of going there with an excuse, she felt angry and offended at the M.C. of the *baile*. Despair and irritation are feelings that remain as a result of a failed mediation that she expected the police to make.

Paula's report raises another issue. As she describes the *baile*, she filled her words with onomatopoeic vocalizations that aimed at reproducing the sound of the party and the DJ's performance. Indirectly, she addresses the kind of music organization that was involved in that evening, that, combined with the loudness and the inappropriate hour, formed a nuisance package she was forced to bear. Her rejection of the *baile* has to do, hence, with her interpretations of the music played there, and how the particular sound organization affected her. In other words, Paula's feelings about the sound of the *baile* are informed also by what kind of music was played there. And this, of course, is not something irrelevant.

5

What music? Tastes, morals and values

When invited to talk about annoying music, people cannot escape from describing their personal tastes. Taste is the starting point for most conversations about being affected or irritated by music in everyday life. As Simon Frith states, 'Part of the pleasure of popular culture is talking about it; part of its meaning is this talk; talk which is run through value judgement' (1996: 8). As such, the interviews done for this book started with general questions about music preferences, answered with abstract references to music genres. Sentences such as 'I like jazz' or 'I don't like pop' were the most frequent entrance to the domain of value judgement. This was not a surprise. In our daily lives, arguments about music are always framed by generic umbrella genre classifications that function as a key organization of the music universe. Thirty-two-year-old Nayha provides a very detailed description of this process, highlighting her uses of each music in her life:

> *Nayha*: I think I've got a quite eclectic taste in music. Most often, when I'm working, I need to listen to music to concentrate but I cannot listen to music with lyrics. So, often I will listen to techno music, like Chicago, electronic music. Something about the beat really helps me to focus. When I walk in places, depending on my mood, I'll listen to folk music sometimes. When I'm feeling a little bit down, and I want to be cheered up, then I will listen to funk and soul, but if I'm feeling tense, unhappy in that mood, then it will be Joan Baez.

Q: Is there any music you don't like?

Nayha: I guess… really, pop music! Generic, run-of-the-mill girl band/boy
band pop irritates me a bit, especially when the lyrics are very much
obviously rhyming, or contradict, or don't make much sense. And
jazz music! But I get less frustrated by that when I'm not trying to
understand it and I can just kind of think about the feeling. I think the
problem is, for example, in Edinburgh you go to somewhere like the
jazz bar and you are trying to dance along to some music and just when
you feel you got it, the rhythm completely changes. I don't know but
maybe culturally there's a little vagueness in jazz, either you get it or
you don't. Sometimes you feel like an outsider with jazz.

Nayha's report resounds several examples presented in Tia DeNora's *Music in
Everyday Life*. Music works for her as a tool that she activates to modulate her
mood and emotions. What is interesting is how she is aware of a whole intimate
system that links feelings and sounds. For her, music is something that works
similar to medicine, taken according to some perceived symptoms to improve
her health. This, of course, is in cases where she controls the sound. If not,
negative adjectives are attached to music genres felt by her as uncomfortable
music experiences, like 'nonsense pop music' or 'undanceable jazz', somehow
detached from her expectations and desires. Washburne and Derko, in the very
beginning of their edited volume about 'bad music', define it as music that is
'somehow unwanted', 'forced upon us in all kinds of possible and impossible
situations' (2004: 1). 'Bad' is a value judgement that irrupts as a result of very
complicated taste and adequacy interpretations, helping the listener to define a
'positioning gesture' about the music s/he listens to (idem: 2). In other words,
'taste is not a stable and inner experience of the subject', but the result of '*affective
relations*, be it with others who share same preferences or with works or artists
that *affect* us' (Janotti Jr. and Pereira de Sá, 2018: 10). Here, again, the auditor's
disposition is a key reference to the value judgement, forming taste evaluations
according to the moment and the background experience and expectations.
Alicia and Peter reported being upset with bad music in audio-visual media:

Peter: I mean, I find it easier to say what sort of music I don't like to
listen to. Country western music, I can't really get converted to it. It

really doesn't work, this kind of pop stuff for teenagers that we have nowadays. It seems to be, like, created by corporates, a machine, as far as I can tell. They actually have sort of electronic voicings. And rap music.

Alicia: One thing we hate is that sort of music you have on TV dramas or documentaries.

Peter: Background music!

Alicia: They particularly sound banal, that music that comes when they are trying to be sensitive: piano chords and so on. It drives us up the wall and he sets the volume control to keep it mute. We just read the subtitles. I think it is just very poor. Poorly written. It's going for easy emotions. Sometimes the music on the television is wonderful. And we think, 'Gosh, that's amazing'.

As trained musicians, they complain about the 'easy emotions' of 'poorly written' music scores, although they sometimes admit the music provided by TV programmes may be 'amazing'. The issue of superficiality is often pointed out as an element of disqualification of music. According to some aesthetic perspectives, a piece of music must correspond to an expectation of profound music experience, able to provide deep emotional immersion to a qualified audience. Moreover, teenage pop songs are referred to as an example of the artificiality of music distributed by corporations, resounding Adornian arguments about the role of the cultural industry in the capitalistic control of desires and thoughts. Although these arguments appear in very brief comments, the rhetoric that feeds these ideas is settled in a far more complex evaluation of what is good and bad in music.

What is important to highlight is that value judgements play a key role in the definition of pleasure and displeasure associated with music experience. Hardly will one talk about annoying music without considering personal tastes together with a very particular evaluation of adequacy. I would like to argue here that this judgement deals with complex thoughts about life in society, identities, individual emotions and values, as well as with shared social codes considered to be 'good' or 'positive'. Therefore, aesthetic judgements are inseparable from moral judgements, defined as a set of accepted rules that one is inclined to follow as a result of both some social constraints and individual desires tied to a usually contradictory interpretation of 'right-and-wrong' definitions.

Moral issues

Stating that music taste is entangled with moral judgement doesn't mean one can assume a direct relation between them. Instead, this entanglement is experienced in multiple ways, according to multiple sets of conditions and contexts in which the music is heard and experienced. As pointed out by the work of Pierre Bourdieu (1984), taste is not detached from social belonging, education and family background. Even considering that our taste is much more unstable than Bourdieusian interpretation suggests, and that it usually incorporates elements that seem to be 'dissonant' with the expected taste of our group belonging (Lahire, 2007), its construction is closely connected to our life experiences, shared values and culture.

Hence, taste in music has to do with knowledge, memories and belonging, activating an important role in the acts of recognition and interpretation. Moreover, taste is dynamic and changeable. As such, it needs to be performed, reinforced, talked about and socially exhibited. The performance is materialized in acts such as listening to recordings, attending shows and concerts, buying products from preferred artists and discussing the value of songs, albums, shows and so on (Hennion, 2001). The shaping and reshaping of our tastes are elaborated daily not only towards music repertoires we like but also, and mostly, against songs, artists and sounds we reject.

Defining a music experience as annoying is the final movement of a corporal and intellectual activity of interpreting ideas about the music heard, which is, in turn, socialized in taste performances that are done to express and elaborate on these interpretations. Final? Perhaps not. The definition of annoyance in music is part of a continuous process of interpretations and judgements about music, developed individually and socially, bodily and mentally. Obviously, this interpretation is not only aesthetically or socially constructed, but also framed through moral and ethical beliefs and, consequently, is strongly affected by them. The moral realm is the realm of social rules and conventions, a pivotal set of thoughts over which our daily life is experienced. It is a moving terrain constantly challenged and reshaped according to several changing conditions and contexts throughout our lives. Music has an important role in sharing moral thoughts and defying them.

For instance, a song that states 'let's kill the cop' or something similar is judged according to ideas about life and death, murder, violence and power. This judgement is also mixed with shared ideas about coercive police power, its oppressing attitude and its role as a repressive force of the state. At first, most people would agree that killing anyone is wrong, but this wrongness can be shifted according to social conditions, which is the contradictory activity of moral judgement. Furthermore, music may have a dramatizing function, staging an act that is acknowledged to be obviously wrong as a means of exposing it, criticizing it and preventing it. 'Let's kill the cop' is a sentence that may refer to a resistance position, or even to an act that should be put aside. This dramatizing effect depends on other elements of the music experience – which, as we all know, cannot be restricted to the lyrics – involving the arrangement, the genre, the voicing, the broader position and behaviour of the artist, the social and physical place where it is played and several other aspects that are part of the semiosis of music experience and can frame it in one direction or another. Depending on all these variable elements, singing a chorus that stimulates the killing of a cop may also be understood as a joke, a humorous text whose interpretation can lead to the extreme opposite side, resulting in a sentence that highlights that it is wrong to kill any person. All these possible ideas are, then, the raw material to be interpreted and ethically judged as people experience the music playing, making up part of the resulting feeling of pleasure or rejection of this semiosis.

In short, the interpretation of the meaning of a song results from an evaluation of the matching or mismatching between the moral expectancies of the listener and what s/he interprets as being the moral message of the song. Yet this process is cognitive and rational, has a strong emotional and corporal component, and usually is not verbalized. As such, although the majority of the people interviewed were very confident in pointing out music genres and artists they like very much or strongly dislike, most of them were unable to elaborate verbally *why* they like or don't like certain kinds of music. When they do, most of them pointed to moral issues to justify their dislike, though this elaboration was often fragmentary, brief and undeveloped. Mike is an exception, and he did elaborate on a detailed interpretation about the reasons why he doesn't like pop music:

> The first thing [I dislike] is pop music that kids listen to. They may or may not be aware of the context of the music, but it is generally about sex. And these kids of seven, eight, nine years old, they are listening to something for the beat, perhaps. They did not think about [the lyrics]: girl goes into a guy, guy goes into a girl, but it's something that is too basic, and it's not appropriate. I could be too conservative, but it just seems not necessary. The point is the groove, but when they do become aware of the lyrics, eventually, a message is being sent. The girls singing those kinds of things, you know? That's frustrating. I find that sending that message to kids of that age is inadequate. And the more music they listen to, as they get older, as teenagers, they are going into this rap, hip hop, R&B: it's too sensual. It sends the wrong message about relationships. When you have a child in your home, you want him to grow up respecting others not to see others as sexual objects. And it is repeated, played over and over and over.

His description is illuminating. The aesthetic disapproval about pop music is due to his moral judgement. Although he mentioned the repetition as an (aesthetic) element of his rejection of pop, the main problem for him is the way the music deals with sexuality. His concern about the 'message' being sent to kids through the music is pointed towards the lyrics. Of course, it is important to be aware that the sexual message is not only in the lyrics. Sex in pop songs is a constituent element of the genre, highlighted in verses and choruses but emphatically reinforced in the corporal movements of singers, in the intonation of the singing, in choreographies, clothes (or their absence) and in the very experience of pop music concerts, where interpersonal relations are highly mediated through sexual appeal, dancing, gazing and seducing. However, it is undeniable that the verbal component of pop songs operates as a kind of guide to narratives, stories and moral aspects of music experience. Popular songs are usually songs about love, seduction and sex. The desire to be close to a beloved one and the regrets for a split are the most common themes found in the lyrics of such songs. Of course, this is not exclusive to the popular music market. The whole commercial world is informed and processed according to love-and-sex metaphors and suggestions. Sex sells. From cars to cosmetics, from soaps to songs, the sex appeal in advertisements seems to be unavoidable. Moral concerns and restrictions towards sexuality are, hence, the most important part of the public debate, as sexuality represents a key aspect of social life, ranging from personal desires to socially accepted rules and widely spread in cultural narratives about love, marriage and family. Music is an artefact that is activated by social groups and individuals to perform, think and elaborate on ideas about sex and love. Ideas about what is wrong and right about sex and love.

If this is true for almost all commercial music, it is undoubtedly more intense in the mainstream pop realm, where it assumes a guiding role, framing the moral interpretation of the aesthetic experience. It is precisely this guiding role that perturbs Mike as he associates listening/singing to pop with being inadequate to young children. Even though he assumes that kids may not understand what exactly is meant by the lyrics they sing, he is worried about the way the ideas are kept circulating in children's minds, structuring their behaviour and even their future relations.

The problem of the lyrics is also pointed out by Luane, quoted in previous chapters. Despite being a teenager, and thus generally expected to like pop and danceable music genres, Luane is concerned about the contents and the message spread by the lyrics. In her words:

> But I am also concerned with the lyrics. You can't listen to the beat and put the lyrics aside. And certain lyrics are impossible, you just can't follow them. Funk lyrics are very repetitive. Nowadays, teenagers are drawn to successful hitmakers, like an MC who gets all the girls and so on. Children, too, because that's trendy. Mass culture listens to funk, pagode. In the old days, people listened to MPB a lot. I like MPB very much. Legião Urbana. Legião's lyrics are very present-day; back then, homosexuality was being discussed for the first time. Before, there was too much repression of everything and people wanted to speak, expose themselves, and people felt repressed. Today, people repress themselves.

It is very interesting the way she defines music connected with moral structures of society across time. She identifies in the lyrics by some artists and songs of the past elements of a desired social debate, which is compared with today's lyrics that she can't listen to. Her example of the Brazilian rock group Legião Urbana is symptomatic. It was a very successful group in the 1980s, led by gay singer Renato Russo, who was also the composer of many songs launched by the group. His songs addressed same-sex love in narratives and stories that, in Luane's perception, helped people to accept homosexuality in a time when it was strongly repressed. Seventeen-year-old Luane was born after Renato Russo's death (1960–96) but listening to his songs allows her to interpret moral aspects of society in previous decades, and even to observe the relevance of past ideas in present-day society. All this is directed to her by the lyrics. She reinforces it as she describes her preferences in music towards genres that presumably have more complex lyrics (aesthetic criteria), with messages that help challenge moral prejudices. By doing so, she organizes the musical universe by comparing genres according to her taste. The 'MPB' she mentioned refers to the term 'Música Popular Brasileira' (which means 'Brazilian popular music' in Portuguese) defined as a category in the Brazilian music market in which songwriters of high prestige are usually located, artists such as Chico Buarque, Caetano Veloso and Tom Jobim, who developed a complex set of procedures in their compositions and, therefore, are acknowledged by cultural critics as 'good'. MPB and classic Brazilian rock are genres Luane associates with a mythical past of Brazilian popular music history, when, according to her, people used to listen to 'better' music. In her interpretation, 'today's' lyrics are led by fashion, by the repetition of direct sexual messages that circulate around 'boys taking girls'. In her thoughts, mass culture is responsible for these repeated messages to teenagers and children, but she did not develop, like Mike, the possible moral miseducation related to the shared fashionable taste. What is worth noting is that both of them are overconcerned with the lyrics, dismissing other elements of the music experience. This is not unusual. People are often very attentive to the lyrics in their talks about music and their value judgement. Lyrics are the guide. An even more radical emphasis in the lyrics is provided by Messias, who makes a distinction between gospel music and electronic beat:

I like gospel music – I only listen to gospel music. My wife is not so keen on gospel. She says the preachers yell. What I really love is His word [God's word]. I also love romantic songs. Lyrics say a lot. They make you go back to the past and become a more romantic man, something that doesn't exist today. Romance makes the man better. Women believe in love. I like old *brega*, I like Fábio Jr., Roberto, Chitãozinho and Xororó, Leandro and Leonardo. I play the guitar because of romanticism. Electronic music is noisier than melodies. I can't stand it. Only here, when they play it in the square. They always do it on the weekends, I can't stand it anymore. It is a very unbearable noise, it has no lyrics at all. It's like funk and the music from Bahia, but these are easier to understand. Contrarily, electronic music is more noise than music itself. In my point of view, that is not music. It is music, but I think it's not. It annoys me in this sense.

His taste is totally framed by the lyrics as he, being an evangelical, is worried about the 'message', the 'word' of God. Interestingly, in his way of thinking, the lyrics are the element that defines something as 'music', in opposition to 'noise', as discussed in Chapter 1. Being able to 'understand' is the path he admits using for his highly personal definition of what is or is not 'music'. When referring to electronic music, Messias mixes the lyrics with the sound, rejecting it as 'non-music'. Even though he admits his classification is not consensual, he seeks, in the definition of 'music', a path to elaborate aesthetically and morally on the value of his unpleasant experience. Again, this distinction about what is 'music' is part of a broader process of judging the value of the sonic experience, which, in his case, is strongly dependent on the message sent by the lyrics. The power of romantic lyrics is, hence, a moral power that makes people better in their existence.

Mike, Luane and Messias all point to the role of music in spreading and framing ideas about life. Our subjective experience with music is framed within social rules and constraints that shape our way of thinking and our behaviour. It is activated through memories and thoughts that split what is considered right or wrong, acceptable or unacceptable, good or bad. Once music is 'a form of thought and action in the world' (Blacking, 1995), the experience with music is not passive, but rather an activity through which people elaborate on lifestyles and behaviours. Music experience may be challenging as it defies settled ideas constructed through our life, which may be disturbing and uncomfortable. Mike's concerns about the sexual education of kids are the result of a mismatch between moral behaviours and discourses that he considers as adequate to children and the set of ideas he finds in pop music. Similarly, Luane's interpretation that some lyrics from the 1980s were 'better' than today's songs results from her particular perception that MPB and classic rock songs were able to elaborate on social prejudices towards the construction of an egalitarian world. Messias also frames his taste and values around the religious aspect, searching, in the lyrics, for an adequate message according to the writings of the Bible.

Sexual, humanistic or religious values are put forward by them as elements of the aesthetic and ethic judgement of songs, shaping the way they listen to the music. Inadequate behaviours described in the lyrics are, then, considered to be offensive and disturbing, in a movement that ends up classifying unwanted music as annoying. The difference between these cases and some narratives dealt with in previous chapters of this book is that this nuisance is not only provoked by the situation, the leakage, the space, the neighbourhood or by background music as such, but is the result of an undesired music experience that forces them to deal with undesired values and ideas.

Moreover, regardless of the overtly accepted idea that music experience must be taken as a whole, encompassing the sound, the dance, the context, the resonance, the sociability and so on, their moral complaints about unwanted music are directed towards the lyrics. The problem of the lyrics can be taken in two overlapping dimensions. First, it is addressed towards specific songs that may be considered offensive and disturbing. In these cases, it is the experience that provides the situation for people to judge the music through the interpretation of the verbal message. Of course, this can only happen when the auditor is able to understand the language used in the song. If not, the disturbing aspect of the experience may be hidden or only suggested in visual and sounded fragments. The second dimension I'd like to address in depth is that the moral problems that come mostly through the lyrics are considered to be a defining feature of certain music genres. In this case, it is not the experience itself that produces repulsion to challenging lyrics, but an accumulated knowledge about a set of songs and artists. This process is far more complex because it activates a set of preconceived ideas about right or wrong together with the homogenization of a vast repertoire into a pejorative classification. Again, genres are taken as a kind of reservoir of 'bad lyrics', becoming targets of rejections and prejudices.

Music genres and hierarchies

The music universe is separated into units of classification that help listeners and fans to identify and select their tastes and preferences. The most effective term to assign these separations is the idea of 'genre', a metaphor borrowed from biology and used in the cultural realm by artistic languages such as literature, visual arts, cinema and music. It was transported to music classification both as a market share strategy and as a social divide (Negus 1999). It is not my objective here to develop a broad theory of music genres (which has already been done by several brilliant works) but to highlight that this separation works as a shortcut to verbalizing music rejections and segregating people. As Fabian Holt argues, 'Genre is a fundamental structuring force in musical life' (2007: 2), and 'discourse plays a major role in genre making' (idem: 3). In his approach, the author suggests not searching for definitions of genres, but for an understanding of them (Holt 2007: 8), which is done in his book through ethnographic work. Similarly, my point here is not to define what people mean when they mention a genre as annoying, but to explore the very fact that people use genre classification to talk about likes and dislikes. Genres provide sets of ideas, expectations and moods that are recognized as desirable and pleasurable for some people and as boring or irritating for others. As such, music nuisance is associated with people's discourse on music genres. Despite the largely accepted agreement in cultural studies that genre classifications are usually blurred, the narratives of most interviewees pointed to a division of the music universe into blocks of music practises defined through genre names. Moreover, some narratives about these blocks suggest that people use genre classification to understand, map and bother other people. The case reported by Bel is interesting:

I hate *sertanejo* music. This has something to do with when I was a teenager and my dad liked *sertanejo* while I wanted to be totally different. Teasing your father, all that teenager stuff – and my dad said we didn't know how to pick good music. Because, for my dad, rock music is the pits, all the more when it is foreign. We listened to rock music, and to protest. I mocked the music he liked. I think that was the reason why, and also because our friends thought *sertanejo* sucked and one wants to belong to the tribe. We bashed it and this is something that has been engraved in me. Right, I am not open. I can't like *sertanejo* because, where I grew up, cool people don't like it. (Bel)

The opposition between rock and *sertanejo*[1] (Brazilian country music) is described as a distinction between her generation and her father's, as well as a tool for being part of her friends' group. For Bel, labelling *sertanejo* as the kind of music her father liked produces a double process of attaching a set of ideas and behaviours to him and his lifestyle and setting her apart from him. Value judgements in music are acts that help people to establish a place in the world and a source of self-recognition (Frith, 1996: 72). Her identity as a young girl both as an individual and as part of a group would be filled partially by her proximity to rock music and distance from *sertanejo*. Interestingly, after more than two decades, forty-two-year-old Bel still feels blocked from *sertanejo* and associates this dislike with her teenage time. Of course, we cannot deny that music genres carry ideas and stereotypes that may explain in part her rejection of the style. After living in several cities in the country, Bel moved to Rio de Janeiro and reported being well adapted in the most famous and cosmopolitan city of Brazil. In this sense, her set of shared codes and values are, nowadays, far away from the idea of the wealthy countryside described in *sertanejo* lyrics. Hence, her refusal of the genre is due to a more complex process than simply the memories of a teenage girl trying to irritate her father. Genre classification is also a cultural classification, which works as a shortcut to (un)shared sounds, ideas and codes.

But there is another layer in genre division within the music market. Classifying means producing a hierarchy. The low evaluation Bel applies

---

[1] The word *sertanejo* refers to a very successful music genre in Brazil that resulted from a merge between rural country music from the first half of the twentieth century and pop styles inspired largely by Nashville American country groups. It has been the mainstream pop music genre in Brazil since the 1980s, enjoying long-term hegemony on the country's charts. Not surprisingly, most arguments about 'pop music' in Brazil are redirected to *sertanejo* with very similar connotations – artificiality, market-driven sound, repetition and so on.

to *sertanejo* is not a personal decision constructed exclusively through her background experience and current cultural affiliations. In Brazil, despite its leading role in the music market, *sertanejo* is acknowledged by powerful intellectual social strata of urban population as bad quality music. This is due mostly to its commercial element, being merged with global pop music in several ways (Trotta, 2018). For some critics, *sertanejo* is a worse version of authentic country music – labelled '*caipira*' – which has abandoned its rural heritage to embrace the global pop market (Alonso, 2015: 23). In doing so, the artists classified as *sertanejo* have lost their authenticity and, hence, their aesthetic and moral value. Not surprisingly, *sertanejo*, as well as 'pop', was among the most cited genres associated with annoying music.

Expanding the case of *sertanejo* to a wider music universe, it is possible to state that hierarchies in the cultural field are not constructed in a desert. Instead, the struggles to affirm the cultural (hence, social, aesthetic and moral) value of music genres operate within the limits of social stratification and the relative power that social groups have in it. Intellectuals, journalists, critics, conservatories, music schools, skilled musicians and aesthetically recognized artists are more likely to have their taste and value criteria accepted and shared than minor artists, low-educated audiences or unskilled amateur musicians (Araújo, 2002). Therefore, the criteria applied to judge a piece of music as 'good', despite being possibly contested, has a few general rules overtly accepted. Without denying the huge universe of conflicts that involves the aesthetic judgement of every music genre separately and wholly, the force of the narrative that positions classical music as well as jazz, *bossa nova*, and classic rock – just to mention a few – in a high-value hierarchy within the music genres is highly consensual. Similarly, the disqualification of genres such as rap, hip hop and 'pop' is widely shared worldwide. Not surprisingly, 'pop music' was mentioned in several interviews, both in Brazil (with local fusion between pop and other local genres, like *funk* and *sertanejo* itself) and in Scotland. The description of Alec goes in this direction:

> Pop. There are many things that I don't like in pop. It is related to consumerism. I feel that pop music is meant either for teenagers or extremely consumerist people and I am neither of those. I understand teenagers liking pop but

when it is an adult liking pop I find it a bit disturbing. I definitely think it is age-oriented. It seems to be done in order to make money exclusively.

The artificiality Alec finds in pop music is a key issue in cultural judgement about annoying music. Part of alleged nuisance caused by unwanted music is described as related to its lack of authenticity. Beyond the context, the disturbing element in music is usually associated with a low value attributed to consumerist behaviour or adolescent fashion. 'Pop' is an umbrella term that joins several of these disqualifications. According to Thiago Soares, debates about pop music are usually organized on two axes: the idea of 'pop culture' and what he calls the 'aesthetic of entertainment' (Soares, 2015: 22). Ideas of superficiality, leisure and joy constitute the shared semantic of pop, together with the culture industry's agency in formatting, producing and distributing its products. In pop music, the artistic element circulates as a commodity, and for some people, in doing so, it loses its value, bringing the economic engine to the foreground. Fabian Holt reports being reluctant to define pop music as a genre 'in the strict sense', yet he assumes that it works as a category that refers to mainstream production of several genres and that, sometimes, it may function as a genre in its capacity for complex labelling practices (Holt, 2007: 17–18). For the purpose of our discussion, the attachment of the category to a genre classification is not very important, once we agree it works as a term that defines a general value distinction and is associated with ideas and behaviour that can be judged as positive or negative. Jason Lee Oakes argues that 'the boundaries of pop music are absurdly far-reaching, extending to include from Cole Porter to the Carpenters to Christina Aguilera' (Oakes, 2004: 54). And all these artists and songs are touched with a kind of 'madness' (idem). What I am trying to develop here is that this set of ideas that supports the classification of pop as something bad is a moral judgement that results from a broader understanding about life in society, which, by its turn, is interpreted by the listener as part of the aesthetic evaluation of the music experience. This moral framing dismisses both the lack of authenticity and the commodification heard in pop music. While interpreting the struggle between jazz and rock in specialized magazines, Matt Brennan observes that, despite their alleged differences, both genres share a 'common underlying ideology' of being 'authentic musical cultures contrasted against mass-produced, manufactured commercial "pop", actively turning a blind eye to their own obvious participation in music as a form of commercial production' (Brennan, 2017: 14). The point is that people judge music sometimes considering a kind of continuum that links two opposite realms: the authentic and the commercial. Although it is a controversial criterion to evaluate music, the two-pole system frequently appears in talks that try to elaborate on value. Authenticity is usually associated with positive ethics in daily life, being the artistic expression of genuine people or individuals, and therefore highly valued. Inversely, commerciality is acknowledged as a cold, materialistic and artistically irrelevant taste of individualistic individuals, associated with evil capitalism, selfishness and social carelessness. Every music practice nowadays is located in an intermediate space between the two poles and part of the judgement is to evaluate to what extent authenticity plays an important role in the aesthetic experience. Of course, not everyone shares this opposition in that way and, besides, even if we agree with the logic of the two-pole classification of quality (which I personally am not sure about), it is not possible to verify precisely where an artist or music genre is situated. What I would like to highlight is that the 'accusation' of commercialism is a frequent argument for disqualifying a music genre, involved with the clear moral depreciation of those who like and listen to it.

When Alec dismisses 'pop' for its consumerism and exclusive money-making aim, he is using his taste to interpret how people relate to each other and how they behave in the world. This process gets clearer when he admits taste for pop being understandable for younger people but not for elder ones. For him, it is part of teenage sociability and helps youngsters to identify themselves in the world and to be accepted in their social groups, in a movement very similar to the one Isabel reported about the construction of her teenage taste towards rock. As Thiago Soares states in his fascinating book about the uses of pop music in Cuba, 'The idea of being part of a global, cosmopolitan and hegemonic world strongly feeds the construction of pop imaginary. Hence, generation appears as a key to understand the particular forms of values that emerge in specific contexts' (Soares 2018: 122). The author discusses the case of 'Martí', a young transgender Cuban who adopted Anglophone pop music as a means to construct his sexual identity as well as his generational belonging. Through the performative practise of being fan of Lady Gaga and Madonna, Martí challenged the masculine military stereotype of the Cuban revolution, emphasizing his attachment to newer generations, aspiring for changes on the island without necessarily being politically against the goals of the revolution (Soares 2018: 120–124). The case reported by Soares reinforces the importance of pop music as a device in teenagers' identity construction through consumption. However, it is precisely this strong connection between youngsters and pop culture that nurtures its disqualification. As Alec pointed out in his quote, it is accepted that young people use pop as such, but it is expected that, as they grow older, their taste changes towards possibly more elaborate or complex music practises. In the same movement, teenagers and pop are undervalued in the hierarchical system of social and aesthetic classification, which means that growing up should be a path towards putting pop at a distance.

The issue of age as related to music appears again in the interview given by thirty-six-year-old Nelson. He has an administrative job at a public health foundation in Rio de Janeiro and reports listening to music every day. In his interview, he describes an intense disagreement with his wife about music. After mentioning several times during the interview that he hates funk, especially the pop-funk performed by mainstream Brazilian artist Anitta, he explains his musical taste. In his words:

> I don't like funk at all, especially the *proibidão*. In my time, funk had rap in it, a rap montage. Today you don't get montage. It is always the same pornography thing, which is highly accentuated in funk. I consider it extremely distasteful – I can't, I don't, enjoy it. I don't like it. Obviously, it is played at parties and you're a bit cheerful, happy, and sometimes you even dance. The rhythm is very nice; I even think the beat is nice. But it is impossible. You see this new generation contaminated by funk, Anitta. She is horrible, but is a success. That's sad! For someone used to listening to Elton John, Beatles, Bee Gees, and not to mention Guns N' Roses, Aerosmith, Bon Jovi […] My wife loves Anitta. I feel as though I have married a teenager. Today I am used to it, I don't care so much anymore. But it took me a while,

because it is shit. And it is bad because she is part funk, and everyone keeps dancing, tilting their butts – I find that weird. Actually, it is democratic. She listens to funk, Anitta, on the Multishow channel, when she is watching to that horrible show of hers. And she doesn't like rock. So she only hears it when I listen to rock with earplugs. She doesn't use earplugs. Really. Tolerance, right? Marriage. She can't stand it, she says it is very bad. I can't stand it.

Nelson mixes several arguments that appeared in other interviews. First, the moral issue. The main reason for his strong rejection of funk is the high sexuality of it. Although he declares ambiguously that he himself can dance at a party if it is played, assuming that 'the rhythm is cool', he refuses the 'pornographic' lyrics and the strange shaking butts on the dance floor. The slight contradiction between him dancing the cool rhythm and the strangeness of the others' dance can be surpassed in his discourse, once he starts worrying about the lyrics. Again, the verbal interpretation of the music is the most important report element in lowering the value of a whole genre.

Second, the genre classification is done by Nelson via representative artists who are defined as 'good', compared with Anitta, who is assigned the worst adjectives. He declared liking 'rock', and in the list he provides of supposedly 'good' artists, several styles of pop and rock are represented, going from the Beatles to Aerosmith to the Bee Gees. Nelson seems to operate a value hierarchy very common in some identity groups in Brazil in which some Brazilian music genres are opposed to Anglophone rock-like music. His preference for Anglo-American rock and pop highlights an affiliation with a set of ideas related to cosmopolitanism, modernity and technology. As Regev puts it, pop-rock music developed a set of sonic techniques derived from the electric manipulation of timbres and tones provided by electric and electronic instruments and devices (2013: 166–168). Hence, after a long-term process of 'pop-rockification', the atmosphere of pop-rock music became the sound of modernity, an 'aesthetic cosmopolitanism' (Regev 2013: 30). Although Regev doesn't classify pop-rock as a genre, but rather as a 'cultural convention', Nelson seems to apply to the term 'rock' a broader idea that can encompass Anglo-American pop-rock artists and groups, using this classification to set them apart from the music performed by Anitta. This way of thinking allows him to split 'good' (Anglophone pop-rock) and 'bad' (Brazilian funk-pop) music.

The third aspect of Nelson's narrative resounds the age-related issue. Nelson thinks it unacceptable that his wife (presumably in her thirties like him) likes Anitta. Anitta and the pop-funk she represents should only be directed towards teenagers and her taste for it would be a sign of immaturity or underdevelopment in terms of music and, perhaps, other realms. It is possible to speculate – although it is important to highlight that it is speculation – that part of his distaste of pop-funk artists such as Anitta has to do with this domestic disagreement, and possibly that this musical conflict is surrounded by others in their partnership. As we saw in Chapter 2, music is an element of intense home conflicts, sometimes highly disturbing ones. The personal dimension of music taste is taken as a significant feature in the evaluation of the relationship itself, which, in his case, seems to be rather disturbing for him. As Frith argues, 'The point is not that we want friends and lovers like us; but we do need to know that conversation, argument, is possible' (1996:5). It is unclear if Nelson feels unable to have this taste conversation with his wife, once he disqualifies her taste as adolescent and denies any respect to the artist she admires. The issue of personal relations is entangled with negotiations of taste, which leads us to another layer in these classifications, sliding from the genres to the people who produce and like them.

The case of 'funk'

If genres provide a categorization of the musical universe that helps people to define likes and dislikes, some of them are more likely to be mentioned in association with 'annoying music'. In interviews done in Brazil, funk[2] was often cited as agent of disturbance or irritation. I cannot say that this was a total surprise, since it is widely known that funk is usually taken in Brazilian

---

[2]It is important to highlight that the music Brazilian people refer to as 'funk' is not the 1970s African North American style known as 'funk' but a variety of hip hop, notably the Miami bass style, reprocessed in Rio de Janeiro during the 1980s to become a different genre with the same name (Palombini 2014: 99). Hence, the term 'funk' used here always refers to the Brazilian genre.

popular music as an (almost) uncontested example of 'bad music'. According to musicologist Carlos Palombini, one of the most important funk researchers in Brazil, funk is 'among the most cited genres in lists of musical abominations' (2014: 320).

Brazilian funk was created in subaltern parties in the suburbs and *favelas* of Rio de Janeiro in the late 1970s, where North American soul music was played (Oliveira 2017). In a creative process of mixing and editing mostly inspired by the sound of Miami bass, young DJs elaborated remixes that changed the sound of these parties, renaming the music 'funk' and the parties themselves '*bailes funk*'. Pereira de Sá (2007) points to funk in Rio as the first original electronic music created in Brazil, in the late 1980s. The parties (*bailes*) were attended by black poor youngsters and became very popular in the last decade of the twentieth century. Nevertheless, since the 1990s, funk has been portrayed by media coverage as a music practice associated with 'gangs or criminal organizations, imputations of anonymous sexual intercourse in parties, alienation, bad taste, and sexist dances, slang, and lyrics' (Freire Filho and Herschmann 2011: 225). At the same time, this negative media coverage raised curiosity in other social groups, in a paradoxical movement of demonization of funk, which came together with an unintentional glamorization of the genre (Herschmann 2005). What is interesting in this process is that, despite being acknowledged as creative and good danceable music by attendants of the *bailes*, funk has been facing a strong prejudice, being entangled with ideas about poverty, blackness, violence and explicit sexuality. Similar to the definition of social hierarchies regarding *cumbia villera* in Argentina discussed by Pablo Vila and Pablo Semán, funk is largely acknowledged as 'music made by poor people and aesthetically poor' (Semán and Vila 2010: 13). The entanglement between a social prejudice with aesthetic disqualification is the ground of several complaints and disagreements that surround funk music and the *bailes*. Moreover, attached to the strong racial prejudice that is part of daily life in Brazil, we could add that funk is recognized as 'black music, made by black people'. The racialization of social segregations (Alabarces and Silba 2016) mixing class and racial prejudices is the starting point for most depreciation of funk as music and as social movement. The significant 'black' taken as a background of funk (bad) evaluation reinforces the long-time depreciation of blackness as a heritage that comes from the slavery time and is still unfortunately very present in Brazil nowadays.

The high number of interviewees who cited funk as an example while talking about 'annoying music' is a symptom of this disadvantaged position of the genre in Brazilian shared music imaginary (Trotta 2016). However, the background prejudices that feed this imaginary are not addressed in the foreground of these talks. Instead, the argument is usually directed at the ethics portraited by the lyrics, or at the dance, or at the (high) loudness at which funk is usually played. Sixty-eight-year-old Ernani, quoted in the previous chapter, mixes funk with other Brazilian genres to describe his discomfort with 'today's' music:

> There was going to be the Feast of Saint John celebration in the square. But, when we got there, it was playing electronic *forró*, *pagode* and funk. I wanted to listen to one thing and there was another, an offensive, outrageous context. Funk, for instance, and *pagode*, I consider outrageous. Both disseminate despicable human values in my opinion. In the old days, the mainstream media (forty years ago) tried to bring quality musical and cultural productions to the great masses. Humanistic values. Nowadays the mainstream media takes advantage of pretty low-quality stuff which is already successful, like *pagode*, funk, etc. and promotes that. This deeply annoys me.

The way he associates the music with several ideas about human values, mass media and violence is rather complex. The expectancy of finding specific music in a traditional popular celebration at a public space was frustrated by genres he associates with 'low level' music. Although he did not develop what would be these 'despicable human values', the judgement is clearly constructed over his personal ethics references. In this sense, funk is an example of this aggressive and low-quality music that media promotes. Using funk as an example of music that somehow hurts diffuse 'humanistic values' is a common development of the conversation about irritating and annoying music. Sometimes, it is described more directly as a music genre that has strong and undesirable sexism. Messias, the evangelic quoted previously, is very explicit in describing this discomfort:

Funk is 99% offensive toward women. This makes you dislike funk more because it doesn't respect women. Funk from the *favela* communities is 90% very degrading for women. And they attend the bailes [parties] and even like it. For me, women attending these bailes have no value at all. They follow the rhythm and the drinking. To like something that degrades you. That's complicated!

The way he gets upset with the 'demoralization' of women is slightly contradictory with his own judgement about the women that go and enjoy funk. He sees no value in them, yet he regrets the lyrics that are putting them down. The issue here is not only the low quality of the funk music in itself, but a moral judgement about the lifestyle that is perceived as being praised by the lyrics. The stigmatization operates in a double process that homogenizes the whole genre and its audience and incorporates the prejudice that associates funk with inadequate behaviour, criminals and violence.

Funk is so widely spread in the Brazilian music market that there are several styles of it, defined not only according to sound differences but also to the lyrics. A style known as *proibidão* (forbidden funk), for instance, presents the most aggressive and sexist lyrics. Not rarely, the narratives performed in these lyrics are descriptions of violence enacted by drug dealers in their confrontations with the police, speaking overtly about killings and fights. Palombini and Facina define *proibidão* as 'that part of funk music in which the thematic deals with life in the inferior strata of illicit substance commerce, or to the *life in the crime*' (2017: 349). As such, a whole explicit vocabulary of violence is applied in a rough way, emphasizing the violent lifestyle of those poor people surrounded by and involved with drug traffic and the violent 'operations' carried out by the police. The moral limits are intentionally surpassed in these lyrics, which, to a great extent, collaborates with feeding the stigmatization of funk as criminals' music, lower, confrontational, dangerous. Even though these lyrics do not correspond to the totality of funk, *proibidão* is always mentioned as an example of bad quality and unbearable music experience. Some people unify all funk styles as simple variations of *proibidão*, in a simplification of the genre diversity. Notwithstanding, there are people who mentioned funk in a more nuanced way, trying to balance their distaste with identifying differences in artists and songs, and through time. Marise is one of these interviewees who tries to separate funk into moments, where older songs were more enjoyable than present-time examples:

> I like, and even enjoy, funk from the beginning of the nineties, like Claudinho and Buchecha. If it is being played at a party I will dance because I like it. But nowadays funk is very offensive, mainly treating women as something unreal, as objects to be used in a pleasant way… When there are no swear words, every song sounds implicitly offensive, about using women, women have twerked, have been already used. It is very primitive, in the negative sense of the word 'primitive', which is a setback. It is a cultural setback because funk didn't begin like that. Today it has a pejorative trend especially in the matter of sex and the female position in the relationship.

Three things are worth mentioning in her talk. First, the issue of violence. Although she seems to be aware that different styles of funk have different approaches and forms, she only recognizes songs from the past as those she could dance to and take pleasure in. It is as if older funk was not aggressive and time passing has made all artists and songs violent. Time changes our tastes and evaluations about songs, artists and genres. At the same time, past repertoires can function as a kind of archive of memories that fill our life history, feelings and shared moments. It is easier to find interesting or enjoyable a song that has been part of a distant time, even though it could have been rather disturbing at that time. Possibly, the selective narrative Marise develops about old-time funk is an example of this distance time provides.

The second issue is related to gender. In fact, most funk lyrics are constructed on a kind of role separation between genders that puts girls and women as objects to be caught and seduced. This is a quite common masculine narrative about sex, which is conceived like a kind of hunt, where sexual intercourse with women is an achievement more than a pleasurable experience. Therefore, funk lyrics (as in many mainstream pop songs) describe women frequently as inanimate objects, ready to be taken by a virile male. Marise, obviously, refuses this imaginary and rejects current funk songs. Sexism in music is a complex issue that is usually interpreted superficially. The surface of the immediate meaning of the lyrics is often the material people use to condemn songs that have accordingly trespassed an ethic limit. While it is obvious that some lyrics really apply ideas and descriptions that are unacceptably offensive and violent against women, it is necessary to deepen the analysis incorporating the sound, the dance and the music experience as a whole in order to get a more complex picture of the way people deal with sexist lyrics. This is beyond the limits of this book. What I would like to highlight here is that people do feel offended by lyrics and when they do so, they reject the song, the artist and eventually the genre as a whole, many times reinforcing prejudices and segregations.

The last thing I would like to point out in her talk is the issue of primitivism. Sexism and violence are understood by her as elements of a non-civilized code of behaviour, defined negatively as primitive, and retrograde. As was discussed in Chapter 4, the issue of civilization as an adequate lifestyle, opposed to animalistic acts that ought to be controlled both individually and socially, is a permanent concern in daily life, arising often in music experiences. It could be said here that Marise is making a direct association between the whole package that funk brings to the surface – entangling racial, social, generational and moral issues – and the primitivism, in another layer of prejudice against funk and its fans. Although I think this would not be totally wrong, it would be preferable to interpret her feelings towards funk as an elaboration that merges moral and ethical concerns with embodied attraction and repulsion to funk as pleasurable dance music. Funk has become a symbol of bad evaluation, as well as a hub of prejudices. In this sense, a very interesting analysis on Facebook comments about the genre is provided by Pereira de Sá and Cunha (2017: 162), who found that arguments against funk could be grouped into four thematic axes: '(1) racial prejudice, (2) socio-territorial prejudice, (3) aesthetic critique and despise for funk as a cultural manifestation and (4) popularization of funk as a "threat" to the country's progress'. In their research, they highlight how people attack funk as a way to dismiss the social group it represents, mixing social and racial prejudice with aesthetic disqualification.

What is important to our debate about annoying music is how people use musical taste to build social borders and to lower other people. Nelson's complaints about Anitta, in a sense, put together both the set of commercial stereotypes of the artificiality of pop music and the poorness of funk as bad quality music produced by 'lower people'. As Julio Mendívil (2016: 37) puts it, 'If music transmits effectively group or cultural values, ranting against a type of music, ridiculing it or aesthetically disavowing is a very productive way of belittling those who produce it and those who listen to it.' In other words, music taste struggles between individuals or social groups are ways of dealing with broader disagreements, conflicts and disengagements. When music annoys, something does not work well in interhuman interaction.

However, we cannot take the relation between music and people who play it as a direct or mechanical correspondence. If we can admit it is generally true that annoying music is associated by annoyed auditors with annoying people, there are cases that point in the opposite direction or, at least, towards a subtler moral evaluation about those who control the sound. Personal relations are complex, and many different conditionings may produce different reactions and levels of irritation. As we saw in the case quoted in Chapter 2, when Claudia describes her husband's successful intervention in a neighbour's party due to their good relation, personal contact may allow several different reactions and even balance how affected anyone can be with the sound. Several people interviewed pointed to the fact that, at first, annoying music is something one tries to bear. Depending on the situation, the context and how long the annoying music has been playing, the irritation may increase or diminish. My argument in this chapter is that the level of irritation depends as well on the kind of music that is being played, and the momentary interpretations associated to the set of values, shared codes, behaviours, prejudices and moral frames that the music activates while being heard unwantedly. As some reports confirm, if people do not share the codes and the moral framing of invasive music, the nuisance tends to increase. And the opposite may be true.

And what if you like the unwanted music?

A few chapters ago I quoted Nigel complaining about what he called 'the backing track'. According to him, this was one of the most irritating things of contemporary life, stating that 'our entire mode of life got a backing track', which he defined as something 'awful'. However, a few moments later in the same interview, he reported the following case:

One very fascinating thing to me was going to Japan. I was in a station at like 8 o'clock in the morning getting a train to somewhere. So I went to a coffee for a cup of coffee before my train was due to go and they were playing music. It was like Charlie Parker. And it was actually the original. It was absolutely wonderful. And another day I went to the supermarket and they were playing John McLaughin, and then somewhere else they were playing Miles Davis. People don't realize, but this is a totally different culture. When the Americans occupied Japan after the Second World War, they brought their music with them. And the Japanese adopted it. They didn't get rid of it. It is not like here, the synthetic background we have to live with.

More than pointing out his contradictions (which, indeed, are part of our musical and cultural taste), the interesting point here is to highlight that irritation is balanced by taste. In his case, the experience of listening around to Charlie Parker ('the original'!), Miles Davis or John McLaughin – recognized talented jazz players, highly rated in the hierarchical system of quality attribution in music – is defined as 'fascinating'. While opposing iconic jazz with a 'synthetic background', he organizes his taste in genres and, additionally, suggests that the music playing as background in public places does not always need to be irritating. Balanced by the auditor's taste, the music imposed may be surprising and produce a very pleasurable experience. Indeed, in the case of owned public places such as restaurants, shopping centres and train stations, the primary intention of the music chooser is precisely to fill the time and provide a better experience for the customers during their time indoors. The very fact that most people interviewed for this research (and quoted here) report being irritated with imposed music in public places does not eliminate the possibility that other people may be amused by it.

Moreover, Nigel's case points to the role of the auditor's disposition and the overall context in this interpretation. He obviously not only acknowledges jazz music as a legitimate and high-quality cultural production but his feeling of a 'good fit' between the place and the music is also strongly related to the fact he was displaced in a far-away Japan. The experience of displacement – it was not clear if he went to Japan to work or as a tourist – makes us aware of different things that we may not have noticed in our homeland. As such, he elaborates a historical theory about the cultural appropriation Japan has done with North American music heritage, adding a frankly positive value in this narrative. In a very particular rhetoric, this experience allows him to be even more irritated with the artificial 'backing track' heard in Scotland's public places. All this thought development has to do with his taste for jazz and distaste for pop and 'synthetized' music, revealing his senses of belonging in terms of cultural and musical background.

One cause of irritation by music in places where you are not supposed to pay attention to it is that it calls our attention. Following Kassabian (2013), I assume we do not need to listen especially attentively for the music to produce changes in our body and mind. However, the presence of music in closed places is unavoidable, especially if it is loud or if it defies or matches intensively our taste. An interesting situation was described by Peter, quoted in Chapter 3:

> I like pop music, I just don't want to hear it when I am doing my shopping. The thing is that I can't concentrate. I went to buy some snacks. The shop that we go to, they play Classic FM all the time, and, like, we can try to handle that, depending on what it is. There was an interesting piece of music that I've never heard before, three or four cellos. I've gone to this shop to buy snacks and I thought, 'Humm, quite interesting', and so I picked up a pack of something else, and I came home with a completely wrong thing.

In his case, the pleasurable music is, paradoxically, an element that disturbs him, causing disorientation and regret. It can be argued that he is a very sensitive listener – what Judith Becker (2004) would define as a 'deep listener' – but he describes this episode in a mix of auto-fun and shame. For him, it revealed both his activated sensibility – which he said was due to his weak health – and the widespread unavoidable presence of music, disturbing his cognitive abilities. Furthermore, what is interesting in the case is that all this nuisance was caused precisely for his positive evaluation of the aesthetic experience he unwillingly had in the shop. Possibly, if he hadn't liked the music, he would have run away from the shop without buying anything (he reported other cases during his interview with this result). However, liking did not produce a very different consequence, but rather confusion and embarrassment at having bought the wrong product. Taste, again, is an ingredient that changes the relation people have with unchosen music. It changes, further, the threshold of tolerance to it. Take the case reported by Janet:

> So, certain types of music I like and I am more tolerant of them. There is one particular charity shop I was in this morning actually where they seem for some reason to play the music I like. So I find I am able to stay for longer than I would stay where the music I find unpleasant.

Like Nigel, she was surprised to listen to the music she likes in a charity shop. This surprise balances her general idea that such places should not play any music. If we agree that music has the power to change moods and produce corporal reactions, the pleasurable experience with music doesn't need to be provided exclusively by ourselves or intentionally. The reported consequence of Janet's liking the music is that she stayed for longer inside the shop, which is exactly the desired expectation of the one who has chosen the background music. For a brief moment, music was not heard as an intruder in her shopping experience, but as an enjoyable element of it. In other words, listening to music may be a forced experience and still be something judged as pleasurable. The 'original' Miles Davis heard by Nigel in Japan or the 'very interesting' cello ensemble that surprised Peter in a supermarket cannot be simply taken as imposed sound situations, but also as transcending aesthetic experiences that irrupted unexpectedly in daily life.

Nevertheless, this positive evaluation is not consensual. Anthony, for instance, is more reluctant to admit having pleasure in those situations. As he was describing the difficulty of going to restaurants without being bothered by unwanted music ('except the very top ones'), he admitted that good music could be, at best, less annoying:

> If it is music that I like, probably it is going to be less irritating. It might still constitute an interruption, a nuisance factor, if I am trying maybe to read something or communicate with someone. I like to hear music which I choose when I want to hear it. I don't want it forced upon me. But if it is music that I like, obviously it is going to be less of an irritation than otherwise.

For him, the adequacy of the music experience is the most important aspect to have in mind as he listens to any music. It could be argued that he adopts a rational political perspective in these situations – he is an active member of Pipedown campaign, supporting the struggle to eliminate the background music of public places. Therefore, the possibility of pleasure in unchosen music experience can be somehow blocked by him. However, we cannot go too much further in this interpretation. Of course, being subjected to music – with all the corporal engagement it produces – in a place may be discomforting, even if it is music we do like. Possibly, Anthony highlights this imposition as something that he is highly aware of and, therefore, doesn't allow himself to enjoy.

In all these cases, forced music experience that somehow activates pleasure is referred to as an individual process. As music blurs the division between mind and body, personal feelings are activated both physically and psychologically during the experience, which can result in contradictory affects. The disturbance of forced music experience is, hence, defined as an individual issue that may be unbearable if the music is far from one's personal taste, but that can be also minimized in cases where the music is judged as 'good' or 'interesting'. This operation is performed in different ways and grades. Stating that liking the music can be 'less irritating', as Anthony put it, is indeed very different from the longer stay in shop reported by Janet.

Notwithstanding those rather different perspectives, what may be called to attention here is the relative consensus that taste is a key feature in the judgement of annoying music. In being so, likes and dislikes are ways of performing one's individuality socially, which involves being more or less keen to adhere to unwanted music experience. This process intertwines individual and collective frames into the issue of being part of the social and having to deal with other people daily. Mediated through taste in its performative feature, living together is a continuous exercise of embracing and rejecting interpersonal relations, getting closer or farther from other people, keeping desperately your personal privacy in messy and almost always crowded public spaces. Music and sound are agents in this permanent and uneasy activity of sharing spaces with other people.

6

Regarding the sound of the others

Annoying music is not something abstract. Instead, it is grounded in very concrete situations and supported by memories, interpretations and judgements done by people who unwantedly listen to it. It deals with emotions as well as with rationality, entangled with very elaborated moral, aesthetic and contextual judgements. When someone classifies a music experience as 'annoying', what is being brought to the foreground is a relation – a relation, first, between the auditor and the music itself, as an imposed sound in a social space. Music, hence, disturbs the expected acoustic privacy, being an undesired intruder. The relation between the auditor and the music triggers not only her/his affective response to the sounds but also a set of interpretations about it, processed through her/his lifelong concepts and ideas about goodness and badness in terms of music. As we've seen, these ideas are informed by moral and aesthetic frames and prejudices.

Second, 'annoying music' is a judgement that reveals a relationship between the auditor and other people who (supposedly) have the power to control the music, choosing the moment, the artist, the song, the loudness and so on. This 'other' can be another individual, an abstract and impersonal agent or a group. The kind of otherness upon which this relation is being experienced is relevant and, depending on who the other is, the irritation caused by the sound intrusion can be more or less tolerated. In this sense, otherness is a key issue in the interpretation of what is defined as annoying music. Nevertheless, while talking about music that forcibly irrupts in a shared acoustic space, the idea of otherness does not refer necessarily to a distant culture, an exotic population or an ethnic group. The 'other' that imposes his/her presence through the form of sounds is often someone who shares most social markers and spaces. More than a pre-existing other, sometimes it is precisely the music experience or the music disagreement that shapes the otherization, not as a stable identity but as a momentary conflict. Moreover, the music involved in this doesn't need to be heard as 'strange' or part of an unknown repertoire and set of conventions. As can be read in the quotes of interviews used throughout the book, in most cases people are disturbed by music repertoires that may be familiar to the bothered auditor, yet do not coincide with his/her personal taste. Hence, the otherness is related here not exactly to a distant belonging or to a musical other, but to a process of otherization triggered by music experience.

Otherness

In her book *Frames of War*, Judith Butler enquires what a life is. This rather unsettling interrogation leads to the development of the idea that the very apprehension of 'life' is intermingled with operations of power that separate valuable and unworthy lives. In other words, 'certain lives are perceived as lives while others, though apparently living, fail to assume perceptual form as such' (Butler, 2009: 24). This statement is supported mainly through the idea that living is something precarious: a life – every life – is always under threat of death and injuries. The key element, for her, is what happens when a life is lost or, more precisely, what *may* happen in cases where a life is lost. The potential to grieve is a fundamental issue that valuable lives are assured and unworthy lives denied. Lives that 'are not regarded as potentially grievable, and hence valuable' are subjected to 'starvation, underemployment, legal disenfranchisement, and differential exposure to death and violence' (2009: 25). The unequal distribution of grievability across populations helps the author to make a distinction between the precariousness of life, which is a condition of every life, and the precarity of life, a condition of those ungrievable lives, not quite recognized as such. Thinking about life as an unstable idea, Butler highlights the inequalities of power and value worldwide, focusing specifically on radical events such as war, mass migration, famine and torture. The main subject of her book is the precarious lives of populations and dehumanized human beings in these extreme situations. However, it is possible to think about the implications of the othering process in daily situations. For the author, 'precariousness implies living socially', being attached to others as a condition of survival. 'It implies exposure both to those we know and to those we do not know; a dependency on people we know, or barely know, or know not at all' (Butler, 2009: 14). And this is true not only in war but in every moment.

Transporting these thoughts to the realm of sound and music exchanges may be fruitful to add some layers to the nuisance caused by the others' music. If we agree that the precariousness of life is attached to our mutual dependency on each other, then the process of otherization is not simply an effort to protect our personal individuality, but the means to construct it. Unwanted sound produces, hence, in condensed form, the mixed experience of reinforcing the self, the identity and the individual belonging, as well as interpreting, refusing and classifying both the sound heard and those who have control over it. Going further in this direction, these 'others' who are then defined as the source of disturbance have their humanity diminished. Their lives can be, at least for a few seconds or even in the hypothetic fantasy of violence, not worthy. The responses quoted in Chapter 4 that hyperbolically mentioned 'killing' the other are part of this process, an ethically twisted desire to stop the sound through the elimination of the other, who, at that moment, is not regarded as having a grievable life.

While discussing the narratives written by nineteenth-century European travellers who went to Latin America, Ana Maria Ochoa Gautier observes that their perception of the sonic environment found between the tropics was filled with negative adjectives of excess attached not exactly to the sound itself, but to the indigenous people who produced it (Ochoa Gautier, 2014: 32). This radical otherization, according to the author, worked as an affective confirmation of racist theories that denied the recognition of indigenous people as 'human'. Their vocalizations, which intentionally operated through a blurred variation between 'speech, melody and shout', were often compared to animal sounds (2014: 41). From the indigenous perspective, however, the act of sounding like animals could be a means of dealing with the relation between the human and the non-human, between nature and culture. As Viveiros de Castro states, the cosmopolitical theory found in several ethnographic works done in indigenous America is replete with descriptions of

> a universe inhabited by diverse types of actants or subjective agents, human or otherwise – gods, animals, the dead, plants, meteorological phenomena, and often objects and artifacts as well – equipped with the same general ensemble of perspective, appetite, and cognitive dispositions: with the same kind of soul. (Viveiros de Castro, 2014: 56)

Deaf to the achievement of this complex interconnection between human and environment, European writers classified this blurred distinction as a sign of inferiority (Ochoa Gautier, 2014: 61). The auditor's disposition informs not only the interpretation of a sound that is felt as unpleasant but also the affective responses that nourish this interpretation. The animal-like sounds were, according to their reports, loud, stressful and annoying.

Moreover, the sound encounter described by Ochoa Gautier has other layers that are relevant. First, despite the fact that the European travellers had gone to Latin America to be emissaries of the colonial power centre, their lives were radically dependent on the natives not only to guide them through the rivers and forests but also to cook and to provide shelter and transport for them. Their perception of the sonic environment of the colony was merged with this uncomfortable situation of an ambiguous power relation. Their dependency on indigenous people to survive remained as a constant reminder of the precariousness of life, of their vulnerability in that different land. Beyond the cultural difference and the several kinds of prejudice that were the common ground of their perception of the colony, this dependency ought to be considered as they were forced to hear the sounded other. As we've seen in several interviews quoted in previous chapters, forced listening produces angst and anger due to the overtly assumed impossibility to stop it. A powerless position in a given space can sometimes (as may have been the case with nineteenth-century travellers) invert the power hierarchies of social roles.

The idea of space leads us to another layer of the process of otherization through sound. In order to be affected by the others' sound (and music), the auditor must share the same physical space as the sound source or be in one nearby, which adds the issue of positionality to his/her feelings and interpretations towards the sound. One of the most illuminating passages of Ochoa's book is her discussion about the *bogas*, boat workers who transported travellers across Magdalena River, in Colombia. The negative feelings and adjectives written by these European travellers about the sound of the *bogas* are partially due to the fact that these sounds were heard by them as they were stuck in a boat for hours and days. Similar to the report given by Alec (quoted in Chapter 2), forcibly sharing a physical space for while in which unpleasant music is being played is a very annoying situation that can lead to somatic symptoms or to an angry writing style. Again, what is at issue here is a profound negotiation of the power that merges the space, the sound and the relative role of each person within the situation. In several ways, and not only regarding sonic experiences, proximity and distance are important elements in the process of otherization.

In his influential *Orientalism*, Edward Said highlights that all the knowledge and meanings constructed about the 'Orient' have to do with a particular political and economic closeness between Britain, France and the Orient (Said, 2003: 4). Through this close relation – physical, military and economic – ideas about the 'Orient' were developed in a huge corpus of texts that constructed knowledge about the Orient, the 'other'. This way of narrating the geographic power is, hence, a way of settling a 'flexible positional superiority', which puts 'the Westerner in a whole series of possible relationships with the Orient without ever losing him the relative upper hand' (2003: 7). This superiority was challenged during the boat experience of European nineteenth-century travellers, as is recovered in their writings. What is important to our discussion here is that the process of naming and othering a relation implies a power asymmetry in which the very physical position of this named other is highly relevant in defining ways through which this relation will be dealt with. In Said's interpretation, knowledge about the Orient is a key issue in the development of hierarchical power between 'we-Europe' and 'them-Orient', which, geographically, was at first positioned in a contiguous land. How far the other is determines a wide range of possible ways in which otherization could be constructed. The affective responses are also framed through an evaluation of relative closeness or distance, physically speaking. At a distance, it is easier to reduce the other's life to a stereotype, be it a country, a group of people, a culture or an individual. At a (cultural) distance, the singing of the *bogas* can be simply described as half-human.

Distance is also a concern in Susan Sontag's discussion about the 'pain of the others'. While analysing the photographs of tortured bodies or dead soldiers, Sontag states that they can be an invitation to think or to mourn, but it is always possible to turn the page or to change the TV channel (Sontag, 2003: 91). Accordingly, images of atrocities 'have been reproached for being a way of watching suffering at a distance, as if there were some other way of watching' (idem: 92). Thinking about sight, the idea of distance is conceived by Sontag as a necessary position from which something terrible can be seen. In other words, 'sight requires spatial distance'. Distance allows one to 'close the eyes', yet it can produce a strong effect of being aware and enquiring about the other's suffering.

What is interesting to underline here is that sound experience, oppositely, requires physical closeness. Sound must be able to reach our body in order to produce otherization. Moreover, otherization will also be entangled with cultural judgements that are as well crossed with ideas of proximity or distance. In other words, the distance that will frame otherization is also variable: it depends on different cultural and interpersonal conditions experienced together with the sound and the physical distance of its source. The unwanted sound and/or music is, hence, judged and interpreted according to an elaboration on *who* is producing it. Let's take, for instance, this report by Alec. Asked if he remembered situations in which the others' music had irritated him, he describes the following:

> *Alec*: I remember a Spanish guy who lives in the other building. I love *flamenco*, but at three in the morning, it's very bad. And you want to kill the guy. Also because it didn't sound that he was having a party or something. The guy was screaming to annoy me. That was a recent experience that made me really angry. I wanted to shout back, call the police.
>
> *Q*: Did you?

Alec: No, I was only contemplating my options. Luckily it didn't happen that often. It was only one summer. And not so long, [but] enough to wake me up, like twenty minutes or something. And you are really awake and filled with anger. It seems so unnecessary, so disrespectful – I felt he was kind of doing it on purpose, I guess being drunk or intoxicated with something. I think some kind of intoxication must be involved. I can understand if you are hanging out with friend and having a good time and you say, 'Fuck, I'm having a good time'. That can happen and I think overall fair enough, we should all have a chance to enjoy things.

There are several layers of distances that appear in his narrative. The guy is classified as 'Spanish' because of the kind of music he was listening to – '*flamenco*'. Although Alec does not seem to have a prejudice regarding anybody's country origins, the continuity between the music performed and the possible nationality of his annoying neighbour is an interesting element in the process of otherization. He is Spanish, he comes from another culture, he likes other music. Even though Alec states that he himself 'loves' flamenco and highlights that the problem was due to the inappropriate time and loudness of the sound, the Spanish classification is a way to elaborate on an idea about the other. Moreover, the guy (again, we deal here with a predominantly male act of listening to music very loudly) lived in another building. The distance between his window and the music source attested to the inadequate loudness of it and made the act of complaining difficult. So, he thought about calling the police, but he did not. The police, once more, appear as an option, a hope of restoring the silence and the civility of coexistence. Another issue that Alec points to as very irritating was that the neighbour was alone, 'not giving a party or something'. It is significant that the threshold of tolerance is flexible enough to understand particular situations and exceptions. The regularity of the annoyance determines less tolerance towards the sound, as does its duration. Twenty minutes of music exposure is not a properly long period, but twenty minutes during the night was enough to perturb Alec's sleep. Time and space are intermingled in the evaluation of the nuisance. The annoying other constructed through the imposed sound-music is an unstable image that can be more or less settled depending on the distance (it is unlikely that Alec would meet the 'Spanish guy' or would recognize him in street) and the regularity of the occurrence (if *flamenco* was played every night, Alec would possibly have a stronger tendency to call the police or 'to do something' about the music).

This rather trivial situation shows that otherization has a close connection with emotions. As music invades an intimate acoustic space, inevitably it raises feelings that result from a very complicated mix of background knowledge about the music played and personal taste, a judgement about the pertinence of the time and the adequacy of the loudness, an interpretation about how long and how often this sound-music bothers and so on. The resulting feeling is the path through which the otherization will be constructed. Alec was awakened 'filled with anger', he felt disrespected, as if the music was played on purpose to annoy him. The inappropriateness of the time, loudness and the music itself made him aware of his own precariousness. The feeling of being targeted was due to the perception that an agreement had been broken by the selfish 'other' who simply did not care about his neighbour's sleep. Anger and despair are, then, the ground over which the otherness is built. And the idea of respect, again, calls attention to the double-sided nature of this relationship. In other words, if a person feels upset about a sound that irrupts in her/his private space disturbing the desired sound environment, the opposite is also true. The Spanish guy could be very upset if someone complained about his music. He was having fun and, though careless about the music that leaked outside his private space, he felt he had the right to put the music on inside his flat at the level that pleased him.

Strictly speaking, the Spanish guy and Alec are both 'the other'. Though not necessarily reducing the humanity of each other, the negative judgements towards the impersonal other make their lives and desires less important. In Alec's interpretation, he tries to understand the reasons the neighbour may have to play the music that loudly, tries to humanize him. We can't be sure about the motivations of the 'Spanish guy', but, similarly to how Alec tries to humanize him, it is possible that this neighbour would be ashamed if someone were to complain about his sound. As I have been arguing, all these complex feelings and judgements are ephemeral, mostly based in relations that are not necessarily experienced face to face. The difficulty of the process is that, in their own perspective, both the bored auditor targeted by someone's music and the controller of the sound equipment are 'right'.

As has been mentioned several times throughout this book, being 'right' means to claim for 'rights', a diffuse idea that is activated as a source of legitimacy of what is considered proper or adequate behaviour. In these reported cases, 'rights' are sets of accepted and protected codes of conduct designed socially to preserve someone's intimate space. Inscribed and prescribed by the written law, the claim for 'rights' in interpersonal disagreements regarding sound and music is a kind of evocation of a broad rule that ought to be respected. This set of expected behaviour is attached to the idea of citizenship, a condition of someone who has rights.

Rights, citizenship and the law

Living in society implies being subjected to collective agreements and rules that one ought to follow. Within this complex interconnected web of social rules, territory is a key element that provides a range of applicability of these codes and norms. Part of these is formed by social shared practises and modes of behaviours that we usually name 'culture'. Embodied practises such as how to talk, walk and dress, and unwritten codes of language and behaviours, are part of our daily lives, framing our way of being in the world and our exchange with other people.

Another part is formed by a set of written rules that are valid within a territory, which we usually call 'law'. The law is at the same time an abstract set of writings that should be followed and a concrete descriptive code one must obey in order not to be punished. The law is not only indicative but also functions as a threat against misbehaviour. In other words, if one dares to do something the law forbids, s/he will be fined, arrested or expulsed from the place.

Music disagreements usually merge 'law' and 'culture'. The expected behaviour of the one who controls the music is mostly shared as social and cultural 'codes'. As such, multiple sound/music practises may be taken as 'desired' or expected, according to the situation, the place and the specific cultural group involved. On the other side, as we've seen in several interviews, the feeling of being personally disrespected by someone's music involves cultural ideas of adequateness and inappropriateness, as well as background protection supposedly given by the 'law'. As such, the bothered auditor can always claim for the 'law' to restore what s/he understands as 'adequate' behaviour in that place, supported by local legislation.

As 'law' and 'culture' are related to territory, it is important to highlight the interconnection between physical territories, legal systems and cultural specificities. Certain places within cities, states and districts have specific rules (laws) that make up part of the behavioural practises within that locality. However, the nation is the main territory that prescribes legal rights and wrongs. In many countries, the legal system joins national, regional and local laws that deal with the issue of sound, usually imposing restrictions on its production in public spaces. This movement has a long history which became more and more intense during the second half of the nineteenth century in several places around the world. The Bill Michael Bass proposed in London in 1864 (quoted in Chapter 2) is an example, similar to the debates in Holland described by Bijstervelt (2008) and to the legislation described by Natalia Bieletto-Bueno in Mexico City three decades after (2018).

In Scotland, sound problems are dealt with in Part IV, Section 54 of Civic Government Act (1982), which states that any person who produces any sound (music devices and instruments are mentioned specifically) 'so as to give any other person reasonable cause of annoyance and [who] fails to desist on being required to do so by a constable in uniform' may be convicted and fined. The law addresses a relationship between two individuals, the annoying and the annoyed, protecting the latter. In schedule 2A, the law authorizes the constable to 'enter any premises on which he reasonably suspects that instrument or device to be and seize any such instrument or device he finds there'. Again, the effort is to guarantee the right of the citizen to be undisturbed in a given place. In 2004, the Scottish Parliament published the Antisocial Behaviour Act, where we can find a whole part dedicated to 'noise nuisance' (Part 5, Articles 41–54) that reinforces the individual claim as the starting point of any measure authorities can take against the noisemaker. In Article

43/1, it states that investigation must be done 'where a local authority receives a complaint from an individual that excessive noise is being emitted from relevant property during noise control period'. What is interesting here is that the individual triggers the process, supported by a law written to protect the 'social', in a merged rhetoric in which a perpetrator is identified as behaving against the social, or 'antisocial behaviour'. The 'social' is a set of expectancies regarding environmental sound that is allowed or not. The emphasis is on both individuals (perpetrator and victim), but the background support is informed by the 'social'.

The idea of 'social' also appears in Brazilian law as 'public quietness'. In Rio de Janeiro, a law published in 1977 specifically forbids 'noises' produced in 'residential buildings by animals, musical instruments, radio or television' (Article 3/IV) as well as public performance of 'bands, music ensembles or sound reproduction devices' (Article 3/V). Interestingly, the same article also prohibits samba school rehearsals between midnight and seven o'clock in the morning, except thirty days before carnival season, when it is allowed (Article 3/VII). This single permission is a fantastic example of how the flexible movement between law and culture works in the settling of rules and the expected sound environment of a place. Carnival is the most important popular festival in Brazil, especially in Rio de Janeiro. Hence, restrictions to the loud sound during the season could be a highly contradictory rule against a party that is both economically and culturally relevant to the city and the country as a whole. Also, the law tries to acknowledge the importance of loud sound in certain situations such as religious rites, fire and ambulance alarms, urban constructions and music bands in squares and public gardens (Article 4). What is at issue here is that the written law tries to protect the rights of citizens against 'noises' that may be considered 'harmful to health, security or quietness' (Article 1). And it recommends that 'any person who understands her/his peace to be disturbed by unallowed sounds or noises can request authorities to take measures to stop it' (Article 9). On the other hand, the law also points to cultural conditions in which loud sounds have to be tolerated.

Reading the laws that try to regulate sound disagreements in social life raises the unstable issue of individual and collective rights. In extensive research about legislation related to street art in Rio de Janeiro and Montreal,

Jhessica Reia (2017) reinforces that sound and visual occupation of the street is often defined by artists as their right to the city. According to the artists, the state (which includes the law and the police) is usually conceived as a censor, not allowing informal and creative uses of the public space. Going beyond live artistic interventions, sound occupation of social spaces (in loco or leaked through electronic devices) is constantly the subject of disagreements over what rights one has in public city space. And here we come to the concept of citizenship.

Citizenship is not a word often mentioned by people interviewed for this research. Possibly for its close association to political activities such as elections and party organizations, the idea of citizenship in daily life takes the form of a claim for 'rights'. This claim is based on the assumption that a person is part of the state and should be protected by the state system. As Richard Bellamy (2008: 87) puts it, 'Membership of the citizen body gives access to positive or institutional rights offered by a given political community'. The idea of being part of this body is the background of several reactions to unwanted music. Usually, rights are referred to on a positive axis, meaning that one's individual perception of adequateness of music in a given situation is the most important reference to measure it. In these cases, if one has 'rights', the other is 'wrong'.

This means that citizenship in daily life is experienced through individual judgements of what is right and what is wrong, in which the limits between desired behaviours and practices written (the 'law') and unwritten ('culture') are blurred. As such, citizenship is an idea performed in daily acts that reinforce one's belonging to a given territory and its culture, at the same time (supposedly) protected by its legal system.

The performative dimension of citizenship helps us to unveil its unequal distribution across the population. Precarious lives have less means of performing and claiming for their citizenship or, worse, they have part of their citizenship denied in their daily experience. We can recall here the interview of Andrea, who lives in a *favela* in Rio de Janeiro, facing daily threats coming from drug dealers, police and neighbours. Asked if she ever complained about the invasive music, she said she regretted having called the police at all, since they ignored her complaint anyway.

As we've seen, the 'police' is the 'state', the official regulative force who could guarantee her right to privacy and to silence. Instead, the alleged impossibility of having the law respected added another layer of despair for her. It exposes the precarity of her life and the reduced possibility for her to claim for cultural and legal rights. The description of Andrea raises the fact that citizenship is not a block whole that one can have entirely or not. Instead, it is an abstract idea demanded in specific situations by specific persons. As such, citizenship is performed through the claim for rights in very objective moments. Hence, this performance can be more or less effective depending on several other features in the given situation, depending on the positionality of the claimer, the social hierarchies between the actors involved, the local power relations that are involved and so on. According to the legal system in Brazil, Andrea is not less of a citizen than anyone else. Nevertheless, in the cultural realm, her position in social hierarchies denies some of her claims for citizenship.

But the performative dimension of citizenship does not appear exclusively through the claim for rights. Without denying the differential distribution of the power to exercise citizenship, it can be enacted in small daily activities and behaviours. Following the influential work of Nestor Garcia Canclini, one of these ways is through consumption. According to him,

> citizenship is seen not only in relation to rights accorded by state institutions to those born within their territorial jurisdiction, but also as social and cultural practices that confer a sense of belonging, provide a sense of difference, and enable the satisfaction of the needs of those who possess a given language and organize themselves in certain ways. (Garcia Canclini, 2001: 20)

In this sense, cultural practises such as music experience are also part of the exercise of citizenship, shaping ideas, values and behaviours that frame the public debate. In other words, 'the habits and tastes of consumers condition their capacity to become citizens' (Garcia Canclini, 2001: 109). The concept of citizenship entangled with consumption is an interesting path to understanding politics in a mundane way. It enables us to understand small acts of daily life as important elements of a diffuse negotiation of ideas and behaviours, which, though roughly, may be summarized as 'politics'. In this framework, citizenship can be the constant movement of making decisions and debating ideas about life and living together. Music, as several authors point out, is a device through which we can elaborate on these agreements and disagreements. Taste disputes are at the core of these debates, together with the constant judgement about the appropriateness of the sound and the volume.

However, underlining consumption in the daily exercise of citizenship may direct our attention to the personal realm, instead of to collectivity. Although taste is known to be a social and lifelong construct, its immediate elaboration highlights individual selfhood. Therefore, citizenship accessed through consumption leaves the trace of this highly individual conception of 'rights'.

Of course, this is not surprising. Individuality is a key element in the construction of a set of rights understood as such. It is the individual that is the major concern of most law systems, developed to save his/her integrity. One of the most important texts in this regard (if not the most) is 'The Universal Declaration of Human Rights', proclaimed by the United Nations in 1948. In several articles, the individual is the one who is the subject of rights, to be protected from violence, torture, death or freedom restrictions. Explicitly in its Article 12, privacy is defined as a right, protected against any 'arbitrary interference'. Privacy and intimacy are, hence, part of the wider construction of the self, relevant features in maintaining and reinforcing personality.

Notwithstanding, the movement towards an emphasis on the individual and her/his intimacy as a privileged unity of right-claiming did not begin after the World War. In a deep historical debate about the changes in the conception of 'rights' between the state and the 'people', Norberto Bobbio (2004) describes a gradual transformation that begins with the denial of rights to the common citizen in monarchical systems and ends with an inversion in which the individual comes first in a legal state. The idea of liberty as proposed in the French Revolution is a turning point from which human beings are understood as 'free' and 'equal' for the law (Bobbio 2004: 51). It is not my intention here to visit this wide and complex debate about the changes in the idea of 'rights' across history. My point is much more restricted. It is to highlight the way the feeling of being part of an abstract collective body (the 'state') in which one has 'rights' is performed in everyday life as a permanent judgement about others' behaviour. Moreover, the blurred notion of citizenship is embodied in individuals who have a strong tendency to claim for their personal rights when confronted by other people judged as misbehaving. In sound and music disagreements, the self is overvalued and the 'social' is dismissed. Actual people have rights, not the impersonal collectivity.

Let's recall the case of São Salvador Square in Rio, reported in Chapter 2. The constant occupation of the square with musical and cultural activities disturbs residents' private intimacy as the sound forcibly invades their living rooms and bedrooms. In the manifesto (quoted in Chapter 2), they argue they can't sleep, and regret not having the 'basic right' to watch TV, read a book or listen to music they choose. The list of activities that one should be allowed to perform at home implies their demand for a safe acoustic ambience inside their private space (Domínguez Ruiz 2015). The idea of being deprived of this 'fundamental' right of indoor intimate activity is the support for the manifesto. At the end of the text, they claim for the regulative power of the state legal system: 'we just want the law to be enforced'. This case is interesting in understanding how the idea of intimacy is referred to as personal rights. Although they are acting in a group, writing the manifesto and trying to call the attention of the authorities (i.e. the government and the police), the writers have constructed their argument upon the idea that a set of individual rights is being disrespected. As citizens of the city, they claim for the public regulation to guarantee their individual rights.

This case highlights the fact that the claim for rights can hardly be a solution for disagreement, since every right, even those considered 'fundamental rights', is constrained by other rights also listed as fundamental (Bobbio 2004). The 'right' to make music in a public space hurts the 'right' of being at home without external sound interference. In a more balanced way, resident Marina (also quoted in Chapter 2) recognizes this contradictory claim for 'rights' and even acknowledges and attends some events just in front of her window. However, as the noise invades her home 'even on Mondays', she raises the question: 'What about *my* break?'

An unsolved question that raises the issue of individuality and tolerance.

Individuality

Possibly, one of the most important contributions of Tia DeNora's *Music in Everyday Life* is the way she frames the connection of music experience with the construction of the self. In search of what she calls 'music in action', DeNora rejects the idea that music acts simply as a *stimulus* for people's reaction, highlighting the role of people's agency in the construction of the encounter between the music itself and the context, the memories, the expectations and uses people direct to this experience. In her words, the result of this sum 'is greater than its parts' (DeNora 2000: 43). Therefore, individuals *use* music as an 'ordering device at the personal level, as a means for creating, enhancing, sustaining and changing subjective, cognitive, bodily and self-conceptual states' (idem: 49). Some of her interviewees mentioned using music as a resource to recover past experiences, people and emotions, helping them to construct their subjectivities and knowledge about who they are and how they feel and behave in the world. And all these processes not only occur in a symbolic or psychological way, but are also closely related to embodied features of music experience, including modulation and transformations in the energy, timing, arousal, breathing, heart rate and self-perception of pain and pleasure (idem: 76). Hence, people's agency towards music has a very profound power to regulate the mood and bodily sensations that are the basis of self-identity. The force and innovative approach of DeNora's work lies in the emphasis applied to the individual. Most of the cases discussed throughout her book are about music experiences controlled by the interviewees, which allows an overtly positive approach to music's powers. Although the issue of control appears several times in her discussion, it is not properly problematized beyond a few registers of its seriousness. When the author discusses the use of music in stores, for instance, even though sometimes the staff of these stores 'get bored' by the tape repetition forced upon their workplace (DeNora 2000: 137), the major concern of her study is the way music shapes the ambience and bodies within shopping places. As such, she states that 'the retail outlet produces potential sources of identification for the consumer, who may visit such a location as a kind of identity repository, as a storehouse of possible ways of being and possible stances' (idem: 146). Again, the focus here is the individual and the possible experience of producing something with the music played in-store, even being powerless to control the repertoire.

Notwithstanding, thinking about the pervasive and intrusive aspect of music experience, it is possible to add a conflictual perspective in this statement. Music produces the self, but this construction/production is not done always in a smooth ambience: it is constrained by several aspects that shape the way this production will happen. Before, beyond and together with this 'production of the self', as entangled by the personal agency performed by individuals who control the music experience, music *challenges* the self. And it challenges first and foremost, in the permeability it enacts between the borders of the individual, the others and society as a whole (which, in daily life, is always an abstraction).

Living together in society is a continuous process of constructing the self and others, a way to perform individuality among others. The borders between individuals and society are, hence, unclear, permeable and dynamic. As Norbert Elias states, 'individuality' and 'social conditioning' are simply 'two different functions of people in their relation to each other, one of which cannot exist without the other' (2001: 60). As such, isolating the general term 'society' from the individual perspective induces a misinterpretation of the process, suggesting that somehow an individual could be outside the society and society could be a foreign entity in an individual life. As DeNora explores the narratives of people who listen to music intentionally, usually at home, a set of social conditioning factors emerge that play an important role in this experience. They are mostly alone, but refer to memories, past experiences, affects, music repertoires and all sorts of social relations that are indissociable from this 'personal' experience. Moreover, 'home' is not a sealed physical space, and it is subjected to sounds that invade it from the outside as well as to inner sounds (personal, intimate, individual) that may leak and be heard by other neighbours and walkers on the street. The individual listening to music is always crossed by society, by other people around him/her, by constrains, situations and codes of conduct that shape the way this agency will and can be performed. Complaints are, hence, a kind of shortcut to accessing the instability of this ideal listening experience, hardly effectively achieved. What is worth noting is that, within these complaints, the idea of 'individual' rights and the self is usually overemphasized.

In fact, sound and music annoyance is hardly referred to as a problem of 'society'. Usually, the target of the complaints is individualized, even though it may not be a proper individual. When describing situations in which music is an element of disturbance, people direct their anger towards the person who controls the sound, be it for his/her personal wish or due to a role performed in a given place (usually a workplace). Sometimes, if impossible to frame precisely who controls the music, the nuisance assumes an even more irritating form. As an employee of a sports store told me once, the constant pop music in her workplace caused her angst and stress, as she was subjected to that sound that was controlled 'by the central', in a kind of internal radio. Despite an increasing unemployment rate in Brazil, she confessed to thinking daily about quitting the job, as she was getting ill because of the sound. In this case, individual ill-being is described against an impersonal sound control which invaded her body and disturbed her health. One cannot be sure whether, if she could have identified the person who controls the sound, she would have talked to her/him, but surely her anger could have been directed and experienced as an interpersonal relationship. Like I saw in a bookstore while I was paying for a book, the employee stood up to change the music and her colleague immediately asked that it not be 'carnival music' (we were in carnival season in Brazil). The possibility of this kind of direct intermediation lessens the nuisance caused by the music, yet it can be transformed into a personal disagreement between them. In fact, despite the request of the employee, the one who went to change the music – and she seemed to be a manager or something similar – said she would just put carnival music on because it was appropriate to the season! Again, in this very clear case, we confirm that having control over the sound environment is having the power, which, in turn, is related to other layers of power relations between people.

However, what I would like to emphasize here is the role of individuality in these relations. The music disagreements presented in the interviews done for this research resounded many of the (sometimes pessimistic) debates about the overemphasis on the individual in modern societies. Authors such as Arendt, Habermas and Sennett, though through very different perspectives and arguments, point to the idea that the 'public' has declined in importance during the last one or two hundred years (at least). What they mean by 'public' is a general idea of collective encounters that take place outside the private domain, the intimate 'home' and its related social structures such as family, associations, clubs and so on. As 'public' issues became less important, the individual gained a major role in social experience. Sennett associated this movement with the growth of psychology in society, which successfully spread what he calls the 'tyranny of intimacy', according to which the individual's desires, impulses, feelings and well-being are the most important issues in society. In his formulation, society is framed in a 'narcissistic norm' that 'interpret[s] social realities as meaningful when they mirror imagery of the self' (Sennett 2002: 6793/9346). According to this trend, individualism is a feature of modernity, especially the idea of modernity in Western countries, including European colonies and ex-colonies.

The image of Narcissus as used by Sennett is interesting as it both points a pathological characteristic of personal behaviour towards the collectivity and evokes the myth of a selfish character who falls dead due to his own beauty. Interestingly, when Viveiros de Castro discusses anthropology as a path to 'decolonis[ing] the thought', he names this effort 'Anti-Narcissus'. In his words, 'If Oedipus is the protagonist of founding myth of psychoanalysis, our book proposes Narcissus as the candidate for patron saint or tutelary spirit of anthropology' (2014: 43). The anti-narcissistic approach supported by Viveiros de Castro inversely confirms individualistic character as a dominant feature of the Western-modern citizen.

This idea resounds in Muniz Sodré work about '*nagô*' thinking. Trying to construct an alternative interpretation of European philosophy, Sodré discusses African diasporic myths and religious practises in order to point to a less individualistic way of being in the world. This project is developed through a very complicated mix of Ancient Greek and Modern (mostly) German philosophy, psychology and African thinking – the *nagô*. In his multiperspective approach, the author reinterprets the ancient Greek philosophical concept of *Arkhé* to refer to a general principle that encompasses every moment and element of existence. According to him, the African *Arkhé* is felt like an 'irradiation of an active corporeity, from which it comes a force (*axé*) and its modes of communion and differentiation' (Sodré 2017: Chapter 1: 92/105). In '*nagô*' thinking, music is the purest expression of this force (*axé*). Essentially vibrational and rhythmic-oriented through chant and dance, music is conceived as a rite, bodily and affectively expressed to feed the existential force of the group (idem: Chapter 2: 84/137). The holistic interpretation of music and social experience that merges the individual with the group, the private with the public and the thought with the body is an overtly assumed twist in cartesian thinking, a framework that can provide a less unbalanced approach to the self, the other and the social.

What is interesting in Sodré's approach is that music functions as a shortcut to making this entanglement alive in daily experience. Even though he recognizes this in what he calls '*nagô* thinking', there is not any strong split between this framework and what may be called 'civilized Western society' thinking. Instead, Sodré emphasizes the complex merge between these two ways to interpret and live in the world, while overtly praising the *nagô*. However, unless we assume a radical utopic approach, modernity has a major role in ruling daily life in Western countries, including African and Latin American ones. In this sense, the hegemonic set of thoughts that highlight the individual and throw a shadow over the collective may function, inversely, as a shortcut to conflicts. If music enacts a kind of experience that has the potential to blur the limits of the self, the group, the body and the mind, music experience in individualistic cultures can be rather unsettling. The interesting case of football fans who manipulate sound in stadiums as a means of supporting their clubs through a magical thinking that links the vibration with the effectiveness of the athletes' performance is an example of these unclear limits between self and group, reason and emotions (Marra and Trotta 2019).

However, the stadium situation is a rite that is somehow detached from everyday life, in which individual rights and thoughts are taken as the fundamental axis of existence. The individual is the one who has rights, and, especially, the right to play (or not) the music s/he likes. The right to listen to a certain repertoire. The right to increase the loudness or to silence the unwanted. In societies where rights are conceived as an individual privilege, this blurring function of music experience may be undesirable:

Whenever they play loud music, I think, 'She's trespassing [on others'] territory'. She's telling someone else that the territory is all her own. It's just like a dog fighting for territory: 'I'll piss here, you're also pissing here, and we're gonna brawl'. When you play loud music, whether you like it or not, that song annoys me. This person's egocentrism is so powerful that he can't even realize another gets annoyed. He doesn't care about what you think. Simple things, right? Respect and empathy.

In her way of describing the annoying situation, Marise uses this unnamed other to interpret the way interpersonal relations are constructed in current life. The nuisance makes her imagine the character of the other, classifying him/her as an egocentric person who does not care about others. In a sense, this lack of respect and empathy makes this other less human, less respectable. Interestingly, she compared the situation to two dogs' dispute for territory, applying a metaphor that resounds some of the ideas that I am following here: that sound occupies a physical space and, as such, plays the role of a power element in social relations. The idea of territory is central here. Occupying a sound space physically is a way to mark a personal space over others', forcing everyone to bare the sound presence controlled by projective personhood within the space. It is a form of showing the others a certain position and of making explicit your relative power within a physical space. Moreover, the association between this behaviour and animal behaviour is a way of thinking about humanity regarded in these 'simple' things. Humanity here is thought of as a capacity to have empathy towards the other, a conceptual shortcut, again, to the issue of 'respect'. Acting like a dog is, hence, an uncivilized way to perform interpersonal relations, showing rude manners and disrespectful behaviour. The comparison can lead us back to the reports of nineteenth-century writers quoted in Ochoa Gautier's book, reminding us that the dehumanization of the other is not only the result of twisted prejudices in the minds of distant Eurocentric travellers but is at hand daily in people bothered by invasive music. Respect and kindness are acknowledged as human characteristics and their lack, therefore, is defined as non-human, dog-like behaviour.

In her auditor's disposition, Marise does not hesitate to classify the act of listening to loud music regardless of others as an egocentric and individualistic behaviour. Her arguments for that are supported by a set of ideas about desired interpersonal behaviours beyond the law. What she claims is far more internal, a moral code that could provide an embodied behaviour of respect and mutual concern within society. Even though her discursive development is built upon the idea of the self and the individual, what she describes with a touch of despair is her perception that human beings are selfish and do not care about others.

Music experience – forced or chosen – is lived in the middle of the self, the others and the collective. It affords interpretations about what we are, about who the others are and about what society is and should be. Moral disagreements, behavioural issues, personal and group belonging are all activated through music experience. The perception of individuality and otherness is brought to the surface when we listen to music, and particularly when we take part forcibly in musical experience. Conversations about annoying music usually lead to elaborations about interpersonal relations. They are part of the daily exercise of being oneself within society. Therefore, these talks reveal the difficulties of living together.

The difficult task of listening to others

Music, as sound, implies an act of listening performed by the auditor, who judges, classifies and interprets it. The verb 'to listen' refers to the direct involuntary act of being touched by the sounds, but also means to pay attention, to consider, to think about what is being said or heard. Listening is a word applied in everyday language to refer precisely to the capacity of being able to understand the other, feel like him/her, create empathy. Listening to the other is, hence, 'the principle of understanding and a fundamental skill for dialogue' (Domínguez Ruiz 2019: 103). By contrast, blocking the possible interchange often means avoiding listening to the other, ignoring the other's wishes and claims. 'A "dialogue of the deaf" is a kind of interpersonal exchange in which participants can talk and hear each other, but they have no interest in what the other is saying' (idem). In this sense, we can take listening as an attitude, an inclination to consider the worth of what others have to say, feel and care about. If sound and music are two of the most relevant agents for putting people in contact, listening is the action that allows, or not, interpersonal relations, exchanges and affective encounters.

However, it is worth having in mind that these dialogues overlap with several other sounds and claims. Noisy urban environments and crowded spaces produce a messy ambience where listening always involves a selective activity. A walk on big-city streets is an experience that challenges our capacity of sound selection, as we are bombarded with music from stores, car horns and engines, homeless begging for money and a huge number of different noises that we are forced to ignore. Like Lourenço referred to in his interview, quoted in the introduction of this book, city environments are highly stressful, and this makes people less careful and attentive with others, more self-centred and likely to react aggressively. Being reactive and constantly called on to ignore sounds and nearby crowds leads to the development of a typical urban behaviour in which others are seen and heard as threatful, dangerous, unimportant:

> Sometimes, I think we talk too much. I talk too much. I am also trying to improve this so I can listen to others. But due to the fact that I feel that people feel that they are not getting heard, they tend to talk too much. And they end up being selfish – they don't listen to others. We joke that someone says, 'I'm a Scorpio', and the other goes, 'I'm Aquarius'. You didn't ask it and it turns into a dialogue between deaf people. Sometimes, I ask myself, 'Why are there shouting salesmen in chain store ads?' Like the ad from 'Casas Bahia!' [yelling] Why do they need to shout? I think this causes dizziness. You get a little dizzy. And in this consumerist society, where we somehow need to consume, the more you get dizzy, the more you eventually consume something you don't need.

Isabel creates a link which is worth noting. Selfishness is related to a kind of listening disability, a deaf way of dealing with each other. In a very noisy environment, the self is constantly challenged by the sound intrusion which leads to disorientation and mental confusion. 'You buy even things you don't want!' Consumerism is another feature of modern life in big cities that is entangled with this individualistic behaviour, in an unhealthy ambience where people do not listen to each other and are forced to shout to sell products or to be heard. In a reflexive moment, she includes herself in this messy environment, thinking about the need to change her own behaviour, her own habit of speaking too much.

The way Isabel frames her difficulties about daily life highlights a central issue that has been discussed in this book since its first pages. Music and sound negotiations are ways to experience the world and live within it. Using sound as a central element of diagnosis, Isabel manifests a wish that people could be less selfish, which is closely linked to increasing the capacity of listening to the other. It is a dual task that requires a high level of tolerance, both to understand the other and to claim for respect. While discussing the noise complaints in council institutions in Mexico City, Domínguez Ruiz argues that most problems regarding sound are solved in a peaceful way and without intermediaries 'when people are willing to talk, to listen and to cede as a path to negotiate common wellbeing' (2016: 140). That's what Isabel tries to elaborate on, at least in her narrative. And, interestingly, her interpretation about what could be a more harmonious life in society is informed by sound terms. 'Noise' in her talk is taken as a general reference to disturbing communication, something that blocks dialogue mainly due to the idea of loudness. Resounding the debate of Chapter 1, she feels some relative silence must be had in order to enable one to listen to others and, therefore, restore mental health. Elimination of sound excess would partially provide this desired ambience in which it would be possible to live in a more respectful way.

Since urban environments are essentially full of sounds and music, produced by machines, people and electronic devices, it is difficult to imagine interpersonal relations being constructed outside this over-sounded space. The ideal of a less noisy ambience that could allow people to hear each other, as elaborated on by Isabel, may be utopic. Instead, however, we could think about the issue of tolerance as a possible path to balancing interpersonal relations mediated by sound and music. Tolerance that ought to be double-sided, in a perspective that controllers and auditors acknowledge the existence and the life of each other as such, constructing a healthier coexistence. Of course, all the discussion developed in this book makes it clear that this balance is very difficult to achieve.

Epilogue

Music and sound conflicts are usually an issue of tolerance. Tolerance is something flexible enough to encompass a large variety of behaviours and practises in daily life. To what extent one can bear a music-sound played by someone else is impossible to determine. Social relations mediated by coexistence are often exposed to sound disagreements. How people will react to this unpleasurable experience is uncertain. How tolerant you will be to a person that bothers you with her/his sound depends on lots of conditions and contexts of the relationship you have with him/her. While writing the final pages of this book, I got a WhatsApp message from an ex-neighbour of mine, complaining about the tenant of my apartment. Her text is worth transcribing once it reveals a clear set of arguments and issues that have been developed throughout this book:

> Good evening, Felipe. I would like you to convince your tenants to balance the level of the sound which they listen to at max level every single day, mostly at noon and, inexorably, at night. I have given up sitting in the living room or in the back area. I have to shut myself in the bedroom, where, after closing the window and turning the air conditioner on, I can watch TV or read or listen to my own thoughts. And I can only get Netflix on the living room TV. I can't watch it. This is not right. I call them every day on the intercom. Not before trying to withstand it. Now I have asked the doorman to talk to them. They turned it down a bit and turned it up again. I called them. He threatened to call the police on me so they could see how low the sound was! That he was with a colonel and more two or three other

military officers! Harassment? Usually, in the rental contracts, tenants are required to respect the rules of the building, which use is residential, and he teaches dance classes. The music repeats on and on the same part teaching each step... Besides, the dancing shakes the floor downstairs. The dance class is annoying and the long nights of loud music and aggressive responses doesn't enable more tolerance. That is why I am asking for your help as a last attempt at accomplishing a conciliatory solution. Thank you.

The act of sending a message may be taken as a kind of desperate attitude. She is, indeed, explicitly begging for help. After listening to all the interviews done for this research and developing all the issues related to music conflicts, I couldn't have any reaction other than being sympathetic to her claim. For her, the sound that invades her private space disturbs her comfort and safety at home, being an intruder in her own apartment. Moreover, she resounds lots of complaints quoted in this book, highlighting that the dance steps and the music are both annoying. Although she did not use the word 'noise', we can consider the sound experience she reports as a whole, bringing together different qualities of sounds produced in the upper floor. Even though she mentioned the 'music' when referring to the repetition, 'sound' is a general term that merges definitions of 'music' and 'noise', usually with blurred borders between them.

However, what I would like to take as the most significant aspect of her message is the issue of human relations. In her description, several acts were taken in her attempts to minimize the nuisance. First, she tried to bear the sound, then talked directly to the tenant before asking for the doorkeeper to intermediate. She hadn't yet called the police but asked for my help. I wrote her back saying I would talk to him and she, again, reinforced the problem of their relationship:

Thank you. The problem is that the dialogue became very difficult, also with harassment. Besides being the most disturbed dweller, due to the position of my flat, I am also the condominium manager – so I can't tolerate this. Not even if I were deaf, because it sets a precedent that characterizes an anarchic building, where everything is allowed. And this is bad for everyone. Yesterday, he argued that I am the only one who complains. How does he know that? I am the manager and the worst victim. Talking to me is much easier. It is very painful to complain and be harassed. Anyway, the property management firm will send an admonition letter. Hoping that your words and the letter achieve success. I thank you for your attention and effort. All the best.

Once the dialogue is somehow blocked, negotiations regarding the sound between neighbours tend to become more difficult. In this second message, she raised the issue of power relations between them. This, in part, is due to the fact that she is not only the resident affected by the sound, but the owner of two or three apartments in the same building and its administrator. In other words, she is in charge of keeping a good coexistence between neighbours, in charge of the employees and the overall functioning of the building. Hence, although she has relative power within it, she feels powerless towards the intrusive sound of my tenant. Possibly, the issue here goes beyond the sound, to the way people live together in the same building, same street, same block or district. And to how this coexistence can be experienced daily. As she states her difficulty in being tolerant, she indirectly suggests being victimized by the sound and, finally, that her neighbour is acting carelessly. It is, of course, easier to be tolerant with someone you feel is behaving with respect, and, inversely, it is more difficult to tolerate a sound that appears to be played by someone who simply doesn't care about the other. Or, worse, someone who plays it loudly enough to intimidate or to bother the neighbourhood. She used the word 'intimidation' to describe the disagreement, yet I am not sure what sort of intimidation she was referring to. It may be related to the sound itself, or, unlikely but possible, it may be a sort of physical intimidation. It's impossible to know and I did not ask about it.

Nevertheless, like any conflict, it has another point of view. As I was asked to intermediate the disagreement, I wrote to my tenant explaining the situation and asking if he could try to balance his sound, suggesting that he change the position of the sound equipment and perhaps reduce its loudness. He answered:

Hi, Felipe, firstly I don't play it louder than what is allowed by law regarding decibels, she is overreacting in relation to the volume – I know that it is a whim of hers, so she can watch the soap opera, and I don't listen to music after 10 p.m. and it is not even that loud. But I will consider a conciliatory solution anyway, although I am feeling robbed of the legitimate right to listen to music! And I repeat I am attending to the decibels allowed by the law because I have already measured that after she complained. I will change the position of the speakers, yes, because today they are close to the balcony. Despite knowing that I am acting inside the law, I will turn down the volume even more because I don't want to create problems and only intend to have my rights assured, so I won't feel offended by an intolerant person and who uses her power as the condominium manager to impose personal decisions. Although it is a personal matter that should be solved here, she contacted you concerning this matter, which shows how she doesn't care for my perception of the issue. And she only wants me to follow her orders. Maybe if she had asked me to change the position of the speakers instead of telling me to turn the sound off? Everything would be rather different!? Do you understand? I consider myself a conciliatory person, although I am against any kind of arbitrary imposition.

But thank you for your perspective even though you're neutral, but with a perspective that acknowledges both sides. And with practical and clever ideas. You're a musician and know about sound and acoustics, thanks for the suggestions. Best wishes.

From his side, the thing seems to go in the opposite direction. He complains about her intolerance and demonstrates confidence in playing within the law. Her position as administrator of the building is obviously something that is part of the negotiation and something that apparently bothers him, making him feel pressured. In his feelings, her complaints about his sound are understood as 'orders', made by someone in a powerful position. Of course, it is possible to imagine that this interpretation of the disagreement leads him to ignore or even to increase the loudness as a kind of revenge. Powerless towards her role in the building, he is in charge of the sound and weaponizes it within this conflict. But we cannot be sure about that.

Additionally, another remarkable part of his message points to the fact that nobody is comfortable with being accused of intolerance. He highlights this by considering himself a conciliatory person, though opposed to 'arbitrary impositions'. This statement resounds the interview done with Alicia, quoted in previous chapters, when she puts it very clearly that people are keen to be 'good neighbours'. In this particular case, this seems to be true, but only in theory. As we come to practical situations, the threshold of tolerance doesn't work in the same way and other layers of disagreements and conflicts appear within the music and sound negotiations. Despite not wanting to be classified as intolerant, people are engaged in defending their personal 'rights', which involves the right to privacy and acoustic safety, especially at home. Being invaded means having this right blocked and how long and how much one can bear the imposition of a sound is uncertain. On the other side, the 'right' is also the main argument for playing the sound equipment loud enough inside your home. How much is loud enough, again, is not clear. This leads us back to the idea of sound leakage that throws the music inside other people's homes, imposing it. The issue is: who is imposing what on whom?

This very particular disagreement that I was incidentally called on to mediate reveals the ambiguities and complexities of the idea of tolerance towards the other's sound. As my tenant claims for his right to listen to music at home, his neighbour complains that his sound invades her privacy. This sound disagreement escalates, then, to a moral judgement about his or her intolerance and lack of respect. The difficulty of living together and the unbearable situation of having a sound imposed upon your acoustic privacy are experienced as an unsolved permanent conflict. Luckily, it seems that my role as mediator was successful and they finally achieved an agreement regarding the sound leakage. Possibly this was made easier because of an actual (water) leakage that irrupted in the middle of these talks in which both of them acted very politely and civilly.

Listening to others is a hard task. It highlights the precarity of our lives, exposes the messy environment we live in, challenges our tastes, sense of belonging and behaviours. It makes us aware of the interconnection of our lives with other people, beyond our choices and desires. It activates memories and feelings that may be irresistibly unpleasant, highly invasive and disturbing. Therefore, music and sound disagreements force us to face the fact that there is not a ready-made solution to life in society. Everyday life is a never-ending exercise of construction and reconstruction of interchanges with other people and spaces. Interchanges sounded by 'music' and 'noises' we usually do not control. It is a hard and inevitable task.

References

Alabarces, Pablo (2014), *Héroes, machos y patriotas: el fútbol entre la violencia y los medios*, Buenos Aires: Aguilar.

Alabarces, Pablo and Malvina Silba (2016), 'Cumbia Nena: Cumbia Scene, Gender and Class in Argentina', in Julio Mendívil and Christian Spencer (eds), *Made in Latin America: Studies in Popular Music*, 79–88, New York and London: Routledge.

Alonso, Gustavo (2015), *Cowboys do Asfalto*, Rio de Janeiro: Companhia das Letras.

Araújo, Paulo César (2002), *Eu não sou cachorro não: música popular cafona e ditadura militar*, Rio de Janeiro: Record.

Araújo, Samuel and Grupo Musicultura (2006), 'Conflict and Violence as Theoretical Tools in Present-Day Ethnomusicology', *Ethnomusicology*, 50 (2): 287–313.

Araújo, Samuel and Musicultura (2010), 'Sound Praxis: Music, Politics and Violence in Brazil', in John M. O'Connel and Salwa Castelo-Branco (ed.), *Music and Conflict*, 217–31, Urbana: University of Illinois.

Areni, Charles and David Kim (1993), 'Influence of Background Music on Shopping Behaviour', *Advances in Consumer Research*, 20: 336–40.

Attali, Jacques (2009), *Noise: The Political Economy of Music*, Minneapolis/London: University of Minnesota Press.

Babbage, Charles (1864), *Passages from the Life of a Philosopher*, London: Longman, Roberts and Green.

Bass, Michael T. (1864), *Street Music in Metropolis*, London: John Murray.

Becker, Judith (2004), *Deep Listeners: Music, Emotion and Trancing*, Bloomington: Indiana University Press.

Bellamy, Richard (2008), *Citizenship: A Very Short Introduction*, Oxford: Oxford University Press.

Bieletto-Bueno, Natalia (2018), 'De incultos y escandalosos: ruído e clasificación social en el México postrevolucionario', *Resonancias*, 22 (43): 161–78.

Bieletto-Bueno, Natalia (2019), 'Construcción de la marginalidad en los músicos callejeros', *Revista Cultura y Representaciones Sociales*, 14 (27): 309–47.

Bijsterveld, Karin (2008), *Mechanical Sound*, Cambridge, London: MIT Press.

Billig, Michael (2005), 'Comic Racism and Violence', in Michael Pickering and Sharon Lockyer (eds), *Beyond a Joke: The Limits of Humour*, 25–44, New York: Palgrave Macmillan.

Blacking, John (1995), *Music, Culture and Experience*, Chicago and London: Chicago University Press.

Blacking, John (2000), *How Musical Is Man?* Seattle, WA and London: University of Washington Press.

Bobbio, Norberto (2004), *A era dos direitos*, trans. Carlos Nelson Coutinho, Rio de Janeiro: Elsevier.

Born, Georgina, ed. (2013), *Music, Sound and Space*, Cambridge: Cambridge University Press.

Bourdieu, Pierre (1984), *Distinction: A Social Critique of the Judgment of Taste*, Cambridge, MA: Harvard University Press.

Brennan, Matt (2017), *When Genres Collide: Down Beat, Rolling Stone, and the Struggle Between Jazz and Rock*, New York and London: Bloomsbury.

Bull, Michael (2000), *Sounding Out the City*, New York: Oxford.

Bull, Michael (2007), *Sound Moves: iPod Culture and Urban Experience*, New York: Routledge.

Butler, Judith (1990), *Gender Trouble*, New York: Routledge.

Butler, Judith (2009), *Frames of War: When a Life Is Grievable?* London and New York: Verso.

Caiafa, Janice (2006), 'Solidão povoada: viagens silenciosas no metrô do Rio', *Contemporânea*, 4 (2): 45–64.

Caldera, Teresa (2000), *City of Walls: Crime, Segregation and Citizenship in São Paulo*, Berkeley, CA: University of California Press.

Chua, Daniel (2007), 'Rioting with Stravinsky', *Music Analysis*, 26 (2): 59–109.

Connel, John and Chris Gibson (2002), *Sound Tracks: Popular Music, Identity and Place*, New York and London: Routledge.

Connell, Raewyn W. (2005), *Masculinities*, Berkley and Los Angeles: University of California Press.

Cruickshanks, Karen and Terry Willey, Theodore Tweed, Barbara Klein, Ronald Klein, Julie Mares-Perlman, and David Nondahl (1998), 'Prevalence of Hearing Loss in Older Adults in Beaver Dam, Wisconsin', *American Journal of Epidemiology*, 148 (9): 879–86.

Cusick, Suzanne (2006), 'Music as Torture / Music as Weapon', *TRANS – Revista Transcultural de Música* 10. Available at https://www.sibetrans.com/trans/articulo/152/music-as-torture-music-as-weapon.

DaMatta, Roberto (1997), *A casa e a rua*, Rio de Janeiro: Rocco.

Daughtry, J. Martin (2015), *Listening to War*, Oxford: Oxford University Press.

DeNora, Tia (2000), *Music in Everyday Life*, Cambridge, UK: Cambridge University Press.

DeNora, Tia (2013), *Music Asylums: Wellbeing through Music in Everyday Life*, Surrey, UK: Ashgate.

Elias, Norbert (2000), *The Civilizing Process*, Oxford: Blackwell Publishing.

Elias, Norbert (2001), *The Society of Individuals*, New York and London: Continuum.

Fast, Susan and Kip Pegley, eds (2010), *Music, Politics and Violence*, Middletown, CT: Wesleyan University Press.

Fernandes, Cintia, Felipe Trotta, and Micael Herschmann (2015), 'Não pode tocar aqui?' *E-Compós*, 18 (2): 1–15.

Ferreira, Marcus and Livia Almeida (2015), 'Perturbação do trabalho e do sono alheios', *Cadernos de Segurança Pública*, 6: 1–8. Available at http://www.isprevista.rj.gov.br/download/Rev20150704.pdf

Finnegan, Ruth (2003), 'Music, Experience and the Anthropology of Emotion', in M. Clayton, T. Herbert, and R. Middleton (eds), *Cultural Study of Music*, 181–92, New York and London: Routledge.

Freire Filho, João and Micael Herschmann (2011), 'Funk Music Made in Brazil: Media and Moral Panic', in Idelber Avelar and Christopher Dunn (eds), *Brazilian Popular Music and Citizenship*, 223–39, Durham and London: Duke University Press.

Frith, Simon (1996), *Performing Rites: On the Value of Popular Music*, Cambridge, Massachusetts: Harvard University Press.

Frith, Simon (2003), 'Music and Everyday Life', in M. Clayton, T. Herbert and R. Middleton (eds), *Cultural Study of Music*, 92–101, New York and London: Routledge.

Frith, Simon (2004), 'Why Does Music Make People So Cross?' *Nordic Journal of Music Therapy*, 13 (1): 64–9.

Galtung, Johan (1969), 'Violence, Peace, and Peace Research', *Journal of Peace Research*, 6 (3): 167–91.

Garcia Canclini, Nestor (2001), *Consumers and Citizens: Globalization and Multicultural Conflicts*, trans. George Yúdice, Minnapolis and London: University of Minnesota Press.

Garcia, Luiz Henrique Assis and Pedro Marra (2016), 'Praças polifônicas: o som e a música popular como tecnologias de comunicação no espaço público', *Famecos*, 23 (1): 1–24.

Goodman, Steve (2010), *Sonic Warfare*, Cambridge/London: The MIT Press.

Habermas, Jüngen (1991), *The Structural Transformation of Public Sphere*, Cambridge: The MIT Press.

Hallam, Susan (2012), 'The Effects of Background Music to Health and Wellbeing', in *Music, Health and Wellbeing*, Raymond McDonald, Gunter Kreutz and Laura Mitchell (eds), 491-501, Oxford: Oxford University Press.

Hanser, Suzanne (2010), 'Music, Health and Wellbeing', in *Handbook for Music and Emotions*, Juslin, Patrik (ed), 849-878, Oxford: Oxford University Press.

Heller, Michael (2015), 'Between Silence and Pain: Loudness and the Affective Encounter', *Sound Studies*, 1 (1): 40–58.

Hendy, David (2013), *Noise: A Human History of Sound and Listening*, London: Profile Books.

Hennion, Antoine (2001), 'Music Lovers: Taste as Performance', *Theory, Culture, Society*, 18 (5): 1–22.

Herrera, Eduardo (2018), 'Masculinity, Violence, and Deindividuation in Argentine Soccer Chants', *Ethnomusicology*, 62 (3): 470–99.

Herschmann, Micael (2005), *O funk e o hip hop invadem a cena*, Rio de Janeiro: EdUFRJ.

Herschmann, Micael and Cintia Fernandes (2014), *Música nas ruas do Rio de Janeiro*, São Paulo: Intercom.

Hirsch, Lily E. (2012), *Music in American crime prevention and punishment*, University of Michigan Press.

Holt, Fabian (2007), *Genres in Popular Music*, Chicago and London: Chicago University Press.

Janotti Junior, Jeder and Simone Pereira de Sá (2018), 'Revisitando a noção de gênero musical em tempos de cultural digital', *Revista Galaxia*, 41: 128–39.

Johnson, Bruce and Martin Cloonan (2009), *The Dark Side of the Tune*, Surrey: Ashgate.

Juslin, Patrik N. (2016), 'Emotional Reactions to Music', in Susan Hallam, Ian Cross, and Michael Thait (eds), *The Oxford Handbook of Music Psychology*, 2nd edn, 197–215, Oxford: Oxford University Press.

Kassabian, Anahid (2013), *Ubiquitous Listening*, Berkley, Los Angeles, and London: University of California Press.

Kennaway, James (2012), *Bad Vibrations: The History of the Idea of Music as a Cause of Disease*, Farham, UK: Ashgate.

LaBelle, Brandon (2010), *Acoustic Territories*, New York/London: The Continuum International Publishing Group.

Lahire, Bernard (2007), 'Indivíduo e Mistura de Gêneros: Dissonâncias Culturais e distinção de si', *DADOS – Revista de Ciências Sociais*, 50 (4): 795–825.

Lanza, Joseph (1994), *Elevator Music*, London: Quartet Books.

Lopes, Adriana (2011), *Funk-se quem quiser: no batidão negro da cidade carioca*, Rio de Janeiro: Bom Texto/FAPERJ.

Marra, Pedro and Felipe Trotta (2019), 'Sound, Music and Magic in Football Stadiums', *Popular Music*, 38 (1): 73–89.

Martí, Josep (1997), 'When Music Becomes Noise: Sound and Music That People in Barcelona Hear But Don't Want to Listen to', *The World of Music*, 39 (2): 9–17.

Mendívil, Julio (2016), *En contra na música: herramientas para pensar, compreender y vivir las músicas*, Buenos Aires: Gourmet Musical.

Murolo, Norberto (2015), 'Escuchando música en el transporte público', *Revista Brasileira de Ciências da Comunincação (RBCC) – Intercom*, 38 (2): 81–98.

Negus, Keith (1999), *Music Genres and Corporate Cultures*, London and New York: Routledge.

North, Adrian, David Hargreaves, and Amanda Krause (2016), 'Music and Consumer Behavior', in Susan Hallam, Ian Cross e Michael Thaut (eds), *Oxford Handbook of Music Psychology*, Oxford: Oxford University Press.

O'Connel, John M. (2010). 'An Ethnomusicological Approach to Music and Conflict', in John M. O'Connel and Salwa Castelo-Branco (ed.), *Music and Conflict*, 1–16, Urbana: University of Illinois.

Oakes, Jason Lee (2004), 'Pop Music, Racial Imagination, and the Sounds of Cheese: Notes on Loser's Lounge', in Christopher Washburne and Maiken Derko (eds), *Bad Music: the Music We Love to Hate*, 47–64, New York: Routledge.

Ochoa Gautier, Ana Maria (2006), 'Sonic Transculturation, Epistemologies of Purification and the Aural Public Sphere in Latin America', *Social Identities*, 12 (6): 803–25.

Ochoa Gautier, Ana Maria (2014), *Aurality: Listening and Knowledge in Nineteenth-Century Colombia*, Durham and London: Duke University Press.

Oliveira, Luciana Xavier de (2017), *A cena musical da Black Rio*, Salvador: EdUFBA.

Palombini, Carlos (2014), 'Funk carioca and Música soul', in David Horn and John Shepherd (eds), *Bloomsbury Encyclopedia of Popular Music of the World*, 317–24, London, New York: Bloomsbury.

Palombini, Carlos and Adriana Facina (2017), 'O patrão e a padroeira: momentos de perigo na Penha, Rio de Janeiro', *Mana*, 23 (2): 341–70.

Pereira de Sá, Simone (2007), 'Funk carioca: música eletrônica popular brasileira?!' *Revista E-Compós*, 10: 1–18.

Pereira de Sá, Simone (2011), 'Ando meio (des)ligado? Mobilidade e mediação sonora no espaço urbano', *Revista E-Compós*, 14 (2): 1–18.

Pereira de Sá, Simone and Simone E. Cunha (2017), 'Haters Beyond the Hate: Stigma and Prejudice against Funk carioca on Youtube', *Journal of World Popular Music*, 4 (2): 152–70.

Picker, John (2003), *Victorian Soundscapes*, New York: Oxford University Press.

Pickering, Michael and Sharon Lockyer (2005), 'Introduction: the Ethics and Aesthetics of Humour and Comedy', in Michael Pickering and Sharon Lockyer (eds), *Beyond a Joke: The Limits of Humour*, 1–24, New York: Palgrave Macmillan.

Proença Junior, Domício and Jacqueline Muniz (2006), 'Stop or I'll Call the Police!: the Idea of Police, or the Effects of Police Encounters over Time', *The British Journal of Criminology*, 46 (2): 234–57.

Quijano, Anibal (2000), 'Coloniality of Power and Eurocentrism in Latin America', *International Sociology*, 15 (2): 215–32.

Quijano, Anibal (2005), 'Colonialidade do poder, eurocentrismo e América Latina', in Eduardo Lander (ed.), *A colonialidade do saber, eurocentrismo e ciências sociais: perspectivas latino-americanas*, 117–42, Buenos Aires: CLACSO.

Quijano, Anibal (2009), 'Colonialidade do poder e classificação social', in Boaventura de Souza Santos and Maria Paula Menezes (eds), *Epistemologias do Sul*, 73–118, Coimbra: Almedina.

Quintero Rivera, Ángel (2005), *Salsa, Sabor y Control*, México City: Siglo XXI.

Regev, Motti (2013), *Pop-Rock Music*, Cambridge and Malden: Polity Press.

Reía, Jhessica (2017), 'Os palcos efêmeros da cidade: táticas, ilegalismos e regulação da arte de rua em Montreal e no Rio de Janeiro', Ph.D Thesis, Escola de Comunicação (School of Communication), Universidade Federal do Rio de Janeiro (UFRJ).

Rodgers, Nigel and Val Weedon (2012), *Whose Choice Is It?* Unpublished.

Ruiz, Domínguez and Ana Lidia (2015), 'Ruido: intrusión sonora e intimidad acústica', *InMediaciones de la Comunicación*, 10 (10): 118–30.

Ruiz Domínguez and Ana Lidia (2016), 'Vivir juntos, vivir con otros: proximidad sonora y conflicto social', *Letra. Imagen. Sonido L.I.S.*, Año VIII (15): 129–45.

Ruiz Domínguez and Ana Lidia (2019), 'El oído: un sentido, múltiples escuchas. Presentación del dossier Modos de Escucha', *El Oído Pensante*, 7 (2): 92–110.

Said, Edward W. (2003), *Orientalism*, London: Penguin.

Sarlo, Beatriz (2014), *A cidade vista: mercadorias e cultura urbana*, São Paulo: Martins Fontes.

Schafer, Murray (2001), *A Afinação do Mundo* [The Tunning of the World], SP, Brazil: Unesp.

Scott, Kennet B. (2011), 'Politics and the Police in Scotland: The Impact of Devolution', *Crime Law Social Change*, 55: 121–32.

Semán, Pablo y Pablo Vila (2010), 'Introdución', in Pablo Semán and Pablo Vila (eds), *Cumbia: raza, nación, etnia y género en Latinoamérica*, 9–29, Buenos Aires: Gorla.

Sennett, Richard (2002), *The Fall of Public Man*, New York and London: Penguin Books.

Shannon, Claude and Warren Weaver (1964), *The Mathematical Theory of Communication*, Urbana: The University of Illinois Press.

Sloboda, John (2010), 'Music in Everyday Life: The Role of Emotions', in Patrik Juslin (ed.), *Handbook for Music and Emotions*, 493–514, Oxford: Oxford University Press.

Soares, Thiago (2015), 'Percursos para estudos sobre música pop', in Simone Pereira de Sá, Rodrigo Carreiro, and Rogério Ferraraz, *Cultura pop*, 19–34, Brasília: Compós.

Soares, Thiago (2017), *Ninguém é perfeito e a vida é assim: a música brega em Pernambuco*, Recife: Carlos Gomes de Oliveira Filho.

Soares, Thiago (2018), *Música pop en Cuba: globalización, territorios y solidaridad digital*, Barcelona: Editorial UOC/InCom UAB.

Sodré, Muniz (2017), *Pensar nagô*, Petrópolis, RJ, Brazil: Vozes.

Sontag, Susan (2003), *Regarding the Pain of the Others*, New York: Picador.

Souza, Jessé (2001), 'A sociologia dual de Roberto DaMatta', *Revista Brasileira de Ciências Sociais*, 16 (45): 47–67.

Sterne, Jonathan (2003), *The Audible past: cultural origins of sound reproduction*, Durham London: Duke University Press.

Thompson, Marie Suzanne (2014), 'Beyond Unwanted Sound: Noise, Affect and Aesthetic Moralism', PhD thesis, International Centre for Music Studies, Newcastle University.

Torres, Lívia (2017), 'Police Officer Murders Young Girl after an Argument at a Party in the West Zone of Rio de Janeiro', online News Portal *G1*, 8/12/2017. Available at: https ://g1.globo.com/rj/rio-de-janeiro/noticia/pm-mata-jovem-apos-discussao-em-festa-na-zona-oeste-do-rio.ghtml.

Trotta, Felipe (2014), *No Ceará não tem disso não: nordestinidade e macheza no forró contemporâneo*, Rio de Janeiro: Folio Digital.

Trotta, Felipe (2016), 'O funk no Brasil contemporâneo: uma música que incomoda', *Latin Amercia Research Review*, 51 (4): 86–101.

Trotta, Felipe (2018), 'Prejuicios, incomodidades y rechazos: música territorialidades y conclictos en el Brasil contemporáneo', *Anthropologica*, 40: 165–91.

Turino, Thomas (2008), *Music as Social Life: The Politics of Participation*, Chicago/London: The University of Chicago Press.

Västfjäll, Daniel, Patrik Juslin and Terry Hartig (2012), 'Music, Subjective Wellbeing and Health: the role of everyday emotions', in *Music, Health and Wellbeing*, Raymond McDonald, Gunter Kreutz and Laura Mitchell (eds), 415-432, Oxford: Oxford University Press.

Viveiros de Castro, Eduardo (2014), *Cannibal Metaphysics: For a Post-structural Anthropology*, trans. Peter Skafish, Minneapolis, MN: Univocal.

Washburne, Christopher and Maiken Derko (2004), 'Introduction', in Christopher Washburne and Maiken Derko (eds), *Bad Music: The Music We Love to Hate*, 1–10, New York: Routledge.

Weber, Max (2008), 'Politics as Vocation', in John Dreijmanis (ed.) and Gordon C. Wells (trans.), *Max Weber's Complete Writings on Academic and Political Vocations*, 155–208, New York: Algora Publishing.

Wisnik, José Miguel (1999), *O Som e o Sentido: uma outra história das músicas*, São Paulo: Companhia das Letras.

Worden, Robert and Sarah McLean (2017), *Mirage of Police Reform*, Oakland, California: University of California Press.

Zizek, Slavoj (2006), *Sobre la violencia: seis reflexiones marginales*, trans. Antonio José Antón Fernandez, Buenos Aires, Barcelona, and Mexico: Paidós.

Index

Lightning Source UK Ltd.
Milton Keynes UK
UKHW050035160720
366477UK00003BA/169